Issues in the Study of Education

ARTHUR GEEN
MARTIN COOK
SUSAN DAVIS
CHARLIE HARRIS
MARTIN RAWLE

G W A S G
UWIC
P R E S S

© **Arthur Geen 2007**

ISBN 978-1-905617-62-3

Published by UWIC Press
Cyncoed Road
Cardiff CF23 6XD
029 2041 6515
cgrove@uwic.ac.uk

Designed by Andy Dark
Printed by HartleyWilprint

Contents

Contributors

Dr Arthur Geen is Principal Lecturer in Educational Studies at the University of Wales Institute, Cardiff (UWIC). He taught Classics before becoming a lecturer in Education at University College Cardiff where he conducted research and published over a hundred papers in various fields of education. At UWIC he is Programme Director for the BA programme in Educational Studies. Publications include the books *Decision Making and Secondary Education* (University of Wales Press), *Effective Teaching for the Twenty-First Century* (UWIC Press) and *An Introduction to Classical Greek Drama* (UWIC Press) and articles in such journals as *Mentoring and Tutoring*, *Public Administration*, *Curriculum*, *Teacher Development* and *Westminster Studies in Education*.

Martin Cook is Senior Lecturer in Primary Education at the University of Wales Institute, Cardiff. He taught in primary schools in South East Wales for sixteen years, and was a primary school head teacher before joining the staff at UWIC. In 2005 he became a UWIC Teaching Fellow for his work on implementing Assessment for Learning principles in higher education programmes of initial teacher education and training.

Susan Davis is Senior Lecturer in Early Years at the University of Wales Institute, Cardiff. She taught in the field of Early Years education, before becoming a tutor on the CACHE Diploma in Childcare and Education at Coleg Gwent, Ebbw Vale. She has also taught with the Open University on the Early Childhood Studies degree programmes. At UWIC she is the Programme Director for the Foundation Degree in Learning Support.

Charlie Harris is Programme Director for the English and Popular Culture degree at UWIC. In addition to lecturing in English Literature and Language he also teaches Education and Popular Culture courses. Mr Harris is an external examiner for a number of British Universities and a secondary school inspector for English in Wales. His publications have focused on mentoring in schools.

Martin Rawle is Senior Lecturer in Educational Studies at UWIC. He previously taught religious education. At UWIC he has lectured on the undergraduate primary and secondary education courses and the postgraduate masters course. He currently teaches on the BA programme in Educational Studies. He is an Estyn approved inspector for schools covering religious education, personal and social education and key questions. Publications include articles in *Journal of Beliefs and Values* and *UWIC Education Papers*. Conference presentations include *Perceptions of Spirituality and Implementation of Personal and Social Education in Secondary Schools in South East Wales*.

Foreword

It is generally acknowledged that education is a controversial subject. Politicians incessantly debate it, and we seem to have legislation nearly every year. Since Labour came to power there have been at least six major Education Acts. It is not, therefore, surprising that courses are springing up in our universities in the field of Educational Studies. This book has been written for students pursuing programmes of this type. It contains material which is employed at the University of Wales Institute, Cardiff (UWIC), and seeks to stimulate reflection about important aspects of education.

The first chapter is concerned with philosophical influences which have helped to shape the curriculum. The starting point is the Enlightenment of the Eighteenth Century and major intellectual movements are described which have influenced thinking upon education in England and Wales to the present day. Specific areas include: the Enlightenment; Progressive Education; Idealism; Darwinism; Rational Humanism; differing interpretations of "liberal education"; and post-modernism.

The following four chapters examine specific current curricular and pedagogic issues. The first of these is early childhood studies, and in the second chapter the four "traditional" disciplines associated with education – history, philosophy, psychology and sociology – are employed to explore a range of themes concerning the teaching of young children. In the light of this analysis some thoughts are offered on the important developments which are taking place in Wales whereby the subject-centred Key Stage 1 is being replaced with a more child-centred, play-based Foundation Phase.

We next focus upon important issues relating to language and learning, whilst in chapter 4 attention is paid to the curricular requirement that schools promote the spiritual, moral, social and cultural development of their children. The key question is asked: What precisely do we mean by "spirituality"? Four criteria are suggested for the clarification of the concept and their implications for teachers are discussed.

The need for assessment procedures which assist pupils' learning is the topic of the next section. The findings of recent research into "assessment for learning" are summarised and an account is given of the use of techniques of this type in higher education.

In the sixth chapter trends in the educational system of England and Wales are recounted, and a contrast drawn between the thought underlying the Education Act of 1944 and the current "market forces" philosophy of the New Right and the Third Way.

The book concludes with practical advice for students engaged in research within the field of education.

All the contributors teach on the BA (Hons) Educational Studies programme at UWIC.

Arthur Geen
Principal Lecturer in Educational Studies,
University of Wales Institute, Cardiff

March 2007

1 Historical and philosophical perspectives on education

I: INTRODUCTION

This chapter takes a historical and philosophical view of education from the Eighteenth Century to the present. It seeks to examine some of the most important intellectual developments which have influenced thinking upon education from the time of the movement known as the Enlightenment in the Eighteenth Century. An account will be given of the origins of the Progressive movement and of the impact of such philosophies as Idealism and Pragmatism. Attention is also paid to the conflict between the advocates of a pedagogy based upon science and the supporters of a humanistic and liberal education.

II: THE ENLIGHTENMENT

The Enlightenment of the Eighteenth Century was an intellectual movement somewhat akin to the Renaissance. Its emphasis was upon the application of reason to all modes of life. It was concerned to apply "the test of a severely accurate reason to everything and reject outright whatever will not stand the test" (Rogers, 1946, p. 387). "Everything," argued Denis Diderot (1712-1784) in the *Encyclopedia* "must be examined; everything must be shaken up without exception and without circumspection."

Philosophers of the Enlightenment saw the Renaissance as the first part of a process of which their movement was the climax - "the great drama of the disenchantment of the European mind" (Gay, 1967, p. 279). Leading figures in the movement include Francois Marie Arouet, better known by his pen name of Voltaire (1694-1778), Claude-Adrien Helvetius (1715-1771) and Charles Montesquieu (1689 – 1755). In addition there was the group of which Diderot (1713-1784) and D'Alembert (1717-1783) were members, which worked upon the compilation of an encyclopedia purporting to contain the sum of human knowledge to that time.

The chief arguments of Enlightenment philosophers were that:

(a) All beliefs should be the subject of critical scrutiny and could be accepted only on the basis of reason and evidence. No beliefs could be held merely on the basis of authority, for example, the Church or writers of a past age.

(b) All superstitions should therefore be abandoned.

(c) It was possible to detect regularity and order in the universe.

(d) Similarly, there existed a uniformity underlying the nature of man. As the philosopher David Hume (1711-1776) wrote: "There is a great uniformity among the actions of men, in all nations and ages, and ... human nature remains still the same, in its principles and operations. The same motives always produce the same actions" (Bantock, 1980, p. 253). Hence philosophers of the Enlightenment sought to *standardise* man and paid great attention to the concept of the *natural* man. They believed essentially in the *equality* of man rather than in individual differences between people. Equality was a concept of greater importance to them than freedom.

(e) In their view natural man was not an inherently bad creature as had been believed by the Medieval Church. They argued that the purpose of existence was the good life on earth rather than an eternity in heaven after a life of misery. Solely by the use of his reason and experience man was capable of achieving this good life on earth. Hence, there was a belief in progress - that by the disciplined use of his mind man could achieve a paradise on earth.

(f) The starting point for the improvement of man's condition on earth was to be the freeing of his mind from ignorance and superstition and the overthrow of the artificial and corrupt "unnatural" society which prevented his living as "natural" man. Consequently, the Encyclopedists criticised the conventions of the Eighteenth Century, for example, the centralised autocracy of French society, the privileges of the nobility and clergy, and the checks imposed on the liberty of the middle class and lower orders. The Encyclopedists contributed to the spirit of opposition which ultimately found expression in the French Revolution of 1789.

(g) It followed from these assumptions that education was essentially the process of freeing man's mind from ignorance and the development of reason as a means of stimulating human progress.

Summing up the influence of the Enlightenment, Cobban (1957, p. 112) states that, "for all its innate weaknesses, its limited scope and the rising challenge of a world which did not bow to its conception of reason or acknowledge its universal laws, the Enlightenment began a movement, the impact of which on the history of the world it is difficult to overestimate."

III: ROUSSEAU, THE "FATHER OF THE PROGRESSIVE EDUCATION MOVEMENT"

(a) **Works of Rousseau:** Jean-Jacques Rousseau was born in 1712 in Geneva and died in 1778. His main works are:

- *Discourse on the Sciences and the Arts* (1750), in which he contrasts the "natural life" of man with the corrupt society of Eighteenth Century France.

- *The Origin of Inequality among Mankind* (1754), the message of which is that man is basically good, but has been perverted by the corruption of society. Inequality between men has stemmed from the ownership of property, especially land.

- *La Nouvelle Heloise* (1761), in which he depicts the ideal family and the "natural education" of young children.

- *The Social Contract* (1762), which greatly influenced the Jacobins between 1791 and 1793, especially Robespierre. Rousseau begins with the words: "Man is born free; and everywhere he is in chains. Those who think themselves masters of others are indeed greater slaves than they" (Rousseau, 2004, p. 2). He wants a society in which men can live "naturally", casting off the chains of prejudice and artificial social custom. To ensure that we can live in this way and that no-one is enslaved it is necessary to enter into a "social contract" with others as the basis of the organisation of a free society. For example, we may agree to drive on the left side of the road in the interests of the safety of us all. The contract must take into account the "General Will" of the people. This general will is not just majority opinion (or the "Will of All"). The dictate of the general will is that which each individual would see to be the best policy if he were truly to consider both his own and everybody else's interest. At present we are unable to see this "general will" as our views are clouded by artificial society. With the right type of education we can produce adults capable of seeing what their interests really are.

- *Emile* (1762), which is his most important work on education. In it he depicts the upbringing of an imaginary boy, Emile. Rousseau advises his readers to reverse the usual practices of the day "and you will almost always do right" (Rousseau, 1974, p. 58). Although there were some progressive tendencies in Eighteenth Century education, it was for the most part extremely rigid. The teacher was the ultimate authority and the principal teaching method was instruction followed by memorisation and recitation of what had been learned. The curriculum was dominated by the classics – the study of Latin and Ancient Greek - with little time allocated to science. Children were deemed to be bad by nature, and the most obvious way of suppressing the inborn tendency to sin was corporal punishment. Thus, the rod was described by John Brinsley (1585- 1665) as "God's instrument to cure the evils of their condition". A typical example of a lesson of this period is described by Heafford (1967, p. 39):

"The pupils read in turn and during the period the Headmaster seldom said more than the word: 'Next!' when another pupil had to continue. At the most he corrected a word which had been pronounced wrongly or called to someone who had not been following, 'Next !' even though it was not his turn. If he stumbled, he was struck a few times with the cane. For us the Bible was no more than a reader which was only of interest to us because with its help we could show how well and quickly we were able to read".

Other examples of this type of "traditional" education which survived into the Twentieth Century are cited by Geen (2005, pp. 83-84).

(b) **Rousseau's General Theory of Education:** In accordance with the thinking of the Enlightenment Rousseau contrasts the innate goodness of man with the corruption of society. *Natural* man is good, but men are corrupted by the evil of the societies in which they live. "God", he writes, "makes all things good; man meddles with them and they become evil" (Rousseau, 1974, p. 5). The child must therefore be shielded from the evil of society. "You can remove this young tree from the highway and shield it from the crushing force of social conventions" (pp. 5-6).

He therefore recommends a *natural education* in which nature, the teacher and the environment work in harmony. "Education comes to us from nature, from men, or from things. The inner growth of our organs and faculties is the education of nature; the use we learn to make of this growth is the education of men, what we gain by our experience of our surroundings is the education of things " (p. 6).

Although the child must ultimately become a member of society, he must not be corrupted by it during his education. The environment must be controlled so that his original nature is preserved unspoiled. "Forced to combat either nature or society, you must make your choice between the man and the citizen; you cannot train both" (p. 7).

Under this controlled environment, which Rousseau sees essentially as a country setting, the child will be able to develop "naturally". In this process he will pass through certain stages of development and his education must be geared to his natural needs at each stage. "Each age, every station in life, has a perfection, a ripeness of its own" (p. 122). These stages, he believes, repeat the growth of the human race. They are defined as:

(i) *infancy* (*to the age of* 2): This consists of physical education concerned to toughen the body. It represents the "animal stage" of human development.

(ii) *childhood* (*to the age of* 12): Education at this stage is based upon the senses. It corresponds to the "savage" stage of humanity.

(iii) *the ages* 12-15: Between these ages education is concerned with development of the intellect with the emphasis on practical thinking and utility. This correlates with the "rational stage" of humanity and its interest in the physical and scientific world.

(iv) *adolescence* (*the ages* 15-20): This is the period of social, moral, religious and aesthetic education, representing the "social and moral stage" of humanity. A major theme is interaction with other people.

In the book Emile is the child reared by Rousseau, the tutor, in a rural setting. At each stage the child's environment is carefully controlled so that his natural needs are met.

(c) **Infancy**

(i) *Freedom and Natural Development*: The peasant mother is the paradigm for child rearing since she allows the child as much freedom as possible to grow naturally. "Put him in a big cradle, well padded, where he can move easily and safely. As he begins to grow stronger, let him crawl about the room; let him develop and stretch his tiny limbs; you will see him gain strength from day to day" (p. 27).

The child should not encounter resistance from adults, only from the environment. "When children only experience resistance in things and never in the will of man, they do not become rebellious or passionate, and their health is better" (p. 33). Accordingly, there should be no corporal punishment. "Sometimes he is punished for faults before he is aware of them... thus early are the seeds of evil passion sown in his young heart" (p. 16).

(ii) *Education through Experience*: Rousseau argues that the child is born with a capacity for learning but no specific knowledge. The first mental experiences are simply the results of feelings. Children are "only aware of pleasure and pain" (p. 29), for example, the desire for food. As the child grows older, the senses develop and he begins to notice what is around him. These sense experiences are very important, as they are the "raw material" of thought and lead at a later stage to understanding. It is, therefore, very important that children learn from experience and be allowed freedom of action to develop these senses. "He wants to touch and handle everything; do not check these movements which teach him invaluable lessons" (p. 31).

(d) **Childhood:** At this stage of natural development Emile is compared with the savage. His higher mental faculties have not yet emerged and his thinking is restricted to the world of the senses; reason has not yet developed. Education is therefore limited to the concrete type of thinking. Consequently, no verbal instruction will be employed. Education will involve *things* rather than *words*. "Keep the child dependent on things only. By this course of education you will have followed the order of nature" (p. 49).

Freedom is still important. The chief restriction will not be the command of the tutor. "The very words *obey* and *command* will be excluded from his vocabulary, still more those of *duty* and *obligation*" (p. 53). Rather, he will learn the *law of necessity*; he will see the need for acting in a particular way and realise that limitations are imposed on his freedom by nature. For example, if he greedily eats all the biscuits now, there will be none left later. In this way, he learns naturally that if he acts in a certain way various consequences will of necessity follow. "It is in man's nature to bear patiently with the nature of things, but not with the ill-will of another. A child never rebels against 'There is none left'..." (p. 55). No verbal lessons are necessary, and Rousseau condemns the idea that we should reason with children at this stage when the requisite faculty has not yet developed. Where the tutor rejects a request, the refusal should be final and no justification need be given. Punishment should be based on the principle of natural consequences. Hence, if Emile breaks the windows in his room, he has to sleep in a cold room.

As the first step towards the acquisition of understanding of the world is sense perception, Rousseau recommends educational methods involving the senses, for example, clapping one's hands in a dark building to calculate from the noise the size of the room and one's position within it.

(e) **Education 12-15:** Gradually Emile is capable of more sustained attention as he enters the rational stage. Thinking is still primarily concerned with sense-given fact, but he is now able to compare sensations and to reason. His thought is not just restricted to the present; he is able to anticipate and exercise foresight. "From the comparisons of many successive or simultaneous sensations and the judgment arrived at with regard to them, there springs a sort of mixed or complex sensation which I call an idea" (p. 165). The curriculum at this stage therefore focuses upon science, handicraft and practical work. Aesthetic and moral insight are yet to develop, but Emile can understand the use of things and this leads to an understanding of the division of labour and organisation of society. He sees the necessity for work and learns a trade. "He must know not merely what is, but what is useful" (p. 129).

As for pedagogy, Rousseau strongly advocates a heuristic approach in which ideas and understanding enter the mind through the senses. Knowledge is to be acquired not from books but from observation of physical phenomena. "The child who reads ceases to think. ... He is acquiring words, not knowledge". The only book he does recommend is *Robinson Crusoe*, which "supplies the best treatise on an education according to nature". It is, he argues, amusing and instructive. Indeed, Emile is to imagine that he is Robinson Crusoe himself (p. 148). Otherwise, books are to be avoided. He writes: "I hate books; they only teach us to talk about things we know nothing about" (p. 147). Rather, he advises educators to "put the problems before him [the pupil] and let him solve them himself. Let him know nothing because you have told him, but because he has learnt it for himself. Let him not be taught science, let him discover it" (p. 131). Rousseau establishes a number of principles:

(i) *The starting point should always be the environment*, for example, map drawing beginning with the pupil's village and a few obvious landmarks.

(ii) *What is learned should be of utilitarian value*: Emile will not know the position of Peking on the atlas, but he will be able to find his way around the countryside. If he should ask about the value of local geography, Rousseau would arrange for them to become "lost" in a nearby forest and use their knowledge of the environment and position of the sun to find their way again.

(iii) *Instruction should not be used*, "but never ... let him form inaccurate or confused ideas. I care not if he knows nothing provided he is not mistaken" (p. 134).

Rousseau discusses simple observational experiments: the power of amber and wax, when rubbed, to attract straws; properties of magnetism (e.g. the "wax duck" story pp. 135-138); expansion and contraction of liquids and the thermometer; the law of gravity; and the principle of the balance.

(f) **Adolescence:** Until now self-love has been a source of motivation; now interest in other people is an important factor. Emile has to this point been concerned with the physical world. From fifteen he is more concerned with the *moral* world of people.

Rousseau is worried that the boy's natural inclinations may be corrupted by artificial society. Thus, Emile is only gradually introduced into community life. Rousseau proposes:

(i) *the beginning of a social and moral education based on "natural sentiment" to the age of sixteen*: Moral education to sixteen should be based on natural feelings. He argues that:

(1) We do not usually put ourselves in the position of those people who are more fortunate than ourselves, but in the place of those who are to be pitied.

(2) We do not usually pity the misfortunes of others unless we believe that we could suffer in the same way.

(3) The pity we experience for the ills of others is proportionate to the feelings we attribute to them. Emile should, therefore, become accustomed to the plight of those less well off than himself, for example, by visiting hospitals or prisons.

(ii) *a wider moral and religious education based not only upon experience but also upon a study of history at eighteen*;

(iii) *an introduction to the polite society of Paris and the cultivation of taste through literature and the theatre at twenty, i.e. aesthetic education.*

(g) **Marriage And The Education Of Women**: The ideal woman for Emile is Sophy, and in Book V of

Emile Rousseau gives an account of the education which she should receive. In essence, he attributes a subservient role to women. Sophy, representative of the female species, is to be pleasing to man; she should follow and obey him. "The man should be strong and active; the woman should be weak and passive; the one must have both the power and the will; it is enough that the other should offer little resistance ... Woman is specially made for man's delight - it is the law of nature" (p. 322). Sophy's education is accordingly engineered to this end.

He therefore recommends for girls up the age of ten physical training in grace and dressing dolls. Idleness and insubordination should not be tolerated, and they should be stopped in the middle of a game to attend to some household task. "This habitual restraint produces a docility which a woman requires all her life long" (p. 333). From the age of ten their education should focus upon the art of pleasing in terms of dress, deportment, dancing and singing. When Emile meets Sophy she has a good natural disposition, a pleasing but not brilliant mind and a happy character. She is fond of dresses, though disliking expensive clothes, and is adept at household management and needlework. She understands cooking and cleaning and "she knows the prices of food and also how to chose it" (p. 357).

IV: THE IMPACT OF ROUSSEAU: SOME ADVOCATES OF PROGRESSIVE EDUCATION

(a) **Progressive Education in the Nineteenth Century:** During the Nineteenth Century Rousseau's ideas concerning "natural" education were refined and modified by other "progressive" educators who opposed the practices associated with "traditional" teaching. Heinrich Pestalozzi (1746-1827) established various schools and centres for teacher training in Switzerland. His chief works on education include *Leonard and Gertrude* (1780), *How Gertrude Teaches Her Children* (1781) and *Swan Song* (1818). Like Rousseau he saw nature as the guide to education and believed in stages of natural development, which must be noted by the teacher. Knowledge, he argued, depends upon motivational foundations, and teaching should involve activity. Ordinary life experiences can be used to educate the young (Heafford, 1967).

Many people visited Pestalozzi's schools and endeavoured to implement his ideas. Charles Mayo (1792-1846) set up a private school in England along Pestalozzi lines, while in Philadelphia Joseph Neef opened an educational establishment designed to put these principles into practice.

Friedrich Froebel (1782-1852) was also impressed with Pestalozzi's methods and experimented in Germany with the *kindergarten*. His educational ideas are set out in *The Education of Man* (1826). He believed that life is an evolutionary process in which education can play an important part by making people aware of the future betterment of mankind. God is the unifying factor in the universe which consists of small "whole unities". Education is the process by which these unities may be brought together into harmony. In Great Britain and America Froebel Societies were organised in the Nineteenth Century (Lawrence, 1952).

(b) **Progressive Education in the Twentieth Century.** Twentieth Century progressive educators stressed such concepts as the freedom of the child, democracy in education, activity and experience rather than the passive learning of facts, creativity and education according to the interests and needs of the child. The teacher is not seen as an authoritarian figure, but as a group leader, helping pupils decide their own activities. Progressive schools are usually run on democratic lines without teacher imposed rules or punishment systems.

Such themes occur in *The Montessori Method* of Maria Montessori (1870-1952), *Summerhill* by A. S. Neill (1883-1973), *Talks to Parents and Teachers* by Homer Lane (1874-1925) and *On Education* by Bertrand Russell (1872-1970). Sir T.P. Nunn's *Education: Its Data and First Principles* (1920) adopts a realistic and biological view of education, seeing it as a process of self-development. The Hadow Reports (Consultative Committee to the Board of Education, 1931 and 1933) and the Plowden and Gittins Reports (Central Advisory Council for Education [England], 1967 and Central Advisory Council for Education [Wales] 1968) were enthusiastic for a progressive approach. The Plowden Committee wrote that the school should "allow children to be themselves and to develop in the way and at the pace appropriate to them" (p. 187). It argued that the progressive school "lays special stress on individual, on first hand experience and on opportunities for creative work. It insists that knowledge does not fall into neatly separate compartments and that work and play are not opposite but complementary. A child brought up in such an atmosphere at all stages of his education has some hope of becoming a balanced and mature adult and of being able to live in, to contribute to, and to look critically at the society of which he forms a part" (pp. 187-188).

Many of these educational tenets met with criticism from such writers on education as Professor Richard Peters of the Institute of Education of London University (Peters, 1969), R.F.Dearden (1968) and Geoffrey Bantock (1971). Progressive education was also blamed by politicians in the later years of the Twentieth Century for alleged declining educational standards (Boyson, 1975). A Green Paper published in 1977 argued that progressive education had "proved a trap for some less able and experienced teachers who applied the freer methods uncritically or failed to recognise that they require careful planning of the opportunities offered to children and systematic monitoring of the progress of individuals" (DES, 1977, p. 8). In 2005 the leader of the Conservative Party, David Cameron, promised that, if ever he formed a government, it would "scrap the progressive education claptrap that has done so much damage to so many children for so many years" (Stewart, 2005a).

V: IMMANUEL KANT AND IDEALISM

(a) **Kant and "Traditional" and "Progressive" Education:** In many ways Immanuel Kant stands midway between the two movements in education often stereotyped as "traditional" and "progressive". Although influenced by Rousseau (1712-1778) and by Johann Basedow (1723-1790), who established a model school - the Philanthropinum - at Dessau in 1774, Kant puts more stress on discipline, compulsion and obedience than the majority of Eighteenth and Nineteenth Century progressive educators.

He was born in 1724 in Konigsberg, East Prussia, and in 1770 was elected Professor of Logic and Metaphysics at Konigsberg University, a post he held until a few years before his death in 1804. Kant was one of the greatest thinkers of his period. In 1781 he published the *Critique of Pure Reason*, in which he attempted to synthesise the philosophies of rationalism expounded by Rene Descartes (1596-1650), Benedict Spinoza (1632-1677) and Gottfried Leibnitz (1646-1716) and empiricism popularised by John Locke (1632-1704), George Berkeley (1685-1753) and David Hume (1711-1776). Both rationalism and empiricism, he felt, gave a one-sided, distorted account of the structure and content of human knowledge. The year 1788 saw the publication of the *Critique of Practical Reason* and 1790 the completion of his *Critique of Judgement*. Kant died in 1804.

One of the terms of his appointment to the University was that he should lecture on other subsidiary subjects, of which education was one. Although he took as his text a book by a Professor Bock, his lectures were totally independent of that volume, and at a later stage he handed his lecture notes to a friend, Theodor Rink, who had them published as *Uber Pedagogik* (*On Education*). In formulating his ideas on education he was greatly influenced by Rousseau's *Emile*, which had been published in 1762. Kant was renowned as a punctual person, and it is alleged that the only time he deviated from his daily routine was the day that he first read *Emile*.

Important aspects of Kant's philosophy which relate to education are summarised in the following paragraphs.

(b) **The Good Will:** The only absolute good according to Kant is the good will. By "will" he means that part of man which decides upon a course of action. The morality of an action, he asserts, lies not in its results but in the principle with which the will consciously identifies itself, that is to say, the motive. The only good motive is *consciousness of duty*.

(c) **The Categorical Imperative:** What is duty? How do we know it? According to Kant the moral law can be deduced from the following formula of the categorical imperative: "Act only on maxims which you can will to be universal laws". By "maxim" Kant means the principle of action adopted by the agent. The categorical imperative may be paraphrased: "If the maxim of your action cannot be given universal validity without coming into opposition with itself, then it is not moral". He illustrates this with the example of the lie. If, when in distress, I make a false promise, intending to break it later, the source of the maxim is clearly self-love. Now, if this maxim were universalised, it would mean that all persons in distress should make false promises. This would come into opposition with self-love for two reasons:

(i) The value of promises would be abolished and I would suffer together with the rest of society.

(ii) If I were the person to whom the promise was made, my self-love would want that promise to be kept.

Telling lies, therefore, cannot be a moral maxim.

(d) **List of Duties:** From the categorical imperative he derives the following list of duties:

A. DUTIES TO ONESELF AS A RATIONAL BEING

(i) *Obligatory duties to oneself*:

    (1) to preserve oneself (not to commit suicide, not to mutilate or stupefy oneself);

    (2) to be truthful and not to lie;

(3) not to be miserly towards oneself;

(4) to respect oneself and not to be servile.

(ii) *Meritorious duties*:

(1) to seek one's own perfection:

(2) natural perfection;

(3) moral perfection.

B. DUTIES TO OTHERS

(i) *Obligatory duties to others*:

(1) to keep promises;

(2) to be truthful;

(3) to seek to establish a system of positive laws and to obey them;

(4) to respect others, even those who are immoral, though this does not entail revering them.

(ii) *Meritorious duties*:

(1) to promote their happiness;

(2) to be grateful;

(3) to be sympathetic;

(4) to be friendly and sociable (Kant, 1964).

(e) **Phenomena and Noumena:** In *The Critique of Pure Reason* he distinguishes "phenomena" and "noumena". *Phenomena* or "things as they appear" in space and time are the objects of our sense experience and perception. Thus, we can see men's actions as we can see the fall of a tree or the eruption of a geyser. *Phenomena* (singular *phenomenon*) are subject to the scientific laws of nature and can be investigated scientifically. *Noumena* (singular *noumenon*) or "things in themselves" exist but cannot be the object of sense perception. Whilst we can observe men's actions (phenomena), we cannot perceive their motives. Motives cannot be investigated scientifically, as they lack the sensory content which would enable them to be examined in this way.

Human beings are both phenomenal and noumenal:

(i) *The body appears in time and space as a phenomenal self*. It is part of the realm of nature and must comply with the laws of science, for example, cause and effect. Its actions are to this extent determined by natural law.

(ii) *The noumenal self, however, is free*. It is not determined by scientific laws. Rather it entails free will and choice. His proof that the will is free is based on man's consciousness of moral obligation; we may opt to do our duty or not. The noumenal aspect of man involves freedom, autonomy and morality.

(f) **Progress of the Human Race:** Kant contends that progress takes two forms:

(i) *intellectual* - the advancement of learning and understanding;

(ii) *moral* - the improvement of society and man.

Reviewing the Eighteenth Century, he feels that great strides have been made with respect to intellectual development as the result of the growth of science, and he hopes that in years to come man will be able to control his environment and decrease the sum of misery in the world. However, in certain of his works he argues that progress can be achieved only if man's moral development keeps pace with the advancement of scientific knowledge. All knowledge, he says, is useless and even harmful unless backed up by character. Education must help form this character. It will play a major part in achieving the "Kingdom of God on earth".

(g) **Aims of Education:** These he divides into two: physical and practical education.

(i) *Physical education* is linked to the phenomenal world in which man is subject to the laws of nature and science. All aspects which relate to the natural, phenomenal world he calls "physical". Physical education includes nurture, discipline, the cultivation of mental skills and the development of prudence where it does not relate specifically to the learning of maxims for moral action.

(ii) *Practical education* relates to the noumenal world of freedom, autonomy and moral action. From the categorical imperative he has given us a list of duties to ourselves and to others. He has argued that one has the duty to acquire good will, to seek one's own perfection (natural and moral) and to promote the happiness of others. Certain skills and forms of development in the pupil are necessary for this. An important task of education is to help the pupil attain these skills and the character required to fulfil duty. "Man," he writes in *On Education*, "must develop his tendency towards the good. Providence has not placed goodness ready formed in him, but merely as a tendency and without the distinction of moral law. Man's duty is to improve himself: to cultivate his mind; and, when he finds himself going astray, to bring the moral law to bear upon himself" (Kant, 1970, p.182).

(h) **The Five Tasks of Education:** Kant outlines the following five tasks of education:

(i) *NURTURE:* This is essentially the responsibility of parents during the child's infancy. It involves nursing, feeding, caring for and protecting the child. It seeks to maintain life and ensure healthy bodily development.

(ii) *DISCIPLINE:* This is concerned to correct faults, prevent the acquisition of bad habits, restrain unruliness, and keep the will free from domination by the desires. Generally, its aim is to ensure that man's animality does not interfere with the development of his humanity.

In the early years it is necessary for the child to follow rules and orders, even when he is unable to comprehend the reasons behind the rules. As he grows older and is better able to think for himself, there should be a gradual progress towards freedom. He will still be obedient, but by then it will not be to his master's command but to duty. Hence, discipline is *external* in the early stages and *internalised* at a later stage. "Obedience is twofold ... obedience to his master's commands and obedience to what he feels to be a good and reasonable will. In the first stage obedience should be mechanical; at a later stage moral" (p. 194).

(iii) *CULTURE:* This involves the acquisition of certain skills including:

(1) *bodily skills* relating to:

- voluntary movements, for example, running, jumping, swimming;
- use of sense organs, for example, measuring the distance between objects.

With young children some "free" methods involving play and, games may be employed, for example, spinning tops, cutting a reed to make musical instruments and flying kites. Throwing games, he argues, are good for developing the power of sight. However, he is very clear that education cannot be permanently based on play and refers to the suggestion of some progressives that all education should be made entertaining as "an utterly preposterous notion". "A child," he says, "must play, must have his hours of recreation; but he must also learn to work" (p. 188). Nor can all education be based on the interests of the child as some progressive educators have contended.

(2) *skills of perseverance*, for example, putting off present desires in order to achieve some other object or to acquire another skill at a later date. This also involves endeavour and thoroughness, dispositions which must become an important part of the character.

(3) *mental skills:* In *The Critique of Pure Reason* he argues that the mind is active, shaping information gained by the senses through the use of the "forms" of space and time and the categories of causality and substance. In this way man comes to know the phenomenal world.

He accepts the doctrine of formal mental training and believes in the possibility of "transfer of training". Certain mental powers like memory, attention, and anticipation can be developed by appropriate mental exercises. "The general cultivation of the mental faculties ... aims at skill and perfection, and has not for its object the imparting of any particular knowledge, but the general strengthening of the mental faculties" (p. 191).

Kant distinguishes lower and higher powers of the mind:

- Lower powers include cognition, imagination, sense perception, attention and memory.
- Higher powers are:

  - UNDERSTANDING, the faculty that develops knowledge of the general;

  - JUDGEMENT, the application of the general to the particular;

  - REASON: This is the overall power of understanding the connection between the general and the particular. It is through reason that we acquire an insight into principles (p. 192). This may be theoretical or practical (relating to noumena). Theoretical reason cannot be used in determining the nature of noumena.

Kant establishes seven principles for the development of the cognitive faculties:

(A) A certain amount of drill, memorisation and rote learning as well as practice and application is necessary. "What is learnt in a mechanical way is best retained by the memory, and in a great many cases this way is indeed very useful" (p. 190).

(B) Subject matter should be structured and presented at the level of the pupil. "Children should be taught only those things which are suited to their age" (p. 197).

(C) Children must learn the difference between knowledge on the one hand and opinion and belief on the other (p. 191).

(D) Knowledge should be related where possible to application and practice. "In teaching children we must seek insensibly to unite knowledge with the carrying out of that knowledge into practice" (p. 191). Education will, therefore, often involve activity: "The best way of cultivating the mental faculties is to do ourselves all that we wish to accomplish; for instance, by carrying out into practice the grammatical rule which we have learnt. We understand a map best when we are able to draw it out for ourselves. The best way to understand is to do" (p. 193).

(E) The lower cognitive skills are to be developed for the sake of the higher. Thus, memory, imagination and the other mental skills should be developed to promote understanding, judgment and reason. Learning and memory without judgment, he argues, are valueless. A man who has a good memory but no judgment is merely a walking dictionary (p. 189). "Memory must be cultivated early, but we must be careful to cultivate understanding at the same time" (p. 190).

(F) Certain subjects should be included in the curriculum as they are helpful in developing specific mental faculties:

> History is "an excellent means of exercising the understanding in judging rightly" (p. 190).
>
> Languages may help cultivate memory, though conversation methods are preferable (p.190).
>
> Mathematics is useful for putting theory into practice (p. 191).
>
> Novel reading is condemned as it "weakens the memory. For it would be ridiculous to remember novels in order to relate them to others. Therefore all novels should be taken away from children" (p. 190).

(G) Reason is best developed by Socratic questioning. This questioning involves:

> - elenchus, examination or cross-questioning of the pupil on the part of the teacher in order to strip away all false beliefs in the pupils' mind;
>
> - motivation on the part of the learner to find the truth;
>
> - maieutice techne or "mental midwifery". Through further questioning the teacher helps the learner to arrive at the truth.

(4) vocational skills: Kant says little about these beyond the comment that "men need the training of school teaching or instruction to develop the ability necessary to success in the various vocations of life. School teaching bestows upon each member an individual value of his own" (p. 185).

(5) *aesthetic skills:* In *The Critique of Judgment* he states that artistic genius is a worthwhile skill, but it "is a talent for producing that for which no definite rule can be given" (Kant, 1892, p. 189). As much learning involves imitation and as aesthetic genius requires originality, it is, he feels, difficult to see any means by which it can be taught. This is equally true of aesthetic taste, which is basically innate. Any type of education which sought to develop it would involve example and practice before instruction.

(iv) *PRUDENCE:* This is the quality which will enable a person to fit into society. It involves good manners, courtesy, and the ability to control one's temper and other passions without being apathetic. Other aspects of prudence are bravery and the tendency to be good-natured, cheerful and sociable.

The chief methods for inculcating prudence are *instruction*, for example, what constitutes good manners and the duties of citizenship, and *guidance*, helping the pupil to apply knowledge to the practical situation.

(v) *MORAL TRAINING:* This, he writes, must form a key part of education. "It is not enough that a man shall be fitted for any end, but his disposition must be so trained that he shall choose none but good ends - good ends being those which are necessarily appraised by everyone and which may at the same time be the aim of everyone" (Kant, 1970, p. 183). This requires:

(1) *the development of dispositions preliminary to and essential for morality* for example, self-reliance, individuality, independence, the ability to exercise free will, autonomy, and the disposition to act on principles or maxims arrived at after thought and reflection.

(2) *the development of good will*, the disposition to choose only good ends. This involves consciousness of duty in accordance with the moral law.

(3) *the development of dispositions associated with the moral life:* He refers to self-mastery, control of the passions, which entails endurance, bravery, self-denial, patience (having the courage to persevere in the face of adversity), humility (but not servility), respect for persons, and the disposition to treat others as ends and not as means. Honesty, fidelity, friendship and gratitude are also important.

Three main educational methods are recommended to achieve these ends:

(A) *lecturing* - the "dogmatic method".

(B) *questioning* which involves the Socratic paradigm, placing emphasis on the pupil's freedom and positive thought, and *catechism* in which the teacher puts a moral question before the pupil, lets him reply and confirms the answer, if correct. If it is not accurate, the educator provides the appropriate response which the pupil memorises. Reasons must be given once the pupil has reached the stage to appreciate them. Various types of casuistic questions may be put, for example: "A man has a certain debt to pay today, but he sees another man in sore need, and, moved with pity, gives him the money which belongs of right to his creditor. Is this right or wrong?" Questions of this type, he contends, exercise reason and provide moral instruction.

(C) *examples of dutiful actions*, provided that the focus of interest is the action and not the person. Examples may be culled from biography and history but not from novels. "... by comparing similar actions under various circumstances, (the teacher) can begin to exercise the moral judgment of (his) pupils in marking the greater or less moral significance of the actions" (Kant, 1956, p. 158). In *The Doctrine of Virtue* he argues that good examples should not serve as a model, but only as a proof that it is really possible to act in accordance with duty. Bad examples should serve as a warning. In discussing all examples the usual questions will be whether the action was in accordance with a moral principle. If it was, the pupil is asked about the underlying principle and the extent to which the action was performed for the sake of duty. The teacher should serve as an example of moral excellence himself.

VI: IDEALISM AND ITS OPPONENTS

(a) **Idealism and Education:** Kant's ideas were further developed by the German Idealist philosophers Johann Gottlieb Fichte (1762-1814) and Georg Friedrich Hegel (1770-1831). Fichte was concerned with the role and organisation of education in his *Addresses to the German Nation* and his *Aphorisms on Education*. Hegel also discussed education and the state in *Philosophy of Right*.

German Idealism began to emerge in Great Britain as a systematic philosophy in the 1860's and 1870's, mainly through the work of a group of scholars at Balliol College, Oxford, for example, Benjamin Jowett (1817-1897), translator of Plato's dialogues, and, above all, Thomas Hill Green (1836-1882), author of the *Prolegomena to Ethics* and *Lectures on the Principles of Political Organisation*.

From 1870 to about 1920 Idealism was a philosophy of great importance in Britain. Certain of its tenets were in harmony with the philosophy of the Liberal Party. R.B. Haldane (1856-1928), a member of the Liberal governments of Campbell-Bannerman and Asquith (1905-1915), studied in Germany and wrote extensively on Idealist philosophy. Many of the educational reformers and administrators of the period were connected with Balliol and were influenced by Green's ideas, for example, Arthur Acland (1847-1926), Vice-President of the Committee of Council for Education from 1892 to 1895 and Chairman of the Consultative Committee to the Board of Education from 1900 until 1916, Michael Sadler (1861-1943), Director of the Education Department's Office of Special Inquiries from 1895 until 1903, James Bryce (1838-1922), Chairman of the Royal Commission on Secondary Education in 1894-1895, Robert Morant (1863-1920), Permanent Secretary to the Board of Education over the period 1903 to 1911, and H.A.L. Fisher, President of the Board of Education from 1917 until 1922.

Idealism accepts a law-abiding universe dependent upon the perception of mind. Man possesses consciousness, a spiritual quality, which confers reality upon the non-spiritual world of nature and objects. This is a reproduction of an eternal consciousness which may be equated with God, the Absolute Mind, or Spirit, which is striving to develop itself to the full. We should accordingly develop our spiritual consciousness as part of the self-realisation of the eternal consciousness. This may be done by:

(i) *education*, which is seen to a great extent as the process by which man identifies himself with the Absolute Mind. All obstructions should be removed which hinder the development of human consciousness. Education must therefore be available to all.

(ii) *participation in the work of the state which serves as an intermediary between God and man.*

Whereas Fichte and Hegel took an elitist view of the state, Green and the British Idealists tended towards egalitarianism, arguing for a unified educational system in which each individual is able to receive an education according to his or her capacity.

A fuller account of Idealism and its impact upon educational thinking is given by Gordon and White (1979).

(b) **The Decline of Idealism:** Idealism and the optimism of the Enlightenment were challenged by a number of factors in the Twentieth Century. The belief in human progress was difficult to maintain in the light of the carnage of two world wars, genocide, global pollution and uncertainty about the future. Specific modes of thought which challenged conventional Idealism were:

(i) *Marxism*: This grew out of Idealism as Karl Marx (1818-1883) applied certain of Hegel's theories to the sphere of economics and politics. World history is seen to develop in a certain direction as the result of economic forces. Since the early period of "primitive communism" most men have been oppressed by others. Slavery in the Ancient World is an example. At a certain stage of development capitalist society will be overthrown in revolution and there will ultimately be a classless society in which all contribute according to their capacity and are rewarded according to their needs. Education is seen as an important tool in stimulating this revolution.

Paulo Freire's *Pedagogy of the Oppressed* (1972) is a statement of Marxist philosophy in the field of education. Writing in the context of the Third World, he argued that injustice, exploitation, oppression and violence dehumanise many people, who have been indoctrinated to believe in their inferior position. Their only hope of liberation is through an education which enables them to perceive reality objectively and to strip away the myths created by their oppressors, for example, that the oppressors are racially or biologically superior or that God has ordained their position. This Freire calls the process of *conscientisation*. The process of education must also motivate them to act upon this conscientisation.

(ii) *Existentialism*: Associated with such figures as Soren Kierkegaard (1813-1855), Friedrich Nietzsche (1844-1900), Martin Heidegger (1889-1976), Jean-Paul Sartre (1905-1980), Martin Buber (1878-1965), Paul Tillich (1886-1965) and Karl Barth (1886-1968), Existentialism enjoyed a degree of popularity in a Europe dominated by two world wars. It stresses the precariousness of life, realisation of which gives man a sense of dread (angst). The religious assumptions within the Idealism of Green were challenged by Nietzsche, who in *Thus Spoke Zarathustra* proclaims the death of God (Nietzsche, 1969, p. 41, p. 104). In the view of Existentialists there are no set values in the world; we create our own values. Man should plan an authentic existence, being aware of his freedom to choose the values according to which he will live and displaying a sense of caring and responsibility for his actions.

Existentialists protest against conformity and the mass society. They emphasise the dignity of the individual and argue for an education in which the humanities and creative arts form the cornerstone and in which opportunities are provided for contemplation of values and self-expression. The sciences which objectify man are seen to be of lesser importance (Morris, 1966).

(iii) *Freudian psychology*: With its emphasis upon the subconscious, the psychology of Sigmund Freud (1856-1939) challenged the view that human behaviour is the product of rational thought along the line argued by Enlightenment thinkers.

(iv) *Pragmatism*: Pragmatism developed in the later Nineteenth and early Twentieth Centuries and is associated with the American thinkers Charles Sanders Peirce (1839-1914), William James (1842-1910) and John Dewey (1859-1952). It is a philosophy which denies the existence of universal truths. Knowledge is rooted in human experience and is acquired from man's interaction with the environment. Dewey asserts that in order to attain knowledge and to ascertain the truth a person needs to follow the scientific processes of examining data, forming hypotheses, anticipating the consequences of each when implemented, and testing these hypotheses in action. Conclusions are drawn on the basis of observation and the correlation of the actual with the anticipated consequence. He writes: "That which guides us truly is true – demonstrated capacity for such guidance is precisely what is meant by truth .. The hypothesis that works is the *true* one; and *truth* is an abstract noun applied to the collection of cases, actual, foreseen and desired, that receive confirmation of their consequences" (Dewey, 1921, pp. 128-129).

In accordance with the philosophy of Pragamatism, Dewey believes that education should be based upon activity and scientific method. He refers to the concepts of *interaction* and *continuity*. By *interaction* he means the coming together of the objective world and the internal condition of the pupil. The pupil is confronted with some experience which is suited to his ability and capacity. He does not regard it as an intrusion disconnected from his real concerns and attended to only by a reluctant effort of will power. Such interaction will guarantee that he will find something of value in the experience. The principle of interaction requires the educator to have a sympathetic understanding of the learner, noting that children in different environments have different types of experience. For example, the child from the city slum tenement has a different type of experience from the child reared in the cultured home or the country. The teacher must select from the environment only those experiences which have value and are conducive to growth. (Dewey, 1938, p. 40).

Continuity demands that the experiences offered must be fruitful in opening up more and richer possibilities of experience. The pupil will want to move to further problems and additional worthwhile activities. "When and only when development in a particular line conduces to continuing growth does it answer to the criterion of education as growing" (Dewey, 1938, p. 36). For example, when the young child learns to read he opens up great possibilities for further learning in a multitude of subjects. Conversely, if a child is over-indulged, an attitude is created in which he expects people to gratify his desires and caprices in the future. Such experience renders him incapable of applying himself and persevering in order to overcome obstacles. Indeed, the wrong experiences in the chain of continuity can operate "so as to leave a person arrested on a low plane of development, in a way which limits later capacity for growth" (Dewey, 1938, pp. 37-38).

Dewey's system of education is essentially heuristic and scientific. It should begin with the presentation by the teacher of some problem which is within the capacity of the learners and is such that it arouses interest and an active quest for new ideas. The method employed for solving the problem must involve purposeful action and intelligent thought. The Pragmatic method is especially recommended by Dewey "as the pattern and ideal of intelligent exploration and exploitation of the potentialities inherent in experience" (Dewey, 1938, p.86). This means in practice that:

(1) Detailed observation and study of the problem is undertaken. Similarities to and differences from other experiences through which the learner has passed are carefully noted. An example is given in the Plowden Report (Central Advisory Council for Education [England], 1967, pp. 245-247) of a group of children who are puzzled because a block of polystyrene feels warm to the hand.

(2) Possible solutions to the problem are listed and hypotheses are formed. Two hypotheses are formulated in the example given in the Plowden Report:

- Polystyrene produces heat.

- The heat the children feel is reflected from their hands.

(3) The hypotheses are tested by action. The anticipated consequences are compared with the actual consequences of the experiments.

(4) Hypotheses not proving effective are disregarded. Those in which the anticipated consequences correspond with the actual consequences are accepted as correct. In the example cited, the pupils drill a hole in the polystyrene cube, insert a thermometer within it and hang another thermometer outside. The thermometers have the same reading. The first hypothesis – that polystyrene produces heat - is, therefore, ruled out. To test the second hypothesis – that the heat experienced is reflected from their hands - the children hang two thermometers near a heat source. One is shielded by a sheet of polystyrene, while the other has nothing to protect it from the heat. The pupils observe that the thermometer shielded by the polystyrene has a much lower reading than the other. Hence, they conclude that the second hypothesis is confirmed and that polystyrene is an insulator which throws heat back.

Unlike some of the supporters of an education based upon science, Dewey stresses that the past should not be ignored and that subjects like history, classics and literature ought not to be excluded from the curriculum. As the individual relies on past experience in his lifetime to plan present courses of action, so many of the issues of social life today may be resolved with reference to the past (Dewey, 1938, p.77). For example, discussion of political and economic issues requires some knowledge of their historical origins.

Dewey's ideology had an impact upon educational thinking in England and Wales. The 1931 Hadow Report (Consultative Committee to the Board of Education, 1931) stressed that the curriculum should be thought of "in terms of activity and experience, rather than of knowledge to be acquired and facts to be stored" (p. 93 and p. 139) and made specific reference to the work of John Dewey. (p. 93). Moreover, his philosophy brought about change in the teaching of a number of subjects, for example, Latin where the course book *Latin for Today*, which first appeared in Britain in 1934, directly utilised his heuristic methodology. Further examples of the Pragmatic approach in other subjects, for example, English literature and art, are given by Ernest Bayles (1966, pp. 109-140).

VII: SCIENCE, EVOLUTION AND CLASSICAL HUMANISM

(a) **Science and Evolution:** In the Nineteenth Century a number of British educators attacked the dominance of the classics in the curriculum and argued for an education which would be based upon "useful" subjects, of which science was deemed to be paramount. Factors influencing this thinking were:

(i) *the industrial revolution (circa* 1780-1850), which led to a greater demand for a knowledge of science and technology that could not be provided in the traditional classical curriculum. Thus Sir Thomas Wyse (1791-1862) in *Educational Reform* (1837) complained that pupils were fed on "the dry husks of ancient learning, when they should be taking sound and substantial food from the great treasury of modern discovery."

(ii) *the philosophy of Utilitarianism* associated with Jeremy Bentham (1748-1832) , James Mill (1773-1836) and John Stuart Mill (1806-1873). Good, it is argued, consists of whatever increases the happiness of the greatest number. Thus, John Mill believes that the aim of education is to render the individual happy both in himself and in his relations with others. A wide or liberal education is one way of achieving this end. In an address to the students of St. Andrew's University he states that the function of higher education is to offer its students a broad and general education with a balance between the classics and science.

(iii) *the theory of evolution*, which gave great impetus to the agnostic movement and encouraged some writers to advocate a curriculum based primarily on the sciences. In November 1859 Charles Darwin's *On the Origin of Species* was published. The theory of evolution had been discussed for some twenty years before, but Darwin presented a coherent account backed by evidence that it should be considered seriously. Evolution in its most fundamental terms means the unfolding or development of the complex from simpler forms. The basis of the theory is that human origins can be explained by the same natural laws of variation, selection and evolution that apply to all other living forms. Hence, it is claimed, all living species, plants, animals and men, originally sprang from less developed forms of life. They have evolved organs and faculties for life to fit the environment in which they happen to live.

Darwin refers to a "struggle for existence" carried on by living creatures both with the environment and with each other. He defines the term as the "dependence of one being on another, including … not only the life of the individual but success in leaving progeny" (Darwin, 2004, p. 1). It was Herbert Spencer (1820-1903) who coined the phrase "survival of the fittest". Only those creatures survive which possess the armour appropriate for the struggle. The process by which the unfit are eliminated Darwin calls "natural selection". Species evolve and through the principle of heredity transmit these life-preserving organs to later generations. It would, therefore, appear that the ultimate end imposed by nature is life.

Life according to Spencer is a process of perpetual adjustment, as man continually adapts his own nature to be able to cope better with his environment. On the basis of this evolutionary philosophy he endeavours to construct a theory of ethics. Man, he argues, is able to change and adapt to circumstances. He is especially able to change from a savage state to a civilised way of life, repressing selfishness and exhibiting such traits as benevolence and justice, which are derived from the principle of sympathy. Moral rules are those which ensure the development of a harmonious and civilised way of life. His theory of social evolution has elements of hedonism in it, as he argues that under the laws of evolution those actions we find pleasurable are those which have survival value.

(b) **Evolution and Education:** Whereas Darwin is concerned essentially with the scientific aspects of the theory, Spencer applies it to education. He believes that the scientific method is the only road to knowledge. It will ultimately yield universal laws or principles explaining the world in which we live. Causal laws underlie all experience and naturalistic analogies can be drawn between societies and organisms. Both, it is argued, are governed by inherent laws of development and evolution. The individual is seen as part of the social organism and is located within a social context. Science and nature are placed at the centre of all experience. This results in a materialistic philosophy revealed in the belief that social progress and individual well-being depend upon material factors. Scientific laws not only describe but *prescribe*; they underlie moral as well as material order.

Spencer accepts the doctrine of progress and takes a deterministic view of the development of society. He is optimistic that natural laws are good and will lead to the improvement of society. Thus, in *Education: Intellectual, Moral and Physical* he writes that "the laws to which we must submit are both inexorable and beneficent. ... in conforming to them, the process of things is ever towards a greater perfection and a higher happiness" (Spencer, 1878, p. 57). Utopia is indeed achievable. Relations between members of a state will improve and the differences between nations will disappear, thus making war a thing of the past. This will happen as evolution will gradually remove the opposition between individual and social good. Ultimately, as nature's end (life) and man's end (pleasure) move into harmony, "pleasure will eventually accompany every mode of action demanded by social conditions".

(c) **Science, Evolution and the Curriculum:** The following are the principles underlying the curriculum advocated by Spencer:

(i) *Curricular aims*: His overall aim is defined as preparation for complete living. "To prepare us for complete living is the function which education has to discharge" (p.9). What is involved in this "human life"? He lists in order of importance the activities which he feels constitute human life:

- those which directly minister to self-preservation, for example, personal safety;

- those which indirectly minister to self-preservation, for example, earning a living;

- those having for their end the rearing and discipline of offspring, for example, education for parenthood;

- those which are involved in the maintenance of proper social and political relations. This implies an education in citizenship;

- those which fill up the leisure part of life devoted to the gratification of the tastes and feelings, for example, music, poetry, painting and other leisure activities (pp. 9-12).

(ii) *Classification of knowledge*: Spencer distinguishes three types of knowledge:

- Knowledge of *intrinsic* value, which is universally true, for example, the truths of science ("Chlorine is a disinfectant").

- Knowledge of *quasi-intrinsic* value, for example, knowledge of Greek and Latin which is useful in understanding English. Its value, however, is not universal; it remains only as long as English is a language of communication.

- Knowledge of *conventional* value, that is to say, knowledge which is accepted by society as a result of tradition alone, for example, learning historical facts.

Of these types the first is the most important and valuable.

(iii) *The rejection of "useless" subjects*: He wholeheartedly rejects subjects like the Classics on the grounds that they are mere ornaments which serve no useful purpose. He compares them with the coloured beads and trinkets prized by wild tribes instead of objects of utility. "A boy in nine times out of ten applies his Latin and Greek to no practical purposes" (Spencer, 1878, p.2). Other arts subjects are also eliminated from his curriculum, for example, Italian, German, dancing, singing, drawing and history. "The births, deaths and marriages of kings, and other historic trivialities, are committed to memory, not because of any direct benefits that can possibly result from knowing them; but because society considers them parts of a good education - because the absence of such knowledge may bring the contempt of others" (p.4).

(iv) *Curriculum Content*: Spencer's curriculum has five elements derived from his aims:

(1) KNOWLEDGE AND DIRECT SELF-PRESERVATION: Health education must be the most important area of the curriculum. "As the laws of health must be recognised before they can be fully conformed to, the imparting of such knowledge must precede a more rational living." (p.20). He regrets that Englishmen of his day are more ashamed if they cannot pronounce "Iphigeneia" with the correct accent than if they know nothing about the workings of the human body.

(2) KNOWLEDGE AND INDIRECT SELF-PRESERVATION: He admits that the value of the utilitarian subjects of reading, writing and arithmetic is generally appreciated, but otherwise British education is sadly lacking in an understanding of those subjects which are important in industry and commerce - the areas essential to "indirect self-preservation". He makes a specific plea for a greater emphasis on science. It is vital in the industrial world, and "this order of knowledge, which is in great part ignored in our school courses, is the order of knowledge underlying the right performance of those processes by which civilised life is made possible" (p.21).

Included under the generic heading "science" he discusses: *mathematics, mechanics, physics, chemistry, astronomy, geology, biology* and *social science*.

(3) KNOWLEDGE FOR THE REARING AND DISCIPLINE OF OFFSPRING: This, he argues, relates to a study of the "laws of life": *physiology; psychology;* and *ethics*. In practice, he admits that these should not be pursued in great depth, but education ought to enable people to realise that "the development of children in mind and body follows certain laws; that unless these laws are in some degree conformed to by parents, death is inevitable ... and that only when they are completely conformed

to, can a perfect maturity be reached" (p.38).

(4) KNOWLEDGE FOR CITIZENSHIP: This implies political and social studies, especially *descriptive sociology* or the "natural history of society" (p.41). This again requires the application of science, which can help explain such factors as supply and demand and enable us to understand how men act under given circumstances.

(5) KNOWLEDGE FOR LEISURE ACTIVITIES: He refers to the fine arts, literature and the enjoyments of nature. Their value lies in the pleasure they bring us. Without the arts life would lose half its charm. However, he stresses that these subjects are subordinate to the scientific studies discussed above, which make individual and social life possible.

(d) **Classical Humanism: The Concept of Culture:** In opposition to Spencer and his supporters the Classical Humanists of the Nineteenth Century argued that a study of the Classics undertaken in the right way helps the pupil understand many of the problems of the modern world. In their view the value of the subject lies in its close relationship to such subjects as history, literature, philosophy, ethics and politics. One of the main advocates of Classical Humanism was Matthew Arnold (1822-1888), son of Thomas Arnold, pioneering headmaster of Rugby School from 1828 until 1846. Matthew Arnold took as the starting point for his educational philosophy the concept of culture, which implies the following characteristics:

(i) *It aims at our total perfection*: Perfection, he says, involves the development of our humanity to the full. It is "an internal condition, in the growth and predominance of our humanity proper, as distinguished from our animality" (Arnold, 1978, p.47). This is to be achieved through a study of *all* the types of human experience - "art, science, poetry, philosophy, history, as well as of religion, in order to give a greater fullness and certainty to its solution" (p.48). In such a study a person will be concerned with "the best that has been thought and said in the world", that is to say, the best ideas in literature, science, art, religion, etc.

(ii) *It is a process not an abstract body of knowledge*: Culture is not something which is static or fixed. It is dynamic and developing, leading us in the growth of wisdom and beauty. However, this development is not inevitable; it needs a positive effort on the part of the members of a society. It requires us to examine our ideas and habits in the light of change and to select the best course of advance. In this respect, culture is a technique - a method of approach to problems. The cultured man is one who is able *to apply his learning to the problems of life*.

(iii) *It has social implications*: Culture is essentially concerned with contemporary society. The stock of great ideas derived from culture enables man to analyse social problems and in this way to improve the society in which he lives. It is an instrument of social amelioration.

(e) **Classical Humanism and the Curriculum:** Arnold is very much involved in the controversy about the respective roles of the sciences and the humanities in education, and it influences his thinking about the curriculum:

(i) *Aims*: The chief aim of the curriculum, he believes, is to help man achieve culture for the improvement of society. Knowledge acquired in the educational process will be the basis for action to improve society.

(ii) *Curricular content* should consist of both the humanities, which are concerned with man and his works, and the sciences, which explain the natural world. An education based on one area to the exclusion of the other is incomplete and unbalanced. Arnold is, therefore, a supporter of the concept of the liberal education. In his various writings he offers a justification for the inclusion in the curriculum of a range of subjects:

(1) CLASSICS: He sees the Classics, the science of antiquity, as the subject par excellence for the development of culture. He argues that the Nineteenth Century is a complex and confusing period, leading to despair and *ennui*. Other ages have developed similarly and presented the same problems. It follows that a study of these is instructive in understanding our own age, especially where these ages have left us suitable literature. Fifth Century Athens he takes as an example of this. It was, he says, an era of civil security and toleration in which man exhibited a high degree of rationality, intellectual maturity and refinement of taste. The late Roman Republic and the reign of the emperor Augustus are also worthy of study for this reason.

(2) LITERATURE, for example, French and English literature.

(3) RELIGION, which can be a practical guide to life.

(4) SCIENCE: He clashes with Herbert Spencer over the position of science in the curriculum. Arnold especially disagrees with Spencer's contention that it should be the principal focus of education. He suggests that there are four powers for the elevation of human life: conduct; intellect and knowledge; beauty; and social life and manners. Science lies within the sphere of the second – intellect and knowledge - but it is not likely to contribute so much to the others, which are better developed by means of literature and the humanities.

(f) **Higher Education:** J.H. Newman in his *Idea of a University* (1852) argued that the university should concern itself with the diffusion and extension of knowledge rather than its advancement. Research should be conducted elsewhere. The university should provide a liberal as opposed to a utilitarian education, being concerned with *education* as inward endowment rather than with *training* in a *specific skill*.

(g) **Current Controversies:** The conflict between the supporters of "useful" education and the advocates of a "liberal" education continued long after the Nineteenth Century. Examples are:

(i) *Twentieth Century Government Initiatives*: On 18 October 1976, the Prime Minister, James Calllaghan, in a famous speech given at Ruskin College, Oxford, criticised the work of schools on the grounds that they failed to equip pupils to find suitable employment and that they created unfavourable attitudes towards the processes of wealth creation (DES, 1977, p. 34). Since that time both Conservative and Labour governments have sought to create stronger links between schools and industry. Currently, work-related education has become a major part of the National Curriculum at Key Stage 4 in both England and Wales. In Wales the core of the new Welsh Baccalaureate contains thirty hours of *Work-Related Education* and another thirty hours of *Work Experience*. In 2005 the White Paper 14-19 *Education and*

Skills announced plans for the creation of new vocational qualifications (DFES, 2005a), the first batch of which will be available in 2008.

This is a good example of the "utilitarian" view of education. Education is seen as a process whereby young people can be *trained* in specific skills to meet the needs of British industry. It is, in essence, the means by which skills are provided which will be of *immediate value* to the learner in acquiring employment.

(ii) *Supporters of Humanism*: Not all Twentieth Century educators, however, have accepted that their role should be defined in such narrow utilitarian terms. Rational Humanists like Robert M. Hutchins (1936) and Mark Van Doren (1943) argue for a return to the classical/medieval type of education based upon the *trivium* (grammar, rhetoric and dialectic) and the *quadrivium* (arithmetic, geometry, astronomy and music). They take Aristotle's philosophy as their starting point and argue that the aim of education should be to produce "free men" as opposed to trained technocrats. Certain fixed values exist, knowledge of which is essential for the preservation of civilisation. Their programme of education features a study of the great literary works of the past which will teach these values. Education should be divorced from vocational training.

Much the same sentiment is expressed by Cyril Norwood, Chairman of the Secondary Schools Examination Council, when he argues that the first business of the school is "ever to bear in mind that man cannot live by bread alone". Education, as well as transmitting some "useful knowledge", must ultimately be concerned "with values which are independent of time or particular environment" (Secondary School Examinations Council, 1943, p. viii).

Other writers on the curriculum who have advocated a "liberal" rather than a "utilitarian" education include Paul Hirst, Philip Phenix and Charles Bailey. Their philosophies are discussed in the next paragraphs.

VIII: TWENTIETH CENTURY PHILOSOPHIES OF LIBERAL EDUCATION

(a) **Paul Hirst**, Professor of Education at King's College London from 1965 to 1971 and at the University of Cambridge from 1971, first tackled the question of the nature of knowledge and the implications of his epistemology for the curriculum in 1965 in an essay entitled *Liberal Education and the Nature of Knowledge*. This provoked much response, and in 1974 he published a collection of papers on the topic in his book *Knowledge and the Curriculum*. Debate lasted for many years, and Hirst continued to promote his views on a liberal education into the 1980s when the Conservative government imposed the National Curriculum.

(i) *Analysis of Knowledge*: Hirst is concerned to analyse the nature of knowledge of the verbal or propositional type (knowledge *that* something is the case) rather than knowledge of the practical or procedural type (knowing *how* to do something). He argues that verbal knowledge:

(1) CONSISTS OF ACCUMULATED HUMAN EXPERIENCE which mankind has gathered in the past.

(2) IS ORGANISED IN SOME WAY. It is not just a collection of isolated facts but has some organised structure. It consists of "not collections of information, but the complex way of understanding experience which man has achieved, which are publicly specifiable and which are gained through learning" (Hirst, 1974, p. 38). Again, he writes that "to acquire knowledge is to become aware of experience as structured, organised and made meaningful in some quite specific way" (p. 40).

(3) IS NOT UNITARY BUT IS SUBDIVIDED INTO:

- seven primary *FORMS* which are "logically unique". They cannot be subdivided into any other form. To draw an analogy, they resemble primary colours.

- *FIELDS* which draw together certain forms or depend upon the forms in some other way for their existence. To develop further the analogy of colour, the fields resemble secondary or tertiary colours. They are not limited in number like the forms, and new fields are likely to develop. He says: "I see no reason why such organisations of knowledge, which I refer to as 'fields' should not be endlessly constructed" (p. 46).

(ii) *The Forms of Knowledge*: According to Hirst the following criteria distinguish a form of knowledge:

(1) EACH FORM HAS ITS OWN SPECIAL SET OF CONCEPTS: For example, *gravity*, *acceleration*, *hydrogen* and *photosynthesis* are concepts belonging to science; *number*, *integral* and *matrix* are mathematics concepts; *God*, *sin* and *predestination* are concepts from religion; while *ought*, *good* and *wrong* are ethical concepts.

(2) EACH FORM HAS ITS OWN LOGICAL STRUCTURE: In each form the concepts relate in some way to form meaningful statements. They form a network of possible relationships in which experience can be understood. This means that each form has its own logical structure. For example, science has a different structure from the arts. To transfer a concept from one form of knowledge to another would be to break the logical structure and result in nonsense. For example, a teacher may explain the law of gravity in a physics lesson, but to criticise a Dali painting because the objects in it do not obey the law of gravity would be illogical, because gravity is not part of the structure of the arts.

As D.S. Wringe writes (1976, p.73): "We can say that two plus two equals four. We cannot say that two plus two is sinful. We can say that metals expand when heated. We cannot say that the expansion of metals should never be allowed".

(3) EACH FORM HAS ITS OWN SPECIAL TESTS TO SEE WHETHER A STATEMENT IS TRUE OR FALSE: "Each form," Hirst writes, "has distinctive expressions that are testable against experience in accordance with particular criteria that are peculiar to the form" (p. 44). Thus, in science we test whether something is true or false by carrying out an experiment. The majority of metals expand when heated, and this can be confirmed by observation in an experiment. In mathematics we judge truth by reference to formal axioms and proofs. Pythagoras's theorem is demonstrated with reference to the angle sum of a triangle (proof) and the properties of angles formed by the transverse of parallel lines (axiom). "It is," Hirst says, "by the use of such tests that we have come to have the whole domain of knowledge" (p. 40). In other words, each form has its own unique *validation procedure*.

(4) EACH FORM HAS ITS OWN METHOD OF WORKING IN ORDER TO ACQUIRE NEW KNOWLEDGE: In his early publications on the curriculum he added that each form possesses "particular techniques and skills for exploring experience and testing their distinctive expressions" (p. 44). For example, we have scientific technique and artistic technique. It is difficult to distinguish this from the third criterion, and in *Knowledge and the Curriculum* (pp. 85-86) he no longer emphasised this as a separate distinguishing mark for a form of knowledge.

By the use of these criteria he differentiates the following "logically unique" forms:

- mathematics;
- science;
- history;
- the arts;
- ethics;
- religion;
- the social sciences (Hirst, 1974, p. 45).

Within these forms it is possible to detect different branches, for example, chemistry, physics, biology within science, but, according to Hirst, they are related by having essentially the same type of validation procedure.

(iii) *The Fields of Knowledge*: These secondary classifications of knowledge are of three types:

(1) FIELDS BUILT AROUND SOME SPECIAL PHENOMENA OR PURSUIT AND DRAWING TOGETHER DIFFERENT FORMS. "They are formed by building together round specific objects or phenomena, or practical pursuits, knowledge that is characteristically rooted elsewhere in more than one discipline" (pp. 45-46). They are held together by their subject-matter. Medicine is an example. It is concerned with curing illness and involves:

- science in anatomy and physiology;
- mathematics in quantifying blood pressure and biochemical reactions;
- ethics, for example, debate concerning the prolonging of life and the rights of relatives.

(2) THE APPLICATION OF A FORM TO PRACTICAL PURSUITS: Ethics is a form of knowledge concerned with what is good and bad in human conduct. It is possible to apply ethics to a number of practical issues, and this results in the creation of discrete fields of knowledge. "Political, legal and educational theory are perhaps the clearest examples of fields where moral knowledge of a developed kind is to be found" (p. 46).

(3) SECOND-ORDER DISCIPLINES "which are dependent for their existence on the other primary areas", for example, the study of grammar in order to acquire a language.

(iv) *Implications for Education*:

(1) Hirst's aim of education is the development of the rational mind. He argues that this can be achieved only through mastery of the forms of knowledge, as they represent the prime ways of human thinking. Hence, it follows that they must be the objectives of the curriculum.

(2) All pupils must have the opportunity of meeting these forms of knowledge, whatever their ability. To deny anyone access to the forms is to prevent that person's acquiring the rational mind. In *Knowledge and the Curriculum* he writes that "a liberal education approached directly in terms of the disciplines will thus be composed of the study of at least paradigm examples of all the various forms of knowledge" (p. 48).

(3) Although the forms are the curriculum objectives, it does not follow that they must constitute the actual content or the actual subjects taught (p. 137). Nonetheless, the curriculum must be so organised that it enables the pupils to acquire mastery of each of the forms. This may be done through a combination of forms and fields. English, for instance, is a field which involves arts, ethics and the social sciences. Hirst, therefore, believes that the justification for including any subject in the curriculum is to be argued in terms of its role in helping pupils to understand the basic forms of knowledge.

(4) Because the forms overlap (for example, science uses mathematics) he opposes the compartmentalisation of the traditional grammar school curriculum. He writes that "it emphasises the differences between forms of knowledge, and the many important interconnections between them can be forgotten to the impoverishment of them all" (Hirst 1971, p. 247). He argues for some degree of "shading"; where there are logical links between subjects, we should make them apparent in the curriculum. A class reading works by Shakespeare in English could contemporaneously study the Elizabethan Age in history.

However, he has reservations about curriculum integration where topics are taken like "Water" or "Man and Rivers" on the grounds that they blur the distinctive ways of working of the different forms. How, he asks, can children become aware of forms of knowledge if we take a theme like "Hands" involving such elements as physiognomy, the conditions of employment of factory hands and the religious significance of the laying on of hands? (Hirst, 1971, p. 71). He argues that the topic approach "does not permit content to be aimed so directly at central concepts, and other logically distinct features of the various forms of knowledge" (Hirst, 1971, p. 247). The chief value of integrated studies in his view is to arouse interest and motivation in younger and less able children. Once this interest is aroused, however, it is better to move to a curriculum in which the forms are more clearly differentiated.

(5) In his essay "The Logical and Psychological Aspects of Teaching a Subject" (1967) Hirst argues that in teaching any discipline the teacher must make clear two dimensions if the pupils are to be successful in that subject:

- THE STRUCTURE OF THE SUBJECT, that is to say the interrelation of the concepts (criteria [1] and [2] for a form of knowledge listed above);

- THE WAYS OF WORKING OF THE SUBJECT, that is to say the means of validating new information (criteria [3] and [4] for a form of knowledge shown above).

Accordingly, in learning science it is necessary both to acquire a body of knowledge and to undertake experimentation, while in history it is essential to learn certain facts and also to understand the ways in which historians reach conclusions from a study of documents and artifacts.

(b) Charles Bailey in his book *Beyond the Present and the Particular* (1984) takes a different view of liberal education from Hirst.

(i) *Criteria for Liberal Education*: Liberal education, Bailey argues, involves the following criteria:

(1) It should liberate pupils from the confines of their present socio-economic background and liberate them *for* rational autonomy. It must widen their horizons, make them aware of concepts beyond their immediate experience and way of life, offer hitherto unfamiliar perspectives and uncover prejudices and superstitions. At the same time it should enable them to become free moral agents, able to make rational choices and to select courses of action in an intelligent manner.

(2) Liberal education is less concerned with specific knowledge geared towards the acquisition of a restricted range of skills than with knowledge and understanding which are *fundamental and general* and therefore capable of application in different contexts. By way of illustration Bailey argues that pupils may learn now to make toffee either by following a precise recipe, which would be an illiberal and narrow form of instruction, or by experimentation into the properties of sugar when heated to different temperatures, this latter approach enabling them to grasp basic principles that could be applied to other disciplines such as the sciences.

(3) It should involve intrinsically valued ends. Writers like R. S. Peters (1966) refer to activities conducted in schools and colleges for *extrinsic* ends, that is to say for motives outside the process of education itself, preparation for employment being a classic example. They then distinguish these activities from a liberal education, which is *intrinsically valued* in that it brings pupils into contact with what is considered to be good and worthwhile in its own right. An important element of a liberal education is bringing children to an appreciation of human achievements in such fields as literature, music and the fine arts, which are valued for the qualities they reflect rather than for any specific utilitarian purpose they may serve.

(4) Liberal education involves more than the mastery of isolated forms of knowledge or disjointed facts and information; it implies the criterion of organisation so that pupils are able to comprehend the relationship of the subjects they study, where such connections exist. As the Newsom committee (Central Advisory Council for Education [England],1963) noted, the disciplines in the curriculum may appear as "single pieces of a mosaic"; what matters most is not the numbers and colours of the separate pieces but the pattern they make when put together.

(5) Liberal education seeks to develop the rational mind. Pupils will accept as true only those statements for which there is adequate evidence and good reason.

(ii) *Curriculum Content*: Bailey's curriculum is humanistic in emphasis and concentrates upon a study of human understanding, action, achievements and practices and the limitations imposed upon them by the physical world. It consists of the following aspects:

(1) FORMS OF ENQUIRY CONCERNED WITH HUMAN ACTIVITIES:

- ■ the HUMANITIES PROPER: literature, history, morality and religion.

- ■ the MAKINGS AND PRACTICES OF PERSONS:
  -social and political institutions;
  -economic, industrial and commercial institutions;
  -mathematical and logical systems;
  -religion and morality;
  -art, craft and design;
  -literature and drama;,
  -music and dance;
  -games and physical activities.

(2) FORMS OF ENQUIRY CONCERNED WITH THE PHYSICAL WORLD:
  - the workings of the human body;
  -health and medicine;
  -food and nutrition;
  -the behaviour and ecology of animals and plants;
  -simple technologies;
  -astronomy and cosmology;
  -physical geography and meteorology;
  -resources of energy and usable materials, ecology and conservation.

The emphasis is upon human understanding and action, the principal role of the sciences being to create awareness of the natural world in which pupils live and the restrictions it places upon human endeavours.

(c) **Philip Phenix** (1964) constructs an educational programme around six "realms of meaning", which, he claims, are the fundamental forms of human enquiry. Each of the realms can be subdivided into specific curricular areas:

Realms of Meaning	Curricular Areas
Symbolics (communication verbal and non-verbal)	Language, mathematics and non-discursive symbolic forms
Empirics (the testing of hypotheses)	Physical sciences, life sciences and social sciences
Aesthetics (the exploration of form)	Music, visual art, dance and literature
Synnoetics (insight into human identity and personal relationships)	Philosophy, psychology, literature and religion in their existential aspects
Ethics (standards and values underlying human conduct)	Areas of moral and ethical concern
Synoptics (an organised study of man)	History, religion and philosophy

(d) **Her Majesty's Inspectorate** in 1985 published the document *The School Curriculum From 5 to 16* which proposed a curriculum based upon nine "areas of experience". These were:

Aesthetic and creative	Physical
Human and social	Scientific
Linguistic and literary	Spiritual
Mathematical	Technological
Moral	

IX: POST-MODERNISM

The term *modernism* has been used to describe the period in European history which took its origins from the philosophy of the Enlightenment. As we saw at the beginning of the chapter, this intellectual movement stressed rationality, order and a belief in universal laws and values. Freed from ignorance, man could, by the application of reason, improve his lot. Science was very much a key to the creation of this paradise on earth. In the two centuries following the Enlightenment many people continued to insist that, despite the trials and tribulations suffered by the human race, it was still possible to detect progress in human affairs. Although natural catastrophes occurred together with disasters for which mankind was entirely responsible, these crises could usually be endured and the quality of life improved.

However in the later 1970s this view of society was challenged and a different perspective was adopted by philosophers who spoke of the *post-modernist* era. The term "post-modernism" is controversial and not the easiest to define, for its meaning differs within various contexts and it has become something of a "catch-all" term. Part of the difficulty of defining the concept is the continuing contemporary debate within the movement. Though post-modernism incorporates a "broad-church" of exponents there are certain common themes that run through it. Many who claim to be post-modernists believe that no universal solutions can be found to the problems of mankind. Science has, in practice, failed to provide the answers for which its advocates once hoped, and philosophies like Idealism and Maxism which sought to explain the nature of the world have been no more successful. Further attempts, it is argued, to create an objective account of reality or to establish standards of truth are equally doomed to failure (Harvey, 1990; Anderson, 1998).

In the era of modernism it could be contended that theories and philosophies offered valuable insights into the process of education. The doctrines of writers whose thoughts have been recorded in this chapter – Rousseau, Dewey and Hirst – have certainly been discussed avidly over the years and many of their ideas have been put into practice. In the post-modernist world, the claim that philosophies of this type can provide universal guidance is discounted. Emphasis is placed more upon each individual's own personal theory and view of reality. One man's opinion is as valid as his neighbour's. Efficiency has replaced the search for exact knowledge as the way forward. Moreover, the postmodern teacher and pupil are without a universally acknowledged rational strategy by which it is possible to evaluate a preference in relation to judgments of truth, morality, aesthetic experience or objectivity. The assumption is that we can no longer accept the notion of some common denominator such as "Absolute Mind", "God", "Truth" or "Nature" which guarantees the "unity" of the world or neutral, objective thought. Experiences are being transformed by new technologies and changing world conditions.

Post-moderism also has implications for subjects within the curriculum. For example in art there is a move away from realism and the acceptance of post-modern styles such as "pop art", "conceptual art", video and computer art, and improvisation. In music we see techno-sonic effects and minimalism which incorporates silence. In literature post-modernist developments include the cybernetic, the self-reflexive and the magic-realist novel. In science and religious education the old assumptions about transcendence and the nature of time and space are being questioned. There is also a tendency to cross over and merge traditional disciplines which were once segregated, resulting in, for example, multi-media arts. Indeed, the traditional canon of education is being challenged and eroded (Usher and Edwards, 1994; Edwards, 1997; Giroux, 1997).

Nonetheless, it has to be admitted that most schools are still essentially authoritarian in nature, upholding and reasserting traditional values, which runs counter to the central tenets of post-modernism. The growth of "faith schools" is an example of the assertion of a common "truth" and acceptance of a religious "grand-narrative".

2 Early Childhood Studies

I: INTRODUCTION

Early Childhood Studies (ECS) is a relatively new discipline. When subjects are in their infancy, academics and students have, to a certain extent, the luxury of being able to shape the context and conceptualise theoretical material as they wish. This chapter aims to explore the growing popularity of Early Childhood Studies as an academic discipline and to examine key concepts which make up its content. Especial attention will be paid to historical, philosophical, psychological and sociological aspects of the subject. Recent developments with respect to ECS in England and Wales will also be recounted.

It is interesting to note that there is currently no clear "academic" route for the secondary school student who is interested in this area of the curriculum at A level. This is unfortunate, as a pupil can pursue the subject at GCSE. Nonetheless, a vocational route is available in the form of the Diploma in Childcare and Education (DCE) offered by the Council for Awards Children's Care and Education (CACHE), and, in spite of a lack of an A level route, ECS is becoming a popular choice as a University Degree programme. There are currently many ECS programmes offered in Higher Education Institutions (HEIs) in England and Wales.

Furthermore, ECS is a subject in which everyone has some direct experience. We have all been children and have experienced childhood. We have undergone, as Parker-Rees says, "developmental processes which can easily be taken for granted, because they are so commonplace and because they are so effortlessly achieved" (Willan, Parker-Rees and Savage, 2004, p.11). Childhood is a fleeting time and can be a positive or negative experience dependent on circumstances. The author Frank McCourt (1996, p.1) in the bestselling book of his memoirs, *Angela's Ashes*, recalls his childhood in rural Ireland just before the Second World War: "When I look back on my childhood I wonder how I survived at all. It was, of course, a miserable childhood; the happy childhood is hardly worth your while". Fortunately, childhood in the Twenty First Century is now more widely celebrated and cherished; it is seen as a special period of life. Many children have far greater autonomy, independence and sense of worth than did McCourt. Along with a greater appreciation of this special time, people became sufficiently interested to wish to study it in greater detail.

Educators in many countries today have developed an understanding of the importance of early childhood, realising the necessity to engage with children on their level and to value their contributions to society. An outlook of this type will be beneficial to those children fortunate enough to be experiencing their early years in such a climate and, ultimately, those who are yet to experience it. Unfortunately, there are still children in parts of the world whose existence is a bleak experience. By taking into account the global dimension in relation to the study of ECS a person can gain a more balanced view and appreciation of the lives of young children in other countries in the world. For example, children who suffered in the earthquake that hit northern Pakistan on the 8th of October 2005 are currently being cared for in the Meira refugee camp. According to Save the Children, they "have been offered a gleam of light" through receiving an education - many for the first time (www.savethechildren.org).

There is always an element of challenge in developing a new academic study. When pursuing a fledgling subject and one about which all people feel they know something, the student is offered the opportunity to question previously held perceptions and theories. Modes of thinking can be scrutinised and invigorated. New research or innovative practice in such an area may still be regarded as a novelty, and thus may be better funded by the government, for example. Early Childhood Studies can be classified as an academic discipline which covers a range of some of the more traditional academic subjects such as physiology, biology, psychology, sociology, education, health related studies and social science. One of the first universities to offer a degree in this field was Manchester Metropolitan University. Jones, Holmes and Powell (2005) reflect on the changes they have seen in the last ten years since this degree was first delivered and highlight the multi-professional and multi-disciplinary nature of the courses emerging from university departments of health, social work and education. However, a survey of the programmes offered by different educational institutions reveals that they have alternative ideas on content and delivery, and it is consequently difficult to formulate a clear, fixed definition of what ECS should encompass. Children have different personalities, life experiences and developmental paths, and it is this difference that makes the study of early childhood so challenging and exciting. This chapter aims to provide the reader with an insight into a fascinating and very rewarding subject.

II: HISTORICAL PERSPECTIVES

Childhood has been documented in the works of writers over the course of history, and there is a considerable literature concerning the ways in which children have been perceived and regarded in the past. A study of these records reveals a plethora of interesting perceptions on the ways in which societies at different periods of time have viewed the concept of childhood and the ways in which young children should be reared. Some examples are given here of different historical periods with a summary of some of the trends, views and thoughts on the education of young children. As may be expected there is a lack of consensus concerning the extent to which childhood can be viewed as a cherished time or a far less pleasant preparation for adult life. For a fuller account of historical perspectives on childhood the reader is referred to Hugh Cunningham's *The Invention of Childhood* (2006).

(a) **Greek Thought:** Certain of the precepts of Plato (427-347 BC) and Aristotle (384-322 BC) have a surprisingly modern flavour about them. Plato, for example, stresses the importance of children's learning through games rather than in a more formal manner, while both he and Aristotle are extremely concerned about the environment in which the young are raised. They believe that children are easily influenced by what they see around them and like to imitate the behaviour of others. Hence, a major tenet within their thinking on education is the need to protect young children from harmful and corrupting influences. Thus, Plato seeks to ban from his ideal republic any stories which describe undesirable conduct (Plato, 1974, pp. 129-135), while Aristotle in an interesting discussion of the role of music in education emphasises that only morally acceptable melodies and rhythms should be employed (Aristotle, 1962, pp. 313-316). From the earliest age, he continues, it is imperative that children acquire the "right" habits, for "we become just by performing just actions, temperate by performing temperate actions and brave by performing brave actions" (Aristotle, 1953, p. 56).

(b) **The Roman Period:** Artefacts from the Roman era have provided us with many clues about the life of the Roman child. Roman civilisation lasted for more than 1,200 years, beginning around 750 BC. The longevity of this empire has given us an insight into the daily life of young children. The word *familia*, for example, meant more than just "family" to the Romans; it encompassed the whole household: parents, children, grandparents, servants, slaves and possessions.

The man was the absolute head of the family. A newly born child baby would be laid at its father's feet. If the father chose to pick up the child, it would be accepted into the family; otherwise it was left outside to be either adopted or left to perish. Roman childhood experiences were dependent on status and gender. Boys and girls from wealthy families were often taught at home by private tutors. Poor children did not receive an education and were set to work as soon as they were old enough. Girls learned how to manage a house and were deemed available for marriage from twelve years of age.

(c) **Medieval Europe:**

(i) *Archaeological Evidence*: Evidence acquired by archaeologists can provide us with some clues about the life of children in the past, though details of early childhood are more difficult to detect. In 866 the Northumbrian city of Jorvik, now more commonly known as York, had been captured by a marauding Viking army. The Vikings left a good archaeological legacy behind and we can glean some information concerning the life of Viking children from this. At this time there was a high peri-natal mortality, and much evidence has to be acquired from contemporary documents. Archaeologists in Jorvik found little evidence to suggest that children of this period had specific toys. It is thought that they amused themselves by play acting or participating in mock battles. King Alfred wrote in the 880s that children rode on their sticks and played many games in imitation of adults.

Viking children helped their parents in household tasks, farming and acquiring life skills. They did not receive formal education as such, but were taught fighting skills. Indeed, evidence from the time of King Cnut in the early Eleventh Century indicates that children over the age of twelve fought in battles.

(ii) *Historical Documentation*: A survey of historical documentation has led to debate about the actual length or period of childhood. Leyser (1995) looks at medieval theories on the upbringing of children and recounts the views of the scholar Isidore of Seville (*circa* 560-636) that "an individual was an infant until age of seven, a child until fourteen, and an adolescent – or more accurately, youth – until twenty-eight." Children of whatever category were not held in very high regard in medieval times. As Leyser points out, "until they were seven years old, children were considered both to lack moral reasoning and to be in need of particularly close attention" (p.133).

Medieval children from wealthy families were not expected to have a close family relationship; they were usually entrusted into the care of nuns or a foster home at an early age to undertake their education. Poor children of this time were mostly brought up in the family environment where they would be expected to undertake various tasks, which would depend on their circumstances. Many children worked in difficult and often dangerous situations.

Often ideas about the rearing of children were derived from the Bible and classical authors. One Franciscan scholar of the Thirteen Century, John of Wales, offered parents advice on the upbringing of the young and made frequent reference to such authors as Aristotle, Cicero, Seneca, Valerius Maximus, Quintilian, and Saints Jerome and Augustine. Children, he proclaimed, should love, obey and honour their parents, helping them if they should fall into poverty. Other writers on the upbringing of young children like Saint Anselm (1033-1109) utilised their own experiences and memories of childhood (Cunningham, 2006, pp.29-33).

(d) **Eighteenth and Nineteenth Centuries:** Children who were born into wealthy families invariably had a more comfortable existence. However, for all children in the Eighteenth Century life was hard. Poor children had little time for play, though most of the games in which they engaged had remained much the same for centuries. These were based on experiences such as clapping, hopping or using natural materials such as sticks and stones. Picard (2000) examines childhood at this time and compares the experiences of different social classes. Children from wealthy families did have access to toys, though these were mostly home- made, until "in 1760 William Hamley saw the market potential of toys for the better off, and opened a shop called *The Noah's Ark* in Holborn, selling rag dolls and tin soldiers, hoops and wooden horses"(Picard, 2000, p.174). Stories from books often served as the motivation for children's games. For example, Thomas Bewick, who was born in 1753, recalled how in imitation of the natives described in *Robinson Crusoe* "I often, in the morning, set off stark naked across the Fell where I was joined by some associates, who in like manner, ran about like mad things" (Cunningham, 2006, p. 123).

Poor children of this era were most often used as a cheap and replaceable labour force. They were regarded as a commodity, especially when they were able to earn money to bring into the household. Before the advent of good hygiene and modern birth control techniques life expectancy for children was limited. We can examine birth and death rates in England and Wales by analysis of parish registers, and find that in the period 1750 to 1809 life expectancy was forty-one years. Male children had a sixty-nine per cent chance of surviving from birth to fifteen, and females had slightly better odds with seventy-one per cent living to this age. By the late 1990s life expectancy had increased to seventy-three years for males and seventy-nine for females. Both had a ninety-nine per cent chance of surviving from birth to the age of fifteen (Wrigley, 1997). In large cities boys could find themselves apprenticed to a trade, and girls were used as domestic help, maids, or child minders. Boys in the Eighteenth Century also worked on ships or were enrolled into the navy. They would be employed in a variety of occupations, many of which involved risk to life and limb. In 1805, boys as young as ten served at the battle of Trafalgar.

Many poor children's ultimate destination was the workhouse. This was the scourge of the poor. From 1732 paupers had to go into the workhouse if they were to receive any benefits. Homeless or abandoned children were also admitted. Families were split up on entry, as men and women had to live separately. Although technically "inmates" were entitled to be paid for their endeavours, corruption was rife. The Reverend William Bromley conducted an investigation into affairs at St Pancras workhouse in 1803. Waller (2005, p.40) describes how he found "systematic fraud going back years. The twopence in every shilling earned to which the inmates were entitled seldom reached their pockets."

Mortality rates for children living in the workhouse were exceptionally high. Nearly half of infants died before their second birthday. Charles Dickens describes the predicament of Oliver Twist on his entry to the workhouse, referring to "the hungry and destitute situation of the infant orphan" (1859, p. 3). The workhouse system existed in England and Wales until 1930.

Increasing industrialisation was a major development of the Victorian era. Children were employed as chimney sweeps or "climbing boys" as they were more commonly known. The younger and smaller the boy, the more employable he was. Children in 1800s were, of course, much smaller than they are today. Robinson (2005, p.99) compares the average ten year old in 1836 who was 125 cm tall with the average ten year old in 2005 who is 140 cm tall. The average width of a Victorian chimney was a claustrophobic eighteen centimetres and the sweep would often light the fire at the bottom of the chimney to encourage the boy to climb to the very top. In 1875 one eleven-year-old boy, George Brewster, died of suffocation while sweeping chimneys (Cunningham, 2006, p. 156).

The Poor Law legislation of 1834, although an influential piece of legislation, contributed to harsher conditions for poor children. One of the motives underlying the legislation was the concept of "less eligibility" by virtue of which the poor might receive help only if they entered the workhouse, but workhouse conditions had to be harsher than the outside world, the rationale for this being that working had always to be seen as preferable to existing on handouts from the state. Parents were legally enforced to provide for children rather than abandon them, which was common practice at the time. Children were admitted to workhouses under the legislation if they were orphaned or destitute. The law also empowered the authorities in the form of the local parish to provide employment through the workhouse system for children who had no parents to support them.

Social reform was gradually improving the lives of children, but this was to be a slow process. In 1868 the Agricultural Gangs Act prohibited children younger than eight from working on farms. However, this practice still occurred. As late as the 1930s it was still common for families, usually from the industrial cities, to spend six weeks hop picking in Kent. Even very young children helped, working up to twelve hours a day.

The first nursery school in the United Kingdom was set up in 1816 at New Lanark in Scotland by Robert Owen (1771-1858), a philanthropist and social reformer. Owen's project in New Lanark included an infant school, a crèche for the babies of women mill workers and free medical care. His ideas were based on plans for a progressive and enlightened system of education.

The 1870 Education Act was pivotal in that it established elementary schooling for all children, and under further legislation in 1880 this provision was made compulsory for the age range five to thirteen. Moreover, children younger than five were often admitted to schools to protect them from harsh conditions on the streets. Nonetheless, these provisions sometimes had unforeseen consequences as many children under the age of five met with accidents or even death because their elder brothers and sisters were no longer able to care for them. In 1905 the Board of Education ruled that children under the age of five who attended elementary schools should have separate facilities and separate teaching.

(e) **The Development of Nursery Schooling:** In 1911 the McMillan sisters set up an open-air nursery for poor slum children in Deptford. Margaret McMillan (1860-1931) was a committed Christian Socialist who was horrified by the conditions in which working class children were being brought up. She also began to advise parents on hygiene, nutrition, health and education for their children. The Deptford centre included a clinic and remedial gymnasium, which emphasised exercise and outdoor activities. McMillan strongly believed that children needed to be healthy in order for them to learn effectively. The Rachel McMillan Nursery was established in 1917 with places for a hundred children. The rationale of the nursery was the need to spend time outdoors in the health-giving fresh air.

McMillan looked at the link between the home and the nursery environment. She was also aware of the impact of the local community as a major contributor to the child's development and education. She had a very strong social conscience, and recorded her educational philosophy at length in *The Nursery School* (1919). Her views such as the importance of working closely with parents and the effects of positive parenting were ahead of her time.

During the Second World War day nurseries operated on a large scale to enable women to work and thus to support the war effort. Kwon (2002) looks at the role that the Local Education Authority (LEA) nursery schools had in relation to promoting the educational value of play and nursery education. However, decreases in family size in the 1960s resulted in the closure of many maintained day nurseries and Kwon notes that it was "impossible for LEAs to increase the number of nurseries, because the Ministry of Education Circular 8/60 stated that there should be no expansion of nursery school provision" (p.3). Riley (1979, pp. 82-108), on the other hand, feels that Government policy at that time was concerned with the "reconstruction of the family".

Nonetheless, the early 1960s witnessed expansion in the non-maintained sector. The first pre-school playgroups were established around this time. Mothers who were at home with their children wanted to socialise outside the family home with other mothers and their children. The origin of the play group movement may be traced to the endeavours of a young mother called Belle Tutaev who along with a neighbour began a play group in a church hall in London in 1961. In 1972 the White Paper entitled *Education: A Framework for Expansion* (Department for Education and Science [DES], 1972) was published by the then Conservative government. It advocated the provision of nursery education for all who wanted it, though the economic difficulties facing Great Britain during the 1970s meant that this ideal was not realised. During the next two decades nursery and pre-school education continued to be underfunded and was not developed very extensively in many LEAs.

More recently, two significant reports have looked at the benefits of providing children with high quality early years education and care. The Rumbold Report, *Starting with Quality* (DES, 1990), and the Royal Society of Arts Report *Start Right* (Ball, 1994) stressed the benefits of partnership with parents. These documents highlighted the importance of parents' involvement in the education of their children, and in the 1990s initiatives such as the Charter for Parents further encouraged this trend (DES, 1991 and 1994).

III: PHILOSOPHICAL PERSPECTIVES

(a) **The Holistic Dimension:** There is a wealth of published material on child development which takes a philosophical viewpoint. As Wood writes, "theories about how children think and learn have been put forward and debated by philosophers, educators and psychologists for centuries" (Wood, 1988, p. 1). As a consequence, there are many valuable and interesting philosophies and theories, and it is difficult to decide which should be included in this chapter. Only a small selection can be cited here, and the principal rationale for the choice is their advocacy of a "holistic" dimension in child development. This emphasis on valuing the "whole child" runs through the ideas mooted by these educational philosophers.

When studying childhood, the perceptive student will realise that there are many ideas which seem to recur or be re-packaged in some way. Ideas on educating young children can drift in and out of fashion. It is also true that often there is nothing new under the sun as this next section demonstrates. The philosophical ideas detailed below can be just as fresh and relevant to young children today as they were when they were first advocated. An example of this tendency can be found in *Birth to Three Matters*, which is a framework developed by Sure Start and the Department for Education and Skills under the leadership of Professor Lesley Abbott (Abbott, 2002) to provide support and guidance for parents and practitioners in meeting the needs of babies and children to the age of three years.

The framework looks at a wide range of ideas relating to the care and education of young children and identifies four aspects:

- a strong child;
- a skilful communicator;
- a competent learner;
- a healthy child.

One of the key themes which prevails through the documentation is the idea that adults who work with young children, recognise "the 'holistic' nature of development and learning" (p.4). The emphasis on educating the whole child in a holistic way is clearly evident in the ideas of the philosophers quoted in subsequent paragraphs. Four pioneers of early education have been chosen for this section because their ideas are enduring, practical and take account of the sensibilities of young children.

(b) **Four Pioneers in the Study of Early Childhood:**

(i) Freidrich Froebel (1782-1852) is undoubtedly one of the most influential philosophers on early childhood. Born in Thuringia, he studied at the Universities of Jena and Berlin and established an experimental school at Blankenburg based upon the ideas of Heinrich Pestalozzi, who had in turn been influenced by the educational philosophy of Jean-Jacques Rousseau. Froebel developed the idea of the kindergarten as a method of educating young children. The term *kindergarten* means "children's garden". He envisaged the young child as a seed to be developed and nurtured. The learning process was likened to a gradual unfolding of a flower, and this development was overseen by a trained teacher. Hence, he protested at many of the practices of his day:

> We grant space and time to young plants and animals because we know that, in accordance with the laws that live in them, they will develop properly and grow well; young animals and plants are given rest and arbitrary interference with their growth is avoided, because it is known that the opposite practice would disturb their pure unfolding and sound development; but the young human being is looked upon as a piece of wax, a lump of clay, which man can mould into what he pleases (Froebel, 1887, p. 8).

A specific curriculum was to be observed, and children were encouraged to learn through discovery and through the use of certain equipment or "gifts and occupations" which constituted a range of toys and activities made from natural materials.

Froebel viewed childhood as an important stage in overall development. His ideas were very much ahead of the thinking on childhood at that time and they have contributed to many of our modern ideas about the ways in which young children think and learn. He strongly believed in the concept of active learning and learning thorough play, arguing that at this age play, far from being trivial, is serious and deeply significant. The focus of play at this age is the core of the whole future, since in it the entire person is developed and revealed in the most sensitive qualities of the mind.

Froebel's ideas had an important influence on British education. The London School Board appointed lecturers to explain the kindergarten concept to the infant school teachers employed in the area, while the British and Foreign School Society set up a college at Stockwell to train infant school teachers in Froebelian principles. In 1887 the National Froebel Union was constituted (Lawrence, 1969).

Many academics have acknowledged Froebel as an inspiration. Sayeed and Guerin (2000, p.12) view him as the pioneer of the kindergarten and nursery school movement, who saw play as a unifying force between the child, adult(s) and environment. He criticised rote-teaching and instead advocated play as making learning meaningful for children.

Moyles considers Froebel to be a major influence today: "From reading Froebel my interest in play and spirituality and the rooting of learning in real, first-hand experience of the natural world has been developed" (Moyles, 2005, p. 139). Many examples can be given of acceptance of his ideas today. For example, he advocates outside play; a key theme in the ideology of the Foundation Phase planned by the Welsh Assembly Government (WAG) is that the "outdoor classroom" should be an integral part of the early years curriculum. A central idea is that children will be able to access the outdoors and undertake a variety of learning experiences in this "natural" environment. In fact, there is explicit reference in the draft guidance (Welsh Assembly Government, 2003) which states: "the Foundation Phase environment should promote discovery and independence and a greater emphasis on using the outdoor environment as a resource for children's learning" (p. 2).

The "outdoor curriculum" has taken on a momentum of its own. Planning for outdoor learning must now become an integral part of the daily routine for early years settings in Wales. Good outdoor provision can enable children to learn in a creative way and with natural materials. Froebel was passionate about concepts such as the interconnectedness of life, nature and its beauty, as well as the value of sensory and first hand experiences, experiences which are readily available in the outdoors. Edgington examines ways in which early years settings can utilise outdoor play facilities. This does not have to be an expensive process; often, the simplest materials yield the best results. "Outside there is scope to make mess and to work with a wide range of natural and recycled open-ended materials, such as shells, twigs, large pebbles, logs, cardboard boxes, milk crates, tyres, guttering and long carpet-roll tubes" (Edgington, 2004, p. 16). Froebel would have approved.

(ii) *Maria Montessori* (1870 – 1952) was the first woman in Italy to be awarded a medical degree, specialising in paediatrics. Her first medical post fostered her interest in the welfare of deprived children. While working with these children who were often mentally and emotionally disturbed she began to develop her own educational philosophy.

In 1904 she was asked to set up a university programme in the Faculty of Natural Sciences and Medicine in the Pedagogic School of the University of Rome. Her next project in 1907 saw the beginning of the first *Casa dei Bambini* or children's house in Rome. The children who were admitted came from the surrounding slum areas. The emphasis in Montessori's educational system was on play with simple materials such as wooden cylinders and cubes, the teaching staff being encouraged not to intervene directly but rather to observe the children at play. Montessori discovered that the children changed from being shy and withdrawn to becoming communicative and happy.

The Montessori Method (Montessori, 1912) as it became known, relied on the philosophy of scientific observation and individual autonomy and freedom. She felt that education began at birth and that children went through periods of sensitivity in their learning. Adults, she argues, need to be aware of these sensitive periods and provide children with the correct stimulus at the time when they are most interested and motivated.

She thought that children learn in a number of ways, for example, through their senses, through movement and in an environment which is designed for their needs. Hence, desks and chairs need to be at the child's height and tools such as gardening equipment should be provided which are child sized. She believed that children can learn to read and write at an early age. However, they should only be encouraged to do so when they are ready. An important principle in her educational philosophy is the development of self-discipline, which can be achieved through a structured prepared environment where children are given choice and autonomy in the tasks they undertake. At all times teachers should be sensitive to their needs. She contrasts the *annihilated* individual and the *disciplined* individual. The former is compelled to act in a certain way by others; the latter is motivated by an active sense of discipline. He is not conditioned to follow the dictates of other people through coercion, but understands that there are natural limits upon his freedom and that he cannot behave exactly as he wishes if his actions conflict with the interests of others. Thus, she writes:

> The liberty of the child should have as its limit the collective interest; as its *form* what we universally consider good breeding. We must, therefore, check in the child whatever offends or annoys others, or whatever tends towards rough or ill-bred acts (Montessori, 1912, p. 87).

One of the greatest limitations of the Montessori method, however, is its lack of emphasis on role play and imagination in the learning process. This aspect of the philosophy may stem from the fact that Montessori stressed the use of "meaningful tasks" when working with the disadvantaged children in Rome. She felt that imaginative play would distract them from the real world and ultimately militate against their learning.

(iii) *Susan Isaacs* (1885-1948) had a distinguished academic career before being asked to set up an experiment school, the Malting House, by Geoffrey and Margaret Pyke. This she ran from 1924 until 1927, during which time she was able to put into practice new teaching ideas, many of which focused upon play, active learning and meeting children's emotional needs.

Gentle guidance is an important aspect of her educational philosophy. She believes that children make sense of the world in their own right, but need adults who are sensitive to their needs and are never sarcastic or likely to break promises. Children's ideas and fantasies, she maintains, should not be curbed and any questions that they have must be answered with respect. Isaacs argues very eloquently along these lines in her booklet *The Educational Value of the Nursery School* which was published in 1954. In this she establishes a number of ideas on methodology. Under the heading "Real and Active Experience" she points out:

> Another essential for happy development is real and active experience. No one can solve the child's problems for him; only his own moving and exploring and experimenting, his own play with toys suitable for this phase of development can advance his skill and his learning. It is the answers to his, not to our questions, which increase his knowledge (Isaacs, 1954, p. 20).

(iv) *Rudolf Steiner* (1891-1925) was an Austrian academic. He was passionately interested in spirituality and established an ideology based upon anthroposophy. His philosophical ideas were at the heart of the educational model he created. The first Steiner-Waldorf school was established for children of the workforce at the Waldorf-Astoria cigarette factory in Stuttgart in 1919. Pound (2005, p.27) observes that "he aimed for all children to experience both arts and sciences and a balanced experience of what he described as 'thinking, feeling and willing'."

Steiner's philosophy centred on understanding children's individuality and interests. There is a strong emphasis on free play and the use of multi-purpose toys, many of which are made of natural materials. Craft activities are freely available and children are encouraged to sew, draw or knit. Woodworking skills are also taught, and the children are able to use real tools. Outdoor play is a feature, but commercial toys are not provided. Children are allowed to dig in the garden or play on tree trunks or logs. There is also a strong emphasis on creating links with the home environment, and Steiner settings reflect this. On a visit to a Steiner nursery in Cardiff, I observed the lunchtime break during which both children and staff sat and ate together. The table was attractively set out with tablecloth, napkins, cutlery and glasses for water. I had also previously seen the children helping staff to prepare food for the meal.

Steiner's thoughts on education were derived from humanistic philosophy and adopted holistic principles. MacNaughton and Williams (2004, p. 368) point to his emphasis on "the spiritual, physical and intellectual being", noting that these were "equally the concern and responsibility of education."

It is interesting to note that many of the tenets of theorists such as Steiner, whose philosophy was conceived in the early Twentieth Century, are currently popular. One of Steiner's main beliefs was that the nursery environment should foster personal and social development. This is an integral part of the Welsh Assembly Government's Foundation Phase Guidance issued in 2005 (ACCAC, 2005).

(c) **Current Philosophies:** The ideas of learning through activity, discovery and play are currently relevant in the proposals advanced for a Foundation Phase within the National Curriculum in Wales by the Welsh Assembly Government's Department for Education, Lifelong Learning and Skills (2007) The educational thinking which shapes these plans is described in greater detail in section VI below.

IV: PSYCHOLOGICAL PERSPECTIVES

In this account of psychological perspectives we are looking at many different interrelated aspects. Psychology clearly forms a very relevant basis for the study of early childhood. One of its areas is related to the study of children's behaviour and the reasons and rationale underlying their thinking and action. Psychology is also very much concerned with the way children may feel in a given situation and their moods and emotions. Other pertinent concepts include memory and thinking. Again, as social beings, young children must learn to communicate and interact with other people in complex situations and practise behaviours such as co-operation, empathy and respect. Psychological concepts such as motivation, cognitive processes and social behaviour are fascinating and relevant to any study which relates to young children.

(a) **Studies of Child Development:**

(i) *Jean Piaget* (1896-1980) was a prolific writer and theorist on child development. Born in Switzerland, he published his first academic paper (on the albino sparrow) at the age of ten and by the age of fifteen he was a respected zoologist and an authority on molluscs. As one of the first psychologists of the modern era who took children's thoughts seriously, he also wrote at length about his own children's development, especially his daughter, Jacqueline, who was born in 1925. Piaget was a contemporary of Freud, but, whereas Freud was interested in emotional and sexual development, Piaget's studies were concerned with intellectual development. He believed that the child is active in this process, and is able to construct and re-construct his or her view of reality in the light of experiences and increasing knowledge. He felt that there is a natural sequence of development and that children at a particular stage of development are able to take on board and learn new concepts.

Piaget (1977) argued that children proceed through the following four stages from birth to adolescence:

(1) THE SENSORI-MOTOR STAGE which occurs during early babyhood. Babies and toddlers gain knowledge from physical action and through their senses. He suggests that babies are ego-centric, meaning that they are unable to appreciate the viewpoints or the experiences of others.

(2) THE PRE-OPERATIONAL STAGE which lasts from the age of about two to seven years. During this phase children learn to manipulate their own environment and are increasingly aware of the power of words. Logic is gained through situations and interaction with others. Children of this age often make up their own ideas when trying to make sense of the world, especially in relation to scientific concepts. Piaget was interested in the way that they often assign human characteristics to animals or innate objects (animism). For example, children will often blame a table if they run into it.

(3) THE CONCRETE OPERATIONAL STAGE: The hallmark of this stage, which extends from the ages seven to eleven, is the development of logical thought in the child.

(4) THE FORMAL OPERATIONAL STAGE: This stage begins at about the age of twelve. Piaget contends that from this age the child thinks in a more orderly and logical way and is able to use abstract ideas, formulate hypotheses and appreciate the implications of his or her actions in relation to others.

Piaget's theories were extremely influential in the 1960s and 1970s, and his ideas are still debated by educators today, though with the backlash against progressive education in the late 1970s and 1980s, which was described in the last chapter, his ideas went out of fashion within teacher training courses (Neumark, 1996). Criticisms of his work have centred on his lack of emphasis on children's social and emotional development and the fact that his studies are located within the contexts of place and time. Nor has the thinking of all children developed within the age ranges he has outlined. Margaret Donaldson (1978) who was a protégée of Piaget, argues against one of Piaget's key ideas - ego-centrism. She thinks that young children are able to comprehend other people's views and feelings as long as the task makes "human sense" to them. In other words, the situation is within their current level of understanding and life experience.

(ii) *Hy Le Xuan and Jane Loevinger*: Le Xuan and Loevinger (1996) analyse stages in personal development. They are especially concerned with the ego which they see as the "fabric" of character traits, modes of thinking, means of controlling impulses and ways of relating to other people.

The stages they chart are as follows:

(1) PRE-SOCIAL: The baby is guided mainly by reflexes and responses to the environment. Only gradually does she/he come to understand that there is an exterior world separate from her/himself.

(2) IMPULSE: The baby is now aware of other people in the environment to whom she/he relates, but is still dominated by impulse. The main difference from the previous stage is that behaviour is an assertion of the baby's own separate existence as a person. However, she/he is concerned only with her/himself and present concerns and is incapable of engaging in co-operative enterprises with others or in rule-governed behaviour.

(3) SELF-PROTECTION: In this stage impulse gives way to rule-governed behaviour. The child realises that there are rules, obedience to which brings rewards while disobedience results in disapproval and punishment. Rules are seen as fixed and unchanging as part of the furniture of the universe and actions are motivated by self-interest and self-protection. Thus, rules are obeyed for ego-centric reasons.

(4) CONFORMIST: Self-interest is now identified with the interest of the group with which the child associates. The main sanction is the disapproval of members of the group. New qualities are needed such as trust and loyalty.

Le Xuan and Loevinger stress that development at this fourth stage depends upon extending the group with whom the child identifies. As Richard Pring notes:

> A growing person might identify with a relatively small social group of peers with whom there is a feeling of trust, and where there is respect for mutually agreed rules, but remain at the earlier "self-protective" stage in relationship to others: school authorities, parents, the police (Pring, 1983, p.50).

(5) CONSCIENTIOUS: This stage is characterised by a growing awareness of the fallibility of others in the group, realisation of competing values in life, and greater self-questioning and self-evaluation. Courses of action are planned in accordance with long-term goals and objectives and an evaluation of the likely consequences of one's actions. There is a new emphasis on responsibility and critical thinking about one's standards of behaviour.

(6) AUTONOMOUS: Inner conflict still remains as the person becomes aware that decisions have to be taken for which there are no clear solutions and concerning which men of good disposition disagree.

(iii) *Lawrence Kohlberg* (1927-1987) offers the following analysis of cognitive moral development (Kohlberg, 1986, 1987 and 1994):

(1) LEVEL I: PRE-CONVENTIONAL. Here action is motivated by self-interest rather than moral principles. Kohlberg identified two stages. In the first, *heteronomous morality*, the consequences of actions (whether the child receives rewards or punishments) determine the morality of those actions. In the second, which he calls *instrumentalism*, "good" is what maximises one's own interests, although the child recognises the need to accommodate the wishes of other people. Actions therefore, are often of the *quid pro quo* type.

(2) LEVEL II: CONVENTIONAL. Actions are now seen as "good" or "bad" not so much in terms of self-interest but for more objective reasons. Once again, there are two stages. Within the first, *interpersonal relationship and conformity*, the "right" is seen to be whatever gains approval from others and usually relates to conventions concerning one's role, as, for example, a son, daughter or pupil. Thus, trust and loyalty are important concepts. The type of thinking associated with this stage is now extended to society as a whole in the second stage, *social system maintenance*. Conventions are observed and respect is shown for the law and for all authority figures. These conventions are seen

to be justified in terms of the maintenance of society and may be equated with the "social contract" theory of justice propounded in Plato's *Republic* (Plato, 1974, pp. 102-114).

(3) LEVEL III: POST-CONVENTIONAL. At this level the person graduates from conventional thinking to an understanding of the existence of universal moral principles. Conventional rules are challenged when they are thought to conflict with individual rights and the more general values of human welfare. Where conventional laws are upheld, it is because they involve social contracts which can be justified in terms of human well being. At the highest level, there is an understanding of ultimate moral principles which can be universalised, for example, respect for persons and justice.

Kohlberg acknowledges that these stages will not necessarily be reached by everyone. Many people, he feels, do not advance beyond the stage of social system maintenance. Usually the reasons for this are limited intellectual ability and failure to see issues from another person's point of view. Another reason may be that the child has a special need such as autism. Again, some children have limited life experiences and opportunities, which limit their ability to take on board the views and life choices of others.

(b) **Behaviourist Theories of Child Development:** Behaviourist theories were popular until the 1950s. They assume that the child is born with basic biological "drives" which have to be satisfied, of which hunger and thirst are obvious instances. Advocates of behaviourism suggest that babies are attached to their care giver primarily for their own selfish needs. As Flanagan (1996, p. 39) states: "It was thought that healthy psychological development could be assured by well-regulated feeding schedules and attention, and that mothers should avoid 'spoiling' their babies".

This idea of "spoiling" babies by giving them love and attention seems bizarre by today's standards. However, at that time another theorist, the psychoanalyst John Bowlby (1907 -1990), was responsible for further changes in attitudes on child rearing. He carried out research on behalf of the World Health Organisation and produced a number of books and reports such as *Maternal Care and Mental Health* in 1951. Analysing the effects of maternal deprivation on children who had been orphaned during the Second World War, he investigated the nature of the relationship between mother and baby and the consequences of a breakdown in this bond. He discussed the concept of attachment and, like Montessori, sought to identify "critical periods" in a child's development, which he saw as an essential factor in the bonding process. Bowlby argued that maternal attachment was essential for the healthy psychological development of the infant and made reference to the term *monotrophy* which denoted the child's need for a central care giver. His concept of mothering did not exclude fathers or others from this process, but he stressed the need for a special person upon whom the child can rely. He believed that the period when these bonds of attachment were formed was critical for healthy development, and he strongly felt that children who were deprived of this central care giver in the first four years of their life would suffer permanent psychological damage.

More support for Bowlby's ideas came from the work of the Austrian zoologist and animal psychologist Konrad Lorenz. Lorenz undertook a piece of research using a brood of greylag geese goslings, setting up an experiment to prove that young animals attached themselves to a mother figure on hatching. He called this process *imprinting*. The young goslings, on seeing Lorenz when they first hatched from their eggs, followed him around and he became a surrogate mother figure to them. Lorenz felt this process may be replicated in humans, though this is a dubious claim (Lorenz, 1979).

(c) *Benjamin Spock*: One of the most popular writers in the post-war years was Dr Benjamin Spock. His famous book on child development, *The Common Sense Book of Baby and Childcare*, was first published in 1946. Many feel that it was ahead of its time. It gave parents the freedom to make up their own minds about employing various parenting techniques and the autonomy to trust their own instincts as far as bringing up their baby was concerned.

Spock begins with a letter to the reader which contains such inspirational sentiment as:

> You know more than you think you do…. Don't be overawed by what the experts say. Don't be afraid to trust your own common sense (p.1).

His advice was initially resisted by professionals, but embraced by parents. Spock seemed to empathise with and listen to parents. He also respected them and much of his writing was based upon his practical work with parents at the time. Originally he had taught paediatric medicine. However, he felt that the child rearing ideas at the time were rigid, and in a documentary in 1966 within the US public broadcasting series Nova he showed how child-rearing books followed the old paediatric traditions, commenting on such issues as "thumb sucking" and reasons why it was bad for children. Strategies in those days which were designed to deal with children's thumb sucking involved such techniques as painting children's thumbs with iodine, or tying their hands to their cot in order to break these habits. Spock aimed to demolish such ideas and to investigate the reasons why children displayed such behaviours. Following from this process, he sought to discover the best way to deal with such issues.

Many of his tenets were based on the psychoanalytical tradition and the work of Sigmund Freud (1856-1939). Thinking of this type was seen as radical by the establishment of the time. Steven Parker, his co-author of later editions of the book (Spock and Parker, 1998), said in an interview on PBS news hour on 16th March 1998:

> to really understand the success and impact of Dr. Spock you have to remember the context in which he burst upon the scene. Child-rearing advice at the time was an incredibly dismal affair. Parents were told: "Don't touch your child; don't kiss them; don't hug them; feed them on a schedule; let them cry; prepare them for a tough world" by not being emotionally involved.

Amazon.com, which is currently selling the book on-line, claims in its editorial that: "After fifty years [this is] still the best book on child development ever. No parenting library is complete without this childcare classic".

It seems evident that the accessibility of the information and advice on a range of issues was a key factor in the popularity of Spock's book. Whether this advice is still applicable to all children and relevant to a variety of cultural or social situations may be debated. Nonetheless, it marked a turning point in the collective psyche of parents at that time, the key issue being the realisation that the medical paediatric profession did not always know best and that there were many other complementary ways of looking at issues pertinent to children's health and well being.

With the success of this volume publishers realised the existence of a growing market for the consumption of books on the subject of child development, and the Behaviourist and Freudian views from which people like Spock were trying to dissociate themselves were popular throughout the 1950s.

(d) **The Growth of Academic Research into Early Childhood Studies:** This development has been more evident over the last twenty years. Child development and education are intrinsically linked with government policy and procedures. This intervention gives researchers much to study and the outcomes of their surveys can be used to inform or challenge government policy.

There are many examples of studies into early childhood from all over the world that we can use. It is widely believed that early intervention is crucial to success later on in life. Research by Weikart and colleagues in Ypsilanti (1996) concentrated upon the effects of access to early education. They shadowed a sample of children for many years, documenting their academic and social achievements. Findings from this research concluded that children who had received an educational input from pre-school and nursery programmes were more likely to be successful in securing employment and were less likely to be classed as displaying anti-social characteristics. Penn (2005, p.33), however, stresses that Weikart's randomised control trial which studied a group of young people for a period of time is "the only source for all claims that one dollar spent when a child is young saves seven dollars later on".

There are many published and well respected academic journals associated with studies into child development. Organisations such as Training, Advancement and Co-operation in Teaching Young Children (TACTYC) have been established as a forum for child development professionals and publish regular journals, bringing together up to date academic writing in the field with contributors from all over the world.

(e) **Emotional Intelligence, Well being and Positive Dispositions to Learning:** Over the past ten to fifteen years there has been a growing realisation of the link between social and emotional development and academic achievement. Daniel Goleman offered some of the first thoughts on emotional intelligence, which were then further developed by such people as Alfie Kohn (2002). In his books *Emotional Intelligence* (1995) and *Working with Emotional Intelligence* (1998) Goleman highlights the importance of fostering emotional intelligence skills in young children. He stresses that, although ideally the process needs to commence in early childhood, it is never too late for the carer to employ suitable strategies. He points out that our level of emotional intelligence is not fixed genetically; nor does it develop only in early childhood. Unlike intellectual intelligence, which changes little after our teenage years, emotional intelligence seems to be largely learned, and it continues to develop as we progress through life and learn from our experiences. Curtis (2002, p. 51) emphasises the importance of the social and emotional dimension in learning, believing that "high self-esteem and positive self-concept are crucial to children if they are to 'learn how to learn' and achieve their full potential".

Models of good practice in early education such as the Te Whariki curriculum in New Zealand and

Reggio Emilia in Italy have variations on a theme of emotional literacy in their curricula. The Te Whariki curriculum (Ministry of Education of New Zealand, 1996, p.9), for example, seeks to develop children who grow up as "competent and confident learners and communicators, healthy in mind, body and spirit". In the UK private training organisations such as Antidote training (www.antidote.org.uk) are looking at the association between developing emotional literacy and enhancing children's learning potential. Collaborative research undertaken by Antidote and the University of Bristol has shown that there is a connection between "quality" relationships in school and young children's learning potential. Joint collaboration by both organisations has resulted in the ELLI study - Effective Lifelong Learning Inventory (2002). This research concluded that children who have better emotional literacy are more able to learn as the result of such traits as:

- curiosity - asking questions to delve beneath the surface;

- resilience - "giving it a go" and sticking with it;

- creativity - playing with ideas;

- interdependence - working with others effectively and coping on their own.

Antidote also took into account research from a variety of other sources and found interesting evidence of the value of emotional understanding in work undertaken at the University of Delaware. This study sought to evaluate "emotional knowledge" as a long-term predictor for social and academic competence in later life, and the research team found that: "the emotional knowledge of the children at five contributed significantly to the prediction of behaviour problems, social skills and academic competence four years later" (Antidote, 2003, p. 17). They found that emotional knowledge correlated positively with assertion and cooperation and that a lack of emotional knowledge correlated with hyperactivity and internalising behaviour, that is to say, withdrawal (Izard *et al.*, 2001).

The development of emotional intelligence is a gradual process for the young child. In its Foundation Phase guidance material the Welsh Assembly Government has rightly placed especial emphasis upon this aspect of the early years curriculum (ACCAC, 2004). Well being is seen to be closely associated with self-identity and self- esteem. In order to feel happy about who they are and how they fit into groups, children need to develop self-awareness as individuals and as part of wider society. This includes self- esteem, self-knowledge, confidence, feeling valued and accepted by others, an ability to express their views and feelings and make sense of them and an ability to relate to others and work with them (p.8). This is a crucial element in development, and it is no exaggeration to state that young children's development is inextricably bound to their feelings of self-worth and self-esteem. The way in which they view themselves affects their relationships, friendships and the manner in which they think and react in certain situations. Another crucial factor, as Lindon (2005) notes, is that "learning is not all intellectual or rational; feelings are equally important. It is important that children develop in confidence that so they can learn" (p.103).

Young children need to form relationships in a positive way. Ideally, these will start with their family in the earliest years. As we know, this will not be feasible for all young children, and so the next best thing is the influence of the early childhood setting. The best combination for the child is a good balance between experiences at home and in school. Bartholomew and Kennedy (2006) stress the need for staff in early years settings to allay young children's anxieties and develop their emotional confidence. They argue that emotional well being requires relationships which are close, warm and supportive and the ability to express feelings such as joy, sadness frustration and fear.

Carr and Claxton (2002) investigate reasons why some children are more successful in their learning and refer to the notion of positive dispositions to learning, suggesting that some children have characteristics that make them more willing to be learners. The principal factors which contribute to this are:

- taking an interest;
- being involved;
- persisting with difficulty or uncertainty;
- communicating with others;
- taking responsibility

A key aspect of this ideology is that these factors can derive directly from the child's motivation or be acquired from the input and nurture of a skilled practitioner. Some children will need external help to achieve such characteristics.

(f) **Role of the Popular Media in Popularising Ideas on Child Psychology:** In the Twentieth Century ideas on the actual "mechanics" of raising children became more widespread. For example, an article in the magazine *The Nursery World for Mothers and Nurses* in 1925 gave advice to mothers and nurses about "the angel child". Dr E Sloan-Chester, the author of the article, discussed the "quiet" child, whom he referred to as "Mary". Although she may act like an angel and give the parent no trouble, Sloan-Chester expressed concerns about an "introverted" nature, writing that "the very goodness of 'Mary' may be an evidence of physical or psychological inferiority" (p.5). The article proceeded to warn parents that, as we become more aware of psychology, "we no longer classify children as good or bad, normal and abnormal. For one thing we realise that no person is absolutely normal". This leaves us with an interesting idea on which to ponder!

When reading articles from the past, it is easy for us to look at them with a sense of nostalgia and to marvel at the quaintness of some of the ideas they advocate. However, this article is significant in that it was the first of a series of articles on child psychology, which at that time was deemed to be a very new and trendy concept. The article even began with a definition of the meaning of psychology.

Today, with the advent of many "reality" television programmes and associated articles in popular newspapers and magazines, the general public seems to take a great interest in psychology in relation to children's development. There is also much published material on the workings of the human brain, and parents can gain easy access to a vast array of books on child development and parenting. In fact, a whole industry is now present dedicated to child development and behaviour.

For example, there are such programmes as Channel 4's *Super Nanny* with Jo Frost. Ironically, Frost, who has become a global childcare celebrity, has no formal qualifications. She became a nanny on television after responding to a magazine advertisement. The third series of *Super Nanny* began in August 2006, and her book, *Ask Super Nanny*, was published by Hodder and Stoughton in July 2006.

Analysis of the contents of British terrestrial and free view television during the week Saturday 18th March to Friday 24th March 2006 (BBC 1, 2 and 3, ITV 1 and 2 and Channel 5) reveals that there were fifteen programmes directly concerned with babies, childcare, and childrearing, examples being:

- *Nanny 911* – ITV2
- *The House of Tiny Tearaways* – BBC 3
- *Honey, We're Killing the Kids* – BBC3
- *The Seven Year Old Surgeon* – Five
- *Desperate Midwives* – Channel 5
- *Child of Our Time: The Children's Stories* – BBC1
  (Source: *The Guardian* TV Guide).

These programmes are generally aimed at the parents and carers of young children. Whereas some of them are clearly designed to provide entertainment, all of them have a high factual content and give lifestyle advice such as the benefits of good nutrition and exercise. They also provide valuable information on child rearing practices with much of the emphasis on behavioural factors. Some seem to offer "quick fix" solutions, especially those with an interventionist theme such as *Nanny 911*, where an experienced practitioner works with the families of children with behavioural problems. As the duration of the programme is usually one hour, the practitioner is shown successfully resolving a myriad of problems within a very short time scale, a situation which is unlikely to occur in real life.

As a direct contrast, the *Child of Our Time* series of programmes shown on BBC 1 and fronted by Professor Sir Robert Winston, an eminent clinician and child development expert, offers a more scholarly approach to the child rearing process. *The Child of Our Time* programme began transmission in 2000, and research evidence generated during this time has been used to inform childcare and educational practice. Research projects are carried out usually in conjunction with academic institutions such as the University of Kent where members of staff have conducted a research project to investigate the perceptions of four-year-old children concerning ethnicity (www.bbc.co.uk.parenting).

Buzan (2003) in the book *Brain Child* seeks to equip parents with many strategies by virtue of which they, as "smart parents", can make their children "smart kids". The book is one of a collection of publications in which Buzan looks at the capabilities of the brain. It is specifically targeted at parents to help them realise that they can "help maximize their child's all-round development by looking at everything from her point of view" (p. xv), and it is very much based on the simple premise that parents need to support, nurture and encourage their children in order for them to achieve their potential.

V: SOCIOLOGICAL PERSPECTIVES

(a) **Education and Environment:** Sociology "seeks to produce knowledge about the nature of societies and to provide frameworks for understanding social life and social practices" (Bartlett, Burton and Peim, 2001, p. 24). As education involves the transmission of values, customs and forms of knowledge and is concerned with the socialisation of pupils so that they meet the expectations of society, there is a clear relationship between education and sociology. Again, as David Wood (1988, p.12) notes, "childhood is what is termed a social construct". Children are undoubtedly a product of the society in which they are raised.

In the 1920s and 1930s it was psychology rather than sociology which exerted the principal influence upon thinking about the evolution of education in the UK. For example, psychologists like Charles Spearman, Louis Thurstone and Cyril Burt believed that children's learning was dependent upon intelligence, which was innate and could be measured in tests. Different types of school, it was argued, were required for the different types of pupil: the grammar school for the "academic" child; the technical high school for the "technical" pupil; and the secondary modern for the "practical" pupil (Consultative Committee to the Board of Education, 1938; Secondary Schools Examination Council, 1943). In the 1960s this thinking was challenged and it was recognised that the environment had an important role to play in learning. Thus, the Plowden Report of 1967, *Children and Their Primary Schools*, drew attention to areas of England which members of the Committee referred to as *Educational Priority Areas*:

> In a neighbourhood where the jobs people do and the status they hold owe little to their education it is natural for children as they grow older to regard school as a brief prelude to work rather than an avenue to future opportunities. ... We have ourselves seen schools caught in such vicious circles and read accounts of many more. They are quite untypical of schools in the rest of the country. We noted the grim approaches; incessant traffic noise in narrow streets; parked vehicles hemming in the pavements; rubbish dumps on waste land nearby; the absence of green playing spaces on or near the school sites. ... The child from a really impoverished background may well have had a normal satisfactory emotional life. What he often lacks is the opportunity to develop intellectual interests. This shows in poor command of language (Central Advisory Council for Education [England], 1967, pp. 50-51).

Similar developments took place in the USA during the late 1960s and early 1970s of which the Head Start programme is a good example. This revealed a definite relationship between nurturing and empowering children on the one hand and their academic achievement on the other. It found evidence that early intervention made a distinct difference to children's school experience, academic success and future life chances. More recent initiatives in England include Excellence in Cities and Sure Start, while in Wales additional funding has recently been made available to schools with the largest number of disadvantaged pupils through the project known as RAISE (Raising Attainment and Individual Standards in Education). Some £16 million was distributed in 2006 to 614 schools where at least one fifth of pupils were entitled to free school meals. Another important support mechanism for young children in Wales is the Flying Start Scheme. This is a package of support, designed to address inequality in children's earliest years. It builds upon the successes which have been identified in evaluation reports of Sure Start in England and the best practice from other countries.

(b) **The Role of the Parent:** By the late 1990s the political priority was to offer choice and autonomy to parents. The Labour government, first elected in 1997, enshrined this principle in its School Standards and Framework Act of 1998 (See chapter 6). There were two factors in this decision. The importance of the role of the parent in their children's education was recognised, and such research studies as that undertaken by Wolfendale (1983) concluded that parents should be recognised as active, autonomous, individual human beings, active and central to decision making and its implementation. There is a strong European dimension to account for this viewpoint. The relationship between children's educational achievement and parental support was the subject of research undertaken by academics in the Organisation for Economic Operation and Development (OECD), Ravn's paper entitled *Parents in Education - European Perspectives* emphasising the importance of "shared responsibility and of involving parents to conduct activities that will benefit their children."

Another key theme is the view that the school community acts as a type of micro- society. Barnekow Ramussen and Rivett (2000, pp. 61-67) write that "the school, environment, curriculum and surrounding community are potentially a powerful catalyst" in relation to social and ultimately economic change. This dynamic can be realised through parental partnerships with schools which can be beneficial both to the child and the school. Parents need to be encouraged to support their children in ways which best suit them. However, they have different life skills, work commitments and ideas on education and, as Whalley and the Pen Green Centre Team (2004, p.59) note, "since parents are not a homogeneous group, they all have different needs and different starting points. They will want to get involved in their children's early years settings in different ways".

(c) **The Perceptions of Advisers:** In any study of early childhood there are many strands and avenues to explore, and we can legitimately ask whether the academic study of the discipline is largely conducted by members of the middle classes and influenced by their perceptions and outlook. It does seem that in the case of many of the academics and childcare professionals from whom we take advice this may well be true. As we saw earlier in the chapter, eminent professionals such as Professor Sir Robert Winston do doubtless have an impact upon the public's thinking about the upbringing of children. They give guidance and advice to many families in all social categories, but they may have little or no personal experience of living in a council block tenement flat on a limited budget whilst bringing up a baby. Such a situation clearly has both its advantages and limitations.

(d) **Popular Culture:** The author Dave Pelzer has written a number of books retelling his childhood experiences with an abusive mother. In fact, the abuse he suffered was one of the worst cases ever recorded in the USA. As he says, "if I learned anything from my unfortunate childhood it is that there is nothing that can dominate or conquer the human spirit" (2002, p.10). His experiences and those of people like him have brought the study of early childhood into the public arena, and it is more common in the Twenty-First Century for children to be heard and heeded with respect. They now have much more autonomy and are generally held in higher regard as people in their own right.

The publication of texts such as these enable students of ECS to reflect upon real life incidents and develop strategies which can be used to benefit new generations of children. The experiences of those who suffered like Dave Pelzer can provide professionals with knowledge which can then be used to teach others, and in an ideal world valuable lessons can be learned. As the poem by Dorothy Law Nolte (1998) so aptly puts it, "Children learn what they live".

VI: CURRENT DEVELOPMENTS AND ISSUES

(a) **The Integration of Children's Services:** In 2003 the government published the Green Paper *Every Child Matters* (DFES, 2003). This proposed new legislation under which the various services with responsibility for the well being of children would work more closely together than had hitherto been the case. The main provisions of the Green Paper were subsequently written into the Children Act of 2004.

Under section 13 each area in England must establish a Local Safeguarding Children Board, including the local authority, police, strategic health authority and children and family court advisory and support services. Similar arrangements are made in Wales under section 31 of the Act. Under section 12 of the Act (England) and section 29 (Wales) data on each child, including an identity number, should be collected and shared among all professionals working with that child.

Section 17 (England) and section 26 (Wales) require authorities to prepare and publish a children's and young people's plan (CYPP) setting out their strategy for discharging their functions in relation to children and young people, while section 18 (England) and section 27 (Wales) expect them to establish the post of Director of Children's Services. All CYPPs should be in place by April 2008. They should cover a three-year period and set out strategies to enable local authorities and schools to work in partnership with other bodies such as the health and voluntary sectors. Every local authority, National Health Service trust and heath board must appoint a lead director and lead elected member with responsibility for ensuring that there are suitable arrangements for the joint operation of children's services in their locality.

In Wales the Assembly Government is promoting "wrap around care" with the introduction of integrated children's centres, where a range of children's services is housed under one roof. As part of this initiative, a new purpose built integrated centre has been established in Ely, Cardiff. The Welsh Assembly Government has closely examined international evidence which suggests that "inequality in early years education leads to inequality in life chances" (htt://www.learning.wales.gov.uk), and has implemented a programme starting with a £46m. investment to include such developments as free part-time childcare for two year olds to run alongside its existing commitment to three year olds. The scheme will also encompass increased help on the part of health visitors and support for parents.

(b) **The Foundation Phase in Wales:** The publication of *The Learning Country: Foundation Phase* 3-7 (WAG, 2003) marked a major shift in thinking about the early years period in Wales. The Welsh Assembly Government is being innovative and forward thinking because it is concentrating on a pivotal time in young children's development and learning. The document lays out objectives for the period from three to seven years, for example, progressively "to improve the support for, and promotion of, children's rounded development and give them a flying start in life" (WAG, 2003, p.1).

Currently, in Wales, the Foundation Phase Framework for early years provision is being implemented as a pilot scheme. It is intended that it will be statutory for three to five year olds in 2008 and then extend to children aged seven by 2010. It is quite radical in its approach by putting play and active discovery at the heart of the curriculum along with personal and social development and well being. The play-based day will encompass all ages of children from nursery up to year two, concentrating on "the serious business of 'play'." It is argued that "through their play, children practise and consolidate their learning, play with ideas, experiment, take risks, solve problems, and make decisions individually, in small and in large groups" (WAG, 2003, p.2). As we have seen at an earlier stage of this chapter, many early years professionals and theorists have argued long and hard for such opportunities for young children, and there is a wealth of writing which demonstrates the value of play for young children. Susan Isaacs wrote over fifty years ago that it is a psychological need for them and that it is the child's means of living and of understanding life (Isaacs, 1954, p.23).

The Welsh Assembly Government has invested heavily in research into play and an effective early years curriculum framework, and a major study, *Monitoring and Evaluation of the Effective Implementation of the Foundation Phase* (MEEIFP) Project Across Wales (Siraj-Blatchford *et al.*, 2005), has been published. This is a joint research project involving the University of Wales Institute, Cardiff and the Institute of Education of London University, the project team consisting of early childhood experts including Professor Iram Siraj-Blatchford of the Institute of Education of London University and Dr Kathy Sylva from Oxford University. The evaluation report has charted the progress made in the forty-one pilot settings which were chosen by the Welsh Assembly Government to make up the first wave of Foundation Phase early years provision. The report focuses upon a range of issues and identifies the following points as the most prominent strengths in the delivery of the programme during the first year:

- a curriculum based upon play, activity and experiential learning;

- a child-centred curriculum;

- a broader , holistic and more relevant curriculum (p. 5).

The consultation document issued by the Welsh Assembly Government's Department for Education, Lifelong Learning and Skills in January 2007 on the Foundation Phase once again stresses the importance of play. Seven areas of learning are designated within the curriculum: personal and social development, well being and cultural diversity; language, literacy and communication skills; mathematical development; bilingualism; knowledge and understanding of the world; physical development; and creative development. Play-based strategies are integral to the pedagogy envisaged in the consultation paper, though it is acknowledged that there must be a balance between child-initiated activities and structured learning directed by adults. Play, it is argued, helps children to learn through concentration, perseverance and attention to detail - characteristics we normally associate with work. As well as being fundamental to intellectual development, it also enables children to develop self-awareness and to learn the rules of social behaviour. Certain of the ideals of John Dewey and other progressive educators cited in this and the previous chapter seem to be prominent in the minds of the authors of the consultation paper when they write that:

> A well-planned curriculum gives children opportunities to be creatively involved in their own learning which must build on what they already know and can do, their interests and what they understand. Active learning enhances and extends children's development (Welsh Assembly Government Department for Education, Lifelong Learning and Skills, 2007, p. 6).

This is very refreshing to read. If these ideals are extended into every early years setting in Wales, that country will undoubtedly have provision which will be the envy of many others.

Readers will, moreover, note from the seven areas of learning that personal and social development and well being, to which reference has been made earlier in this chapter, constitute a key factor in the Foundation Phase ideology. The 2007 document states that within this area:

> Children learn about themselves, their relationships with other children and adults, both within and beyond the family. They are encouraged to develop their self-esteem, their personal beliefs and moral values. They develop an understanding that others have differing needs, abilities, beliefs and views. The Foundation Phase supports the cultural identity of all children, to celebrate different cultures and help children recognise and gain a positive awareness of their own and other cultures (Welsh Assembly Government Department for Education, Lifelong Learning and Skills, 2007, p. 7).

It will surely prove to be extremely beneficial to children that the Welsh Assembly Government is not only developing and enhancing play opportunities, but is also thinking about the importance of enhancing young children's personal and social development and well being. Young children are naturally sociable. Devereux and Miller (2003, p.213) state that "many parents and teachers would say that the social dimension of learning is the most important one because if children are happy in school they are likely to be more receptive and confident and therefore able to take new learning on board, or at least they will not be afraid to ask for help." This seems to be a very simple idea, but it is such a poignant one. Young children must be nurtured and well equipped with the skills of confidence and positive self-esteem in their earliest years.

Finally, the Draft Framework for Children's Learning (ACCAC, 2004) states that:

> Research evidence also clearly identifies that the experiences to which children have been exposed before they enter education at three years of age have a considerable impact on their development. The Foundation Phase curriculum advocates that positive links between the home and the providers of care and education are fostered and promoted (p. 1).

This idea of a link between home and the nursery environment is very important. As has been shown above, partnership with parents is an important dynamic in ECS. The parent or carer is deeply attached emotionally to his or her child and this can confer many advantages as well as create problems, especially where the parent or carer has difficulty assigning responsibility to nursery staff.

(c) **Personal and Social Development as a Curriculum Area in England:** As we have seen, there has been growing awareness over the past twenty years of the importance of young children's overall holistic development. Dryden *et al.* (2005 p.102) point out that the School Curriculum and Assessment Authority (SCAA) in its document *Desirable Learning Outcomes*, published in 1996 (SCAA, 1996a, p.1), defined the outcomes of early years education in terms of literacy, numeracy and the development of personal and social skills. They argue that this aprrangement gives the impression that literacy and numeracy are more important than social and emotional development. Subsequent English early years curriculum documentation in the form of the *Curriculum Guidance for the Foundation Phase* (Qualifications and Curriculum Authority [QCA], 2000, p. 28) has emphasised emotional development more highly, as there is now a dedicated section entitled *Personal, Social and Emotional Development* with the statement that "successful personal, social and emotional development is critical for very young children in all aspects of their lives."

Drawing overall comparisons between the Foundation Stage in England and the Foundation Phase in Wales is not the task of this chapter. Nonetheless, it is interesting to note that the Foundation Stage profile handbook (QCA, 2000, p. 29) which is designed for use by early years practitioners for assessment purposes has a section on "dispositions and attitudes to learning" in the Personal, Social and Emotional development section. Clearly, these opportunities need to be delivered by knowledgeable, sensitive, well trained staff. Research by Kathy Sylva and her colleagues (2004) on the Effective Provision of Pre-School Education (EPPE) project has found a definite correlation between the quality of adult support and intervention and children's performance.

The actual mechanics of learning must be based on a firm foundation. Children need to build confidence in their abilities. They also need to be able to function effectively in the challenging and very social atmosphere of the classroom. Therefore, the child who is well versed in these coping strategies may be the more effective learner. As Chilton Pierce (2004, p.13) points out, "fear of any kind throws us into an ancient survival mentality that when fully active shuts down our higher modes of evolutionary awareness."

(d) **Research into the Functioning of the Brain:** Academics in the field of ECS are now able to make use of scientific data derived from research into the functioning of the human brain. Scientists are using more sophisticated techniques to discover the inner workings of the brain. This research can be valuable for ECS specialists in a variety of ways. For example, there has been much speculation over a possible relationship between certain vitamin supplements and enhanced brain activity and function. This has been documented in studies relating to the inclusion of dietary supplements such as Omega 3, which is derived from fish oil. These findings have been reported in the media.

Nursery World, the weekly magazine for early years and childcare practitioners, reports that new research has suggested that women who consume high levels of Omega 3 fatty acids during pregnancy have more intelligent and better behaved children. The consequences of such findings could be immense, inspiring the expectant mother to head straight for the supermarket vitamin aisle. On the other hand, feelings of guilt may afflict the mother who did not partake of this vitamin supplement during her pregnancy, even more so, if her child subsequently displayed behavioural problems. The moral dilemmas involved could make a fascinating study in years to come.

VII: CONCLUDING THOUGHTS

If we are to support young children we must learn as much about them as we can. Isaacs (1954, p. 20) felt that "no method of education based upon the notion that the little child is a simple bodily machine or mere creature of habit and reflex response can sustain him in his deepest difficulties". In order to begin the process of understanding young children and their complex development, we need to be able to appreciate the holistic nature of learning in the early years and have a clear idea of the close relationship between feelings and learning. We must also take time to step back, ponder and be aware of the world as it seems through a child's eyes.

The idea of all-round development has been explored throughout this chapter. While it is necessary for children to develop "brain power" and strategies for effective learning, it is also just as important for them to be rounded and happy individuals. Young children need to grow in mind, body and spirit. They need adults who care for them, nurture them and value them as individuals. Martin (2005, p.205) feels that "happy children typically learn and perform better in the classroom than unhappy children". He also muses over the observation that "making people happy is rarely an explicit aim of education". No child's school days will ever be a completely happy experience. We must, however, aim to achieve a balance of provision that goes someway towards meeting this goal.

3 Language and Learning

I: LANGUAGE IN EDUCATION

Language is our chief means of expressing ourselves and it plays a central role in learning. We speak today about the interconnectivity of the Internet but language remains the primary network through which we communicate our thoughts and feelings. Literacy, as a fundamental communication skill that involves talking and listening, reading and writing is clearly a vital part of language. Over the past decade the present government has striven to raise standards by launching the National Literacy Strategy in 1998, but arguments about falling standards continue and the topic of literacy has rarely been out of the headlines. At the time of writing, the *Observer* newspaper leads with the headline:

Classroom revolution in bid to boost 3Rs: English, Maths GCSEs toughened; Employers warn over falling literacy (Temko and Campbell, 2006).

Teachers, especially those suffering from "innovation fatigue", might be forgiven for greeting news of yet another "revolution" with some cynicism, but it is the case that some educationists, for example, Baroness Warnock, have been strongly critical of the government's education policies particularly with regard to school leavers' capacities to write coherently and think critically. This chapter is an exploration of key issues and controversies that have arisen in language and literacy debates over the past few decades. Salient areas such as language and thought, boys' and girls' achievement, speech and writing as well as language change are included and some space is devoted to the much-aired topic of standard English. Ideas of a standard have a particular resonance in Wales with its distinct cultural and linguistic heritage and, bearing in mind issues of language variation in the UK, the emphasis is on those chief sociolinguistic aspects that connect most closely to teaching and learning in today's classrooms.

The selection and coverage of material is in some senses eclectic and the sections offer introductions to an inexperienced student approaching the topics for the first time. Where possible, practical observations for teachers are made and a brief glossary is included to clarify key terminology.

The ability to use and understand language well is one of the most crucial aspects of a person's education and personal development. In school, language is the medium through which all subjects are taught; in most disciplines, especially in the core subject of English, pupils are assessed on the quality of their written and spoken language as well as the content of their work. In the primary and secondary phases of education, the subject of English is now a wide-ranging area of the curriculum which embraces language study together with literature, drama, media and information technology.

Proficient use of language enables the child to communicate ideas effectively and to meet many of the demands of other subjects as they too depend fundamentally on the cognitive and expressive potential of these four modes. In England and Wales the National Curriculum for English centres on four attainment targets: reading and writing as well as speaking and listening. Pupils are expected to progress through the key stages of the National Curriculum so that they become increasingly skilled and sophisticated users of language. This journey, however, is not linear, but is best thought of as a recursive process which involves uneven advancement followed by consolidation and requires the child to weave back and forth between these attainment targets with increasing dexterity and control. How we learn language remains a complex process, and, as Crystal (1997, p. 427) comments: "Literacy is not an all-or-none skill, but a continuum of gradually increasing levels and domains of ability." We should also remember that influences from outside school, for example, language encountered in the home, through peers and the media are at least as important as those within the school.

II: LITERACY ISSUES

Why do we place so much stress on language in education? One of the most influential reports was the Bullock Report in 1975, significantly entitled A *Language for Life* (Committee of Enquiry Appointed by the Secretary of State for Education and Science under the Chairmanship of Sir Alan Bullock, 1975). This influential report was widely acclaimed by teachers but its long-term impact was later questioned. Putting policy into practice is the acid test of any educational initiative and current literacy strategies are coming under similar criticism, as I shall outline shortly. Thoughts about what to do about literacy are strongly influenced by ideology with some favouring a programme-based approach that is often highly structured, while others who take a more liberal line favour a more creative, open-ended approach. In 1988, the Kingman Report (Committee of Inquiry into the Teaching of English Language, 1988), though gentle in tone, marked a move back towards a more top-down, prescriptive approach to literacy; it systematically set out the subject knowledge teachers in training should acquire and, in turn, what pupils needed to know and thus set the stage for things to come.

Put into practice a decade later, the current literacy strategies at Key Stages 1 and 2 and more recently at Key Stage 3 are programme-based with pre-determined outcomes. At Key Stage 3 the adoption of such programmes often means that lessons have five clear elements:

- Identification of prior knowledge;
- Teacher demonstration of a process;
- Shared exploration through activity;
- Via scaffolding pupils' application of new learning;
- Consolidation through discussion/ activity.

These initiatives have been a direct response to perceptions of falling standards in literacy in schools. The rationale behind the Key Stage 3 National Literacy Strategy is clearly stated:

> The Key Stage 3 National Strategy is part of the government's commitment to raise standards in schools. Effective literacy is the key to raising standards across all subjects, and equipping pupils with the skills and knowledge they need for life beyond school. (DFEE, 2001, p.9).

Proponents of programme-based strategies favour explicit teaching objectives that relate to a systematic framework that ensures even coverage of the diverse aspects of the curriculum. Thus, in Year 5 Term 1 of the National Literacy Strategy (NLS) pupils will encounter: (i) novels, stories and poems by significant children's writers; (ii) playscripts; and (iii) concrete poetry, whilst in Term 1 of Year 6 fiction and poetry will involve: classic fiction, poetry and drama by long-established authors, including, where appropriate, study of a Shakespeare play and adaptations of classics on television and film. A generous interpretation of these guidelines might conclude that these are helpful prompts, while a cynic might conclude that the specificity of these guidelines guarantees that they are teacher-proof. More of these strategies shortly. Let us first consider a few of the wider issues connected with language in education.

First, language is closely connected to thought itself, though the precise nature of that relationship has been hotly debated. In the Eighteenth Century, Samuel Johnson stated that "language is the dress of thought" (1954, p.8) but whether thought controls language or language controls thought is beyond the scope of this chapter. Nonetheless, it remains an intriguing issue. A brief instance of some seminal fieldwork regarding linguistic relativity neatly illustrates the complexity of these connections. In the Mid-Twentieth century in the USA, ethnolinguist Lee Whorf (1956) devoted most of his life to studying differences in language, thought and reality. Much of his work involved comparing Native American language with European languages. He contended that nature is dissected along the lines laid down by our native languages. We are met in the world by a kaleidoscopic mass of sensory impressions that have to be organised by our minds. The manner in which we do this is, he asserted, strongly dependent on the categories present and absent in our mother tongue.

Whorf, who had worked as a fire insurance inspector, in seeking to show how language habits influenced thought and behaviour, cited the much quoted anecdote of a garage employee who described oil drums as "empty" and would blithely smoke next to them, when he knew that these containers contained no liquid but were full of dangerous flammable vapours. In this way the term "empty" used by the workers was inadequate for describing in reality the dangerous fullness of the drums.

The patterns and codes within our language community undoubtedly influence the way we can express ourselves, though few today would endorse a strongly deterministic view that denies us the ability to break free of local linguistic constraints. However, the idea that our consciousness, thought patterns and our capacity to communicate ideas may be restricted by the tools and categories of our language has been pervasive in education, particularly when linked to social class. We shall return to exploring the relationship between language and thought later, in connection with notions of language deficit and the work of Bernstein, who provoked a fierce debate in the early 1970s, in which he was interpreted as saying that working class speakers used a "restricted code" which limited their powers of thought and wider communication.

We can think perhaps of many examples in schools where pupils struggle to grasp ideas because they lack the language terms and later, at A level, for instance, to use the specialist terminology of a discipline to express concepts clearly. In their analyses of literature, are students able to use specialist vocabulary confidently to explain literary effects and stylistic features? We should not forget, however, that even at Key Stage 2 (Year 6: Term 2) in the National Literacy Strategy children are expected to be able: "to discuss the way standard English varies in different contexts, for example, why legal language is highly formalised, why questionnaires must be specific."

Do they need the terms to comprehend the ideas or do they understand the ideas but lack the words to communicate their knowledge? Or may both be operative at various stages of their education? Whatever the dominance of one influence over another, as teachers, we certainly need to be aware of the complex reciprocal connections that thought and language share as cognition develops. Lawton's views on these issues still hold true today: "Whether it can be said that language is a determiner of perception, cognition and thought might be disputed, but there is little doubt that it exerts a channelling influence on thought processes" (Lawton, 1968, p. 158). Lawton was also concerned with investigating the variable of social class, and he ascribed much of the waste of potential that he perceived to an "inadequacy of linguistic range and control" on the part of many working-class children. He contended that these linguistic difficulties which accumulated in school related to "wider concerns of motivation and culture" (p. 157). Lawton also felt his experience as a teacher significantly in a grammar school in Kent and then in a secondary modern school in south-east London had been illuminated by the wider questions of language, thought, culture and class that Basil Bernstein's ground-breaking work raised (Bernstein, 1971). More about Bernstein and concepts of linguistic inadequacy follows shortly.

In the era before comprehensive education when selection at the age of eleven meant that around twenty per cent of children were admitted to grammar schools while the remainder were relegated to secondary moderns, much of the focus of Lawton's work centred on social class and opportunity. It is perhaps ironic that in 2006, as we seem to be abandoning the comprehensive ideal (at least in England), similar arguments about academic selection by ability or parental interviews, disadvantaged children and the comparative failure of "working-class" children in the educational system seem all too familiar. Many teachers are sceptical about social inclusion and fear the possible consequences of the creation of independent trust schools which may "cherry-pick" pupils.

The relationship between language acquisition, intellectual development and achievement in school is complex. Language is central to our concept of self and social development in the world. Vygotsky (1986) argued that language was the vehicle that linked the initially separate processes of pre-intellectual thought and inner-speech and, at a certain point early in the child's development, once this fusion had occurred, language had a immense influence on the thought processes. (See also Lee, 1979, pp. 105-106.) Full cognitive development requires extensive social interaction and this social dimension of learning is a central aspect of the English curriculum in many schools. This is not to deny that that in terms of language development, a child's experience outside the school –particularly the influence of peers – is not highly significant here, and more will be said of this later. In the school, mindful of the dimensions of self, social and intellectual development, through pair and group work, whole class discussion and role-play, teachers seek to extend a child's confidence, competence and verbal repertoire. The few tragic instances of pre-pubertal individuals who have been denied exposure to human language underline the social dimension of fluency with respect to learning the mother tongue. The sad case of Genie in 1970 in California, who was isolated from virtually all human contact until the age of thirteen, suggests that these isolated children make limited progress to what may be loosely described as pidgin levels but can never master the full grammar and syntax of their native language. Pinker (1994, p.293) asserts that "acquisition of a normal language is guaranteed for children up to the age of six, is steadily compromised from then until shortly after puberty, and is rare thereafter".

We cannot conclude this section, however, without mentioning boys and literacy, as their lack of performance in English in schools has become a major issue in schools over the decade and more. In many co-educational schools, there are usually greater numbers of girls in more able sets, while a higher proportion of boys is located in classes containing pupils of less academic ability, many possessing individual education plans or statements.

The significance of this issue is indicated by the number and frequency of official reports on the matter. For example, in 1993 OFSTED published a major report entitled *Boys and English* that set out ways of tackling male underachievement in English, and key issues were followed up in 1996 with *Gender Divide: Performance Differences between Boys and Girls at School*. In 2003 a follow-up report stated in its main findings "when boys enter secondary school they are already well behind girls in English, except in a small number of schools, the gap does not close during the secondary years. Boys continue to achieve less well than girls in Key Stage 3 tests and GCSE examinations" (OFSTED, 2003a, p. 3).

There is no reason to suppose that things are different in Wales as many schools in the Principality, in their self-evaluation documents, continue to highlight disparities in achievement between boys and girls. It has long been known that boys tend to stop reading for pleasure earlier than girls and that they have different reading preferences, and, whereas girls will read boys' books, boys are reluctant to read girls' books. Newman (2005) provides an interesting summary of the debate and suggests practical ways in which a "laddish" culture that tends to reject English can be combated. She also offers a useful concluding comment pertinent to the cultural and socio-economic threads found throughout this chapter.

> As the "Boys and English" debate continues, we should remember that gendered identities are shaped in complex, subtle ways, and that laddishness does not necessarily mean a resistance to the subject. As we consider the achievements of boys in English, we must maintain a clear awareness of the subtle and contrasting modes of masculinity expressed by differing socio-economic groups and use that awareness to inform our pedagogy (Newman, 2005, p. 39)

III: POPULAR PERCEPTIONS

What follows is a Hansard transcript from the House of Lords (16th October 1996):

> Lord Quirk: …. many of us have felt for years that the quality of teacher training lies at the

heart of our educational problems…..Is not the plain fact that the writing of sixteen year-olds in 1993 and 1994 was found to be starkly inferior to that of their counterparts in 1980?

Most people, including lords of the realm it seems, have strong views on language, and, because language is all around us, it is easy to express our views about different usage and changes in use. The views expressed are usually strongly negative. However, like the process of evolution itself, language change often naturally occurs where new habits and social, leisure and commercial activities necessitate the need for change and the coinage of new words and phrases. For instance, the Internet and Popular Culture may propel new items such as "pants" (rubbish), "blog" (web log), "papped" (photographed by the paparazzi) or more obvious compounds such as "ringtone" and "combover" into the mainstream. Young people are usually at the forefront of changes that may meet with the general public's disapproval and the disapprobation of the guardians of tradition in language matters. The moral panics that frequently occur with regard to perceptions of the decline and fall of the "Queen's English" feature prominently in the popular press. A brief list of typical bugbears follows:

- The abandonment of traditional grammar teaching (sometime in the 1960s) has led to a decline in standards of speech and writing.

- Deterioration in pupils' literacy has occurred accompanied by a decrease in private reading especially with regard to the classics.

- The undesirable influence of American English through the media ("thru" etc) continues to corrupt our homegrown English.

- The impact of new technologies on language, for example, textspeak has led to a further alarming downturn.

- There has been a rise in swearing and the use of "bad" language.

Many of these problems and perceptions of educational malaise are often attributed to the teaching of English. For example, in one edition of *The Daily Mail* in 2006, the public was informed that in 2005 children of eleven could not spell the simplest words; ninety-seven and ninety per cent respectively of eleven year olds taking Key Stage 2 English National Curriculum tests tripped up over words such as "washing" and "before". Standards, it is suggested, have not risen despite the introduction of the literacy hour in England in 1998, in which teachers' responsibilities include ensuring that pupils can spell. We are also informed that employers are complaining that they have to spend millions on remedial lessons for staff who left school lacking basic literacy and numeracy skills. The deterioration in language skills is attributed to advances in technology and use of the ever-present mobile in the hands of youngsters. *The Mail* continued:

> Literary experts have already drawn a link between the cult of text messaging and the decline of spelling and grammar. Exam boards are warning that GCSE Language students are increasingly using text language such as "2" for "too", "gr8" for "great" and "u" for "you" (Clark, 2006, p.7).

Andrews (2006) in a wide-ranging international study of the value of grammar teaching, points out that there is still little evidence to demonstrate that the teaching of formal grammar is effective, though teaching sentence combination does show a positive effect on the writing of five to sixteen-year olds.

However, concerns about a collapse in standards of literacy are not the preserve of the popular press and the anxieties are not confined to jeremiahs on standards in schools. *The Times Higher Education Supplement* in February 2006 ran an article which reported the views of 250 university admissions staff whose opinions on academic standards suggested that today's students are falling behind those of students ten years ago. Referring to poor literacy skills, several tutors commented:

> They can't even write in sentences. Their spelling is appalling. They can't be understood. They cut and paste essays from the web. Reading books is a skill that has been lost (Wilde, *et al.* 2005, p. 14).

Technology with its attraction of easy communication- some might say facile- lies at the centre of these new anxieties about language and literacy. And these anxieties extend to content as well as the innovative orthography of texting. At the time of writing a damning report on young people's ability to express themselves in writing is about to be published by the Royal Literary Fund. At the centre of many of the criticisms about students' inadequacies are accusations that:

- A "tick-box" culture exists especially in secondary schools where pupils are spoon-fed and rewarded for bits of information and knowledge.

- Social and cultural changes together with reliance on the Internet have led to a situation whereby pupils are unable to "find their way around a book".

- Universities, however, still demand written assignments and sustained analysis of text.

The report continues:

> Many students have difficulty not just in structuring a sentence, but in structuring paragraphs or essays as a whole….they seem to have had very little experience of writing. In consequence, their essays are often incoherent not only at the level of the sentence but also in their overall argument. Absent, in may cases, is any sense of confident fluency, of knowing how to mount an argument, how to articulate it with clarity and consistency and how to see it through to a decent conclusion (Spurling, 2006, p. 7).

These findings, which strongly suggest that current strategies are failing, are the result of the work of 230 professional writers in seventy-one universities and indicate high levels of dissatisfaction with outcomes of concerted government-led initiatives over the last two decades. Julia Strong wrote in *Literacy Today* in June 2002:

> The problem with the literacy strategies is that they are created by people with no sense of joy of the written word ... I remember a time when documents on the subject of English teaching were written by people of genuine accomplishment and solid, well-rounded knowledge of the field - I'm thinking of the Bullock Report. But now we have this sort of half-baked drivel slapped down in front of us, like greasy food on a dirty plate brought to us by a drunken waiter... (Strong, 2002, p. 14).

Aware, no doubt, of its detractors, the Department for Education and Skills (DFES) has commissioned evaluations, for example, Beard (1998) and Harrison (2002) of the effectiveness of recent literacy initiatives. The evaluation undertaken by Harrison (2002) is systematic and tackles many of key issues raised by critics of these schemes, though he is broadly supportive of the new rigour which is characteristic of approaches to literacy in many schools in England. (Some schools in Wales voluntarily follow these schemes.) Harrison (2002, p. 3) makes the following points:

- As we do not yet have a unified theory of language, how do we measure the success of such initiatives which cannot be measured simply?

- The research on the teaching sequence - the five elements in lessons - is unequivocally positive.

- There are reservations regarding the strategy's recommendations for pedagogy with regard to the teaching of grammar. Though the strategy has moved to the teaching of grammar in context, there are still issues concerning the ways in which grammar may be taught effectively.

- Changing literacy standards is not a skills issue: it is a systems issue. Harrison with regard to more imaginative approaches (p. 34) goes on to explain that research carried out by Langer (2001) in the USA showed that teachers in "schools that were beating the odds were in touch with their students, their profession, their colleagues, and society at large. …. They did not take a curriculum off the shelf and apply it to their students uncritically…."

Harrison's word "uncritically" seems central to the debate here; language learning is a complex and dynamic process for which there are no ready-made solutions. What emerges from the debate is the need for each teacher to weigh up the linguistic potential of every individual in a class in a particular locality and devise effective and exciting lessons as freethinking professionals. And, most importantly, we should not lose sight of the enormous potential of creativity at all levels in English. Stevens (2005) offers a useful discussion of how more imaginative approaches to literacy can include the Key Stage 3 National Literacy Strategy so that meaning and creativity are breathed into the framework. It seems reasonable to conclude that all teachers should adopt a flexible approach to the subject so that we make it our own; the mechanistic implementation of top-down strategies is a soulless and futile enterprise that will ultimately do little for teachers and pupils alike.

IV: LANGUAGE AS A SYSTEM

At a descriptive level, all the language varieties we find in Britain are closely connected to the regional, cultural or social origins of the speakers of those areas. At this point we also need to be aware that linguists who take the *descriptive* approach see all forms of usage as equally valid and worthy of study. Descriptive linguists focus on the language as it is now; this approach is usually synonymous with the synchronic approach, that is, it is concerned with the study of language as it appears at a given period in time, usually the present. The focus on descriptive linguistics followed the pioneering work of Saussure (1983) who asserted that it was vital that language be viewed as an interconnected system rather than as individual items, in the same way that we might consider a game of chess and all its pieces. A snapshot of the chessboard with a game in progress at a particular time is *synchronic*, but once a piece is moved it has an effect on the whole of the game and the relationship between pieces that would require diachronic (or historical) analysis. Additionally, the *diachronic* approach focuses on historical linguistics, which may trace the development and evolution of language over time.

Before Saussure's insights, linguists would spend their time furthering enquiries into the discovery that the Indo-European language tree connected Ancient Sanskrit in India to modern languages in Europe. Much of their work was necessarily centred on written texts and often involved detailed study of language forms from the past. At the turn of the Twentieth Century, Saussure's radical departure was to ask his students to turn away from these fixed points in the evolution of language and to explore instead the current state of language in the period from 1903 to 1907 by analysing the spoken word in his newly conceived "Course in General Linguistics". We shall shortly explore writing and speech in its educational context today.

V: LANGUAGE CHANGE

In addition to the regional varieties of language all teachers need to be aware of the continual process of change in language. We also need to be cautious of assuming that in the past some Golden Age existed in which our language was pure and stable. Change signifies life. As Weimann observes, "language change characterises every living language. If a language does not change it is dead (cf. classical Latin or Greek). Language change is an essential property of language" (Weimann, 1995, p. 16).

Such linguists as Pei (1965) divide language change into four basic categories; I have added my own examples to illustrate these.

(a) **Sound change**, for example, "beard" – post vocalic "r" or the "gh" of "nigh". It is worth noting that English spelling retains the now silent sounds (cf. knead and gnaw) These sounds were once pronounced in the spoken language but their presence is now confined to the written word. It is interesting to note, however, that in some accents of English, for example, in American and Scottish English, the post-vocalic r is still sounded and the possible influence of accents on children's spelling should be borne in mind.

(b) **Semantic change**, for example, the word "ignorant" in Shakespeare (which was used neutrally in the sense of simply "not knowing") or the word "awesome" in the last decade. Changes that occur in speech can occur rapidly but will take longer to become consolidated in writing.

(c) **Morphological change:** Morphology involves the study of systems of categories and rules regarding word formation and interpretation. We have dropped the "st" from "thou sayst" which is now restricted to Biblical and dialect usage. Again, we should note that some of these second personal singular forms still exist in dialect form, for example, in dialects of Yorkshire, and that these may too influence children's home language and impact on their language usage generally. Teachers need to recognise these features and be sensitive to local language forms. Teachers should also note that a morpheme is the smallest unit of meaning: for example, put simply *tap* is the singular form- with the simple addition of the letter *s*, we have the plural form *taps*.

(d) **Syntactical changes:** We no longer use negative constructions in the way that Shakespeare did, for example, in *King Lear* (2:2:125): "I am too old to learn: Call not your stocks for me". We might say today: "Do not call for the stocks for me", though the device of the stocks used to confine the ankles of disorderly offenders would probably need some explanation.

(e) **Lexical change:** To these categories we should also add *lexical change* (see Crystal, 1997 for a fuller discussion), which includes changes in vocabulary, for instance, new words and phrases. Examples are:

■   a "shoe-in" for a "cinch";

■   "suits" meaning bosses in smart attire.

Further examples include the conversion of a word from one class to another; for example, when a verb is used as a noun. Thus, in a Radio 4 programme on 27th Feb 2006 a police spokesperson said that it was "a big ask" to request men to come forward to rule themselves out as suspects to a crime. Conversely, nouns are frequently used as verbs, for example:

"The critics ***rubbished*** Brown's book."

"How can I ***access*** this material?"

"These findings must be ***factored*** and ***evidenced*** before they can be published in a research report."

It seems that Jespersen's prediction in 1946 that non-standard varieties would be reduced as nationalism and centralisation increased may well have come true to some extent. However, dialects are still very much with us, though the regional versions we hear on television "soap operas" are usually presented as simplified versions that add local colour without the complexity of real life. Language is intrinsically dynamic and in Britain today there continue to be different varieties of language all around us. These varieties are usually connected with social stratification and geography. But these varieties are not monoliths. For instance, Received Pronunciation (RP), the traditional marker of the ruling class, has undergone subtle changes since its clipped tones of the 1950s and there has been considerable debate whether regional dialects are still as strong and distinctive or whether they have been subject to levelling. Williams and Kerswill (1999, p. 141) define dialect levelling as "a process whereby differences between regional varieties are reduced, features which make varieties distinctive disappear, and new features emerge which are adopted by speakers over a wide geographical area." Undoubtedly, since the Second World War, there has been a great deal of immigration and social mobility which has led to the dispersal and mixing of accents and dialects that were formally more separated. Similarly, Aitchison suggests that in the last century there has been a gradual move towards homogenisation: "Although a considerable number of local accents are still found in Britain, dialects are dying out, due to the influence of education, radio and television" (Aitchison, 2003, p.115).

Let us remind ourselves that the term "dialect" can be a loose one but is normally taken to embrace the difference in grammar and lexis (or vocabulary) rather than the distinctive accent of a particular region. Thus, a dialect is the localised form of a language used over an identifiable regional area that is distinct from the standard form. On this basis, we can consider American English as a different dialect from British English, and, though there is less variation over a far greater geographical area, there are, of course, different varieties of American English (Crystal, 1997, p. 312).

A useful way of illustrating the distinction between accent and dialect follows which also raises issues concerning the actual nature of a dialect. In the 1990s, the emergence of a new variety of language, that of "Estuary English" was identified. This type of English seems to be largely based on accent, as its grammar conforms to the standard. It is a variety found largely in the Home Counties of England. Kerswill (1996) suggests it may be advancing northwards from this base, though Crystal (1995) is more sceptical of its encroachment. Typical features of this accent are more glottal stops for /t/ as in "butter" and increasing use of vocalised /l/ as in "hill" that produces sounds approximating to "hiw". Przedlacka's (2001) authoritative study suggests that it may be an over-simplification to regard Estuary English as a distinct dialect halfway between Cockney and Received Pronunciation. It seems more likely that this new variety presents itself as a loose conglomeration of modified regional speech that indicates a growing trend in our global village:

Jane Setter of the English Language Pronunciation Unit describes it thus:

> Estuary English is an umbrella term for a number of accents of (loosely) the South East of England which have some similar accent features. For example, varieties which come under Estuary tend to have a vocalised /l/ in syllable final position (which means /l/ is realised as a vowel similar to the one in "foot", e.g. "milk", "apple"); use glottal stop inter-vocalically and syllable finally (e.g. "butter", "cat"), and so on. But there is actually quite a lot of difference among varieties which fall under the Estuary umbrella (Rhodes, 2005).

There is a good deal of evidence from Kerswill (1996) and others that the language of young people in London is powerful in influencing speech patterns throughout the UK. However, the BBC Voices project (2004-6) found that many regional accents are still holding their own and that Estuary English is not taking over throughout the country. The researchers involved also felt that immigration was among the factors leading to the new diversity of language in Britain today. David Crystal, consultant to the project, comments: "Some of the old rural dialects have disappeared as that way of life has dwindled, but they are being replaced by a new range of dialects from ethnic groups as they settle into communities" (Crystal, 2005, p.1).

It is also interesting to note that adolescents are the richest source of innovation in language and that we might expect London with its rich social mix to act as the epicentre of linguistic change. Roughly one third of London's primary schoolchildren have languages other than English and there is evidence (Kerswill and Williams 2005) to suggest that a multiracial vernacular is emerging among young Londoners and that this may be impacting on mainstream speech. Another fascinating perspective on people who drive change forward comes from Tagliamonte (2005) in Canada. In her research in Toronto she found that: "One of the most pervasive findings of sociolinguistics is that, when you have language changing, women tend to lead the change. They pick up the new form and they carry it forward probably about a generation ahead of the guys" (Tagliamonte, 2005, p1).

Finally, all teachers hear and see continual evidence of language change all around them, and we should be wary of simply assuming that change equates with deterioration. There are no good reasons to assume that the contemporary state of the language is any less effective as a tool of communication than earlier ones.

VI: STANDARD MODELS?

One of the most controversial topics in discussions of language involves the notion of a standard model. Given the complex social, cultural and political history of the British Isles, this is not surprising. We have already discussed descriptive approaches in relation to language, and many linguists argue that all languages, and dialects too, are equally good in that they are able to meet the social and communicative needs of their speakers. Many teachers were outraged when early versions of the National Curriculum for English in the late 1980s threatened to prescribe spoken standard norms for children. At the time there was much discussion whether the imposition of such norms should extend outside the classroom to children's informal usage in the playground. Many teachers questioned the notion of insensitive intervention in any context. However, that such interference in children's leisure activities could be contemplated was perhaps a measure of popular perceptions of a sharp decline in standards of English in schools generally; a slant that was convenient to the political agenda of market-driven reform at the time. More specifically, a survey conducted by Hudson and Holmes in 1995 found that in a small-scale investigation of spoken English used by eleven and fifteen year olds:

- Thirty-two per cent of speakers did not use any non- standard forms.
- Girls used fewer non-standard forms than boys at both ages.
- Almost every non-standard form was used by some speakers alongside its standard equivalent by "choice" rather than out of ignorance.

The emphasis in the National Curriculum is now rightly on standard English in its written form and includes recognition of variation in speech, though this does not mean that teachers should not provide some encouragement and indeed direct instruction regarding the norms of Standard Spoken English (SSE). Standard English may be usefully defined as:

> that variety of English which is used in print and which is normally taught in schools and to non-native speakers learning the language. It is also the variety which is generally spoken by educated people and used in the broadcast media and other similar public situations.

Standard English is in reality spoken in many regional and international accents without any communication problems. Wales has its own distinct linguistic heritage that has produced a range of regional accents and dialects in both English and Welsh. Interestingly, Crystal (1995, p.110) points out that, if we argue standard English is a dialect, then it should be seen as a special one as it has no regional base in Britain. It has particular grammar forms that broadly conform to the standard grammar of the language; it is socially acceptable and is expected and appropriate in formal public contexts. But, when we listen to speakers of Standard English, there will be nothing in their vocabulary or grammar that connects them to a particular part of the country. Of course, all speakers have accents, but Standard English has nothing to do with pronunciation. Notions of prestige that indicate a speaker's social position and educational background are also indicated in someone's ability to communicate in a standard form that is widely understood. Interestingly, Crystal points out that in reality few speakers other than radio newscasters, for example, use it when they talk: "Most of us speak a variety of regional English or an admixture of standard and regional Englishes... More than anywhere else, Standard English is to be found in print" (Crystal, 1995, p. 110).

More of speech and writing shortly. Many teachers of English and other subjects feel that part of their role as educators is to make pupils increasingly aware of these correct forms and the situations in which such usage, either in spoken or written contexts, is appropriate. At the same time, they may wish to help pupils to be increasingly confident about the variety of language that they bring to the classroom. The National Literacy Strategy is quite specific, however, in stating that in the third term of Year 5 pupils should be taught grammatical awareness, which includes "avoidance of non-standard dialect words". Fixed notions of a single standard are further complicated by the fact that English is now a world language in which standard British English and American English strongly influence the English of other nations to varying degrees.

To return to the UK and the debate about Standard English in schools, much of the tension has stemmed from deep-rooted divisions between descriptivists and prescriptivists. Descriptivists, as we have seen, strive to adopt an objective position from which they view a language and its varieties as systems. Prescriptivists, on the other hand, take a more judgemental approach and contend that certain varieties of language have more value than others. Over the last hundred years from Fowler (1906) to Truss (2003) there has been a long line of those who are keen to lay down rules about what is correct and incorrect. As the term suggests, they may wish to prescribe that some forms of language are preferable to others and may argue that certain usages, particularly those that are non-standard, should be avoided. Honey is the most outspoken of these authority figures and he unashamedly defends traditional notions of "good English" and refutes the notion that all languages and varieties of them are equally acceptable in school contexts. In chapter three of his book, significantly entitled *Language is Power: The Story of Standard English and its Enemies*, he declaims:

> This book ... is about the way the linguistic dogma has been used in order to oppose an emphasis on Standard English in Britain and North America. Assumptions about the special value of Standard English cannot be supported if, as the dogma goes on to state, not only all languages, but all varieties of a language, are equally good (Honey, 1997, p. 21).

The strength of Honey's views is evident, though in my experience there are few, if any, teachers of English, who do not see the value and empowerment that proficient use of Standard English can offer a pupil. Equally, however, we should not lack the sensitivity to respond appropriately to the linguistic varieties that pupils bring with them to the classroom. On a practical note, it is my view that Standard

English cannot be effectively and efficiently taught unless the teacher has a clear understanding of the small but significant differences between Standard English and the local dialect norms of a particular region.

VII: PRESTIGE AND STANDARD VARIETIES

It is possible to find companies that offer elocution lessons and coaching to soften one's accent. We should, however, distinguish clearly between the skills of effective verbal communication such as clarity which these enterprises claim to develop, usually with a view to improving one's job prospects, and the desirability of retaining the badges of personal and cultural identity that regional accents bestow on speakers. In a devolved United Kingdom, issues of social and ethnic identity have been widely debated and the variety of language we use is a key indicator of our social identity. Variation in language is an evident feature of community life and often signals social and cultural identities that all teachers should respect and explore in classrooms. Issues of clarity also relate to the key skill of communication, whilst language diversity should be a feature of the English curriculum as the sections in the National Curriculum regarding language development specify.

One thing is certain; we have certainly moved on from the societal constraints of post-war Britain which Beryl Bainbridge recalls:

> In those far off days (1940s), it was considered important for people to talk properly; even a job as a shop assistant required a knowledge of the correct pronunciation of Standard English. Consequently, I was later sent to elocution lessons …in Liverpool, where I intoned "How now, brown cow" and "Claire has fair hair" (Bainbridge, 2005, p. 3).

Indeed, this extract highlights a common misunderstanding regarding the term "standard" since we can pronounce Standard English in any accent. If we were to look for the accent that certainly a generation ago carried great prestige, then pure Received Pronunciation (RP) would no doubt have been our benchmark. Crystal (1995) points out, however, that nowadays few people speak what may be termed pure Received Pronunciation and that many people speak with modified Received Pronunciation. What is also subsumed in Bainbridge's observations, of course, are notions of social prestige that continues to make up a great deal of Britain's social and cultural history. It also brings to mind a line from Shaw's Preface to *Pygmalion* (1916) which was itself a satire on the typical preoccupations with social class of the England of that period. Here again language variation is connected with working on one's accent with a view to being more upwardly mobile in a highly stratified society.

> Finally, and for the encouragement of people troubled with accents that cut them off from all high employment, I may add that the change wrought by Professor Higgins in the flower girl is neither impossible nor uncommon (Shaw, 2003, p. 1).

It is perhaps significant that George Bernard Shaw chose a young woman as the protagonist of his linguistic experiment; sociolinguists have noted that women use more standard forms than men. Men use more "stigmatised forms", for example, double negatives ("I ain't got none.") and tend to have stronger regional accents when social class is stable. Wardhaugh (1993, p.314) offers the example of schoolgirls in Scotland who pronounce the /t/ in words like "water" and "got" more often than boys who prefer to substitute a glottal stop /ʔ/ as in "butter" and "bottle". There is also the phenomenon of covert prestige. In both America and Britain "an association between working-class speech and masculinity and 'toughness' has been noted…The covert prestige of working-class speech obviously attracts men rather than women" (Coupland and Jaworski, 1997, pp. 284-285). This is a key point for all teachers to note in relation to interactions in the classroom between teacher and pupils and well as pupil to pupil interchanges.

We may argue that these "norms" are further reinforced by the repeated image of hard-men on television and cinema, from John Wayne cowboy films to Vinnie Jones's macho centrepiece *Lock, Stock and Smoking Barrel* in 1998. Romaine (1994) notes that women have more status consciousness and concern for politeness, whilst other studies show that in mixed-sex conversation men interrupt women more. These last two points have undoubted significance for teachers when class discussions take place and some management of talk is required in the classroom to maintain an ethos that encourages all pupils to speak and be heard. In this context, though, we should also beware of the stereotypes of the "co-operative" female and the "assertive" male.

It is also evident that perceptions of the role of teachers in the eyes of more conservative members of the general public, often with support from the media with respect to the teaching of English, may lead to beliefs that Standard English should be imposed as a prescriptive norm in schools. The majority of primary school teachers are increasingly women, and they undoubtedly play a leading role in standardising the language norms of children. In 1974 Trudgill suggested that some males may associate standard speech with femininity and that middle-class speech may carry feminine connotations because schools, which generally support middle-class speech, are staffed largely by women. In 2006, in secondary schools in England and Wales, only about twenty-two per cent of full-time teachers are men, while in primary schools the percentage is as low as fifteen.

There are also issues here of gender and status in that such linguistic features as taking turns in conversations may be perceived by boys as belonging to women's language in situations when males may see themselves in a subordinate position in terms of classroom interaction. The negative prestige of non-standard forms can be a typical response from some pupils, boys and girls alike, and, in my experience, may be a simple reaction against school norms in general rather than expressions of class or gender solidarity. However, these tendencies need to be borne in mind in relation to teachers' interaction with pupils and the development of effective classroom management strategies. Studies also show that women are more sensitive to the use of standard forms and to the wider social implications of speech. In addition, they tend to be more conservative when standard forms carry more status but they can also be innovators, as they will generally shift according to style and where change is more socially appropriate as social situations are rarely static. We should, however, be aware of the dangers that these generalisations embody, as it is simplistic to see all female language interactions and events as basically co-operative as opposed to the competitive communications of boys. In all classrooms reality is far more nuanced, and many of these largely adult tendencies will be represented to greater or lesser extents with the age groups of children taught. For example, Labov's much cited 1972 study of adult New Yorkers' pronunciation of /r/ in such words as "car" and "park" found, amongst other fascinating features, that lower middle-class speakers are more consciously aware of speech as an indicator of social class and make a concerted effort to improve their status (Labov, 1972b, pp. 43-70).

However, as a teacher, one would clearly need to be cautious about assuming that the same reflective and "corrective" procedures are operating with children who are still less self-aware than adults and coming to terms with their linguistic and social identities. Secondary age pupils are more likely to display instances of greater awareness with regard to the language they use in connection with their developing identity, though here too negative prestige and toughness as well as the kudos of the subculture begin to emerge. For instance, Hudson and Holmes (1995, p. 16) found that in their survey of 350 eleven and fifteen year olds there was "no evidence of a decrease in NSE [non Standard English] usage with age; in fact, our figures show the contrary trend".

Finally, Chambers (2003, p. 159) in a cross-cultural study that involved the Middle-East, where females generally occupy socially inferior positions to men, points out that most people of both genders, when asked to evaluate speakers who use standard and non-standard forms, judge standard speakers more positively and accord higher economic status to them. Nevertheless, there is the fact that Britain is made up from four distinct nations each with its own linguistic traditions, and, as Chambers has noted particularly in connection with dialect, covert prestige clings to those varieties with no less tenacity than overt prestige attaches itself to the standard. As teachers, however, we need to be aware that non-standard usage in the classroom may be observable in vernacular forms that are based on local dialect and that other forms may be more the product of popular culture and contemporary slang. For example, "dumb" may be used to describe "a dumb (foolish) idea", an increasingly popular American usage, whereas "dull" in South Wales dialect can also be used to express the same notion. Each form may carry a particular cachet, though, as we have seen, both non-standard forms may be more prevalent in the speech and writing of boys rather than girls, even when their social class is similar. We shall move on to consider social class and language shortly.

VIII: LANGUAGE DEPRIVATION AND EDUCATIONAL DISADVANTAGE

... the "celebration" of children's home language and environment by educationalists was seldom whole-hearted. Wilkinson, for instance, while passionately asserting the validity of non-standard accents, nevertheless designated working class homes sites of "language deprivation" because of the fragmentation of family life brought about by shift work, "school and canteen feeding" and too much television (1965, p. 46). This negative stereotyping of the language of working class families was fuelled subsequently by (misinterpretations of) Basil Bernstein's (1971) work on restricted and elaborated codes (Stierer and Maybin, 1994, p.141).

It is now rare to find references to deficit theory in current literature on language in education, but the topic merits some brief discussion here in relation to the current initiatives promoting assessment for learning, particularly with respect to ways in which teachers respond to and evaluate children's spoken and written language. It is also worthy of scrutiny in relation to issues of institutional racism and concomitant attitudes to language and cultural diversity. To recapitulate, from the 1960s onwards the idea that working class children might be as linguistically impoverished as they were socially disadvantaged became an area of heated discourse. As Stierer and Maybin (1994) have indicated in the quotation above, in the early seventies Bernstein's ideas (1971) that postulated the existence of separate codes (restricted and elaborated) were taken to suggest that working-class school children, because of their reliance on a restricted code, simply did not possess the type and range of language to express abstract thought and consequently to succeed in school. Whether or not these ideas were misinterpreted, such suggestions were in any case swiftly countered by Labov (1972a), who argued that non-standard language was an equally powerful and effective means for thinking and that middle-class standard language could be less direct and more verbose. He convincingly demonstrated that Larry, a speaker of non-standard Negro English (NNE) who used what approximated to the restricted code, was not only a very skilful speaker but also that he could articulate complex ideas regarding the existence of God and other metaphysical concepts. (It should be noted that the term "Black English" has now largely replaced the designation "Non-standard Negro English".)

Though Bernstein refined his views several times, most notably to assert that working class children might occasionally use the elaborated code, it is worth exploring his basic position in relation to his idea that there were two different linguistic codes operating in the English repertoire – the restricted code and the elaborated code- and that these were linked to the logical thought and expression required in the school system. The key differences are as follows:

- In the elaborated code, syntax is more formally correct and corresponds more closely to Standard English.

- The restricted code relies on intimacy and often uses deixis to the extent that its content is strongly localised and context-dependent.

- The elaborated code is more effective in conveying abstract ideas and factual information, whereas the restricted code can convey attitudes and feelings.

- Greater use of a variety of connectives is found in the elaborated code; the restricted code typically relies on simpler coordination terms such as "and" and "but".

- In the elaborated code we find more subordinate clauses and fewer unfinished sentences, whilst the restricted code has simpler syntax and more clichés.

Crucially, Bernstein alleged, working class children generally operated in the restricted code and this had far-reaching educational implications in that the school system relies heavily on children's ability to use the elaborated code in formal speech situations and in most writing tasks, particularly in examinations. The elaborate code was deemed to be a more effective mode of communication for these tasks, as it is more explicit and independent; the restricted coded relied more heavily on assumptions about knowledge shared by speakers and thus was less useful once a speaker was outside the local situation. It should be borne in mind that the restricted code does not refer to restricted vocabulary but rather to its range and "framing" of ideas that often rely on a "taken for granted" underpinning.

Many of these differences were said to have arisen from the different ways that children were spoken to in the home by their parents. Bernstein asserted thatlower class mothers used elaborated code less frequently when speaking to their children and that these differences in the process of socialisation had negative impacts on the working-class children's modes of communication in school. Middle class children could use both codes; but they could switch between more intimate situations of family and friends, which were best served by the restricted code, to the more public mode that the elaborated code provided. It also needs to be said that Bernstein was fully aware of the reaction his theory was attracting from both left and right at the time of the publication of his ideas. The right saw his theories as justifying ideas of "high" culture while the left predominantly saw the work as yet another stereotype of the working-class from a middle-class perspective.

These ideas were sometimes extended to assessment. In what were thought at the time to be standardised tests to determine vocabulary and grammar, working class children generally scored lower in educational tests (Holmes, 1992). Typically, children from working class backgrounds would be interviewed individually in formal test situations and would often respond monosyllabically. Many teachers who find themselves talking to strange children in formal situations on a one-to-one basis will be familiar with this tendency. Middle-class children tended to do much better in these situations, and Holmes pointed out that pupils from more affluent backgrounds were generally better able to interact and respond explicitly in the ways that the testers anticipated. Sociolinguists gradually produced evidence that there were significant differences in the ways the tests were perceived and received by the children. As Holmes has written, "an adult stranger using the standard dialect would be more likely to resemble the friend of your mother or father if you were a middle class child" (Holmes, 1992, p. 361).

It was also concluded that middle-class children were more confident and skilful when it came to displaying what they knew in these formal situations. Working class children were less familiar with social contexts that required them to be explicit verbally and thus wrongly conveyed the impression that they were verbally impoverished. Subsequent research by Michaels (1981) in the USA indicated that Afro-American children were highly adept verbally with their friends, and in the UK Wells (1979) discovered similar high levels of proficiency with young children from lower social backgrounds in their familiar home situations. It should also be noted that in written tests the language used was generally closer to that used by middle-class children and that answers by children were marked wrongly if they responded in the vernacular and supplied answers that did not correspond with the predetermined marking schedule.

To summarise, we may conclude that it is unwise to assume that in the classroom there are simple, sure-fire ways of assessing a child's linguistic ability. The perils of deficit theory lie in attempts to blame the child and his/her home conditions for shortcomings in language rather than to put into practice effective educational programmes to promote language development for all children. In today's busy classrooms, teachers are required to assess children frequently and, consequently, where practicable, they need to observe pupils in a number of different oral and written situations, both formal and informal, before any secure or summative judgement can be made about their linguistic capabilities. Teachers are, however, pragmatic people, and many of them know that the skilful use of role-play and drama as well as opportunities for personal and creative writing can often reveal the hidden language potential of their pupils.

IX: SPEECH AND WRITING

Every language has more than one variety, and this is particularly the case in the way a language is spoken. Much has been said of the influences that the home and peer group have on the language of children, and it is therefore useful, as we move towards the final sections of this chapter, to examine some of the key differences between speech and writing together with their educational implications. The National Curriculum for Wales (ACCAC, 2000a) is quite explicit that pupils should "be given opportunities to consider the development of English, including: current influences on spoken and written language; [and] the differences between speech and writing" (ACCAC, 2000a).

Teachers of English are expected to develop pupils' understanding of how language operates in a wide range of situations and make them aware of the key differences between speech and writing. The ability to speak appears to be innate (Pinker, 1994) whereas writing, as all teachers will know, requires a lengthy period of apprenticeship. Pupils' first efforts in writing usually build on the spoken model, particularly in the first few years of education when their writing is often close to their talk. In writing, from the outset we are encouraged to write in sentences; the National Literacy Strategy at Key Stage 1 (Year 1: Term 1) states that: "pupils should be taught to use awareness of the grammar of a sentence and to begin using full stops to demarcate a sentence" (DFEE, 1997b, p.20) and in the first term of Year 3 "to write in complete sentences" (DFEE, 1997b, p.33). Many teachers are intuitively aware, however, that it does not normally make sense to apply the unit of the fully-formed sentence to normal speech, and this difference should alert us to the fact that, though the grammars of spoken and written English are close, they are not one and the same. Put simply, speech is not a less well-formed version of writing.

Most teachers are now adopt a pragmatic approach broadly in line with the National Curriculum, whereby standard forms of grammar and syntax are emphasised in their evaluations of pupils' written language, whilst greater latitude is exercised in relation to their spoken forms. Teachers, like most of us, often feel more knowledgeable about written English in terms of its codified grammar and notions of correctness. For example, instances of the double negative ("You ain't seen nothing yet." "I ain't got none.") present themselves as clear candidates for the red pen. Writing also has the advantage of being static and permanent, whilst, unless we take the trouble to record speech, it is transient and often elusive when we try to assess it formally.

Moreover, as we have seen, spoken language has dialects and a range of accents which undoubtedly make the assessment of oral language more complex. Still more significantly, we may not be aware that spoken language operates on different grammatical principles from those of written language, as research by McCarthy and Carter (1996) has begun to demonstrate. The differences regarding the structural principles in accordance with which spoken language operates are highly significant and have important implications for today's classrooms. Since the sixties, the use of talk has been recognised as a powerful tool for learning and effective teachers take advantage of the immediacy and power of talk as a powerful vehicle for learning. In terms of structure, however, the spontaneous nature of talk means that many of the most productive exchanges may be unplanned beyond outlines and broad intentions. Speech is characterised by its prosodic features, especially the use of intonation, and through subtle changes in pitch and volume we can signal fine distinctions that go beyond the roughcast of print. Put another way, the limited range of punctuation marks such as capitals, layouts and question marks means that the nuances of speech cannot be clearly expressed in writing. We shall shortly return to a further consideration of these structural differences. Anyone who has attempted to create dialogue in creative writing will know that it is particularly difficult to represent intonation even with skilful use of punctuation and other orthographical tricks.

Novelists like Dickens and Emily Bronte have famously attempted to capture the complex qualities of accents and dialects through a variety of representations on the page. Here is an instance of how a writer strives to capture the voices of Cockney and Irish low-life in the early Nineteenth Century. We also create our own imagined version of this interchange complete with intonation:

"What 'ave we 'ere, boys?" said a voice.

"A werry respectable gen'leman to be aht on a night like this, an 'in St Giles an' al'", said another.

"For why's you fetched your doxy down our way, mister gentleman?" said another, Irish-accented this time (Thompson, 2006, p. 201).

Imaginative interpretations of Shakespeare's plays have built on the range of meanings that bare words on the page cannot simply encompass. Lady Macbeth's, "What, in our house?" is an oft-cited example of how intonation can signify a range of meanings:

MacDuff: O Banquo, Banquo,

                Our royal master's murdered!

Lady Macbeth: Woe, alas!

                What, in our house?

Banquo: Too cruel anywhere. Too cruel anywhere.

X: THE SPOKEN AND WRITTEN WORD: THE QUESTION OF PRIMACY

Over the centuries there has been no clear agreement whether the spoken or the written word should be accorded the status of "primacy". As we saw in connection with Saussure, earlier perspectives tended to stress the dominance of the written word, and Johnson, writing in the Eighteenth Century in the Preface to his dictionary, may be expressing a generally held view: "For pronunciation, the best general rule is to consider those as the most elegant speakers who deviate least from written words" (Johnson, 1755, p.1).

Johnson's observation hints at the common belief that spoken language is basically a lesser version of written language. The authority and status of the written word stems, of course, from its long association with political and economic power, the Church and the Law, respected literature and formal examination systems. The lore of the written word has held a certain potency since the time of the early scribes and the invention of writing circa 3,200 B.C. Furthermore, as Halliday suggests, "linguistics has played a part in sanctifying the written language and traditional grammar was a theory of written language" (Halliday, 1989, p. 97).

Many theorists, for instance, Bloomfield (1933), Saussure (1983), Bakhtin (1986) have, from different standpoints, argued for the supremacy of the spoken word. Saussure was quite explicit here: "The more inadequately writing represents what it ought to represent, the stronger is the tendency to give it priority over the spoken language. Grammarians are desperately eager to draw our attention to the written form" (Saussure, 1983, p. 29).

An astute overview of the primacy debate is provided by Hughes (1996) in which three broad camps are identified:

(a) That of Saussure and Bloomfield who conclude that writing is a subsidiary form of language.

(b) Linguists such as M.A.K. Halliday who see the two forms as complementary systems; social and cultural contexts determine which mode is the more appropriate for the purposes of communication.

(c) Those linguists like Olson (1994) and Goody (1987) who award primacy to the position of writing and its influence on cognitive thought.

As Kress (1982) indicates, however, though many linguists recognised the primacy of the spoken language, "this work confined itself to the sound-aspects of speech, and did not look at the grammatical organisation of speech as a mode of language" (p. 37). His study is concerned primarily with the different structural organisation of speech and writing and offers a wealth of insights regarding the many differences between speech and writing, particularly with regard to the structure, character and function of spoken language. Speech, he observes, was often seen as substandard, less well regarded and less correct particularly in its lower class forms. These viewpoints relate to earlier discussions regarding prestige. Kress also mentions a factor that often lies at the heart of learning in the classroom- the presence of an audience; this is a significant variable in communication so that "language is generated mutually in the interaction, with both participants contributing to the text, which is consequently not a single-speaker text" (Kress 1982, p. 19).

He too asserts that the structures of writing and speech need to be perceived as different. Besides intonation, another key characteristic of the verbal channel, and one that was central in the positing of a "restricted" code, is that of shared knowledge in which the speaker judges what is known and unknown to the listener. The social dimension of talk creates its own structures, some of which are dictated by its interactive nature; components which may be deemed redundant purely in terms of the information they impart are, in fact, important from an interactional viewpoint. Phatic elements, for example, such as greetings and small talk establish relationships and play a vital part in the ethos of school life and its impact on learning. At this point a table from Czerniewska (1985, p. 31) is helpful in providing a useful summary of the key differences between speech and writing.

The Oral Channel	The Written Channel
1: Sounds.	Letters.
2: Intonation patterns and changes in pitch and stress to convey attitudes.	No direct counterpart, though underlining words, parentheses, punctuation (e.g. exclamation marks) and capital letters can convey similar meanings.
3: Non-verbal gestures, eye-contact.	No direct counterpart, though different types of handwriting might express different meanings.
4: No direct equivalents, though changes in pitch and speed may express equivalent meanings.	Punctuation marks such as dashes, question marks and dots; different types of handwriting or typefaces.
5: Pauses and silence.	Gaps and dashes.
6: Expressions to indicate topic, e.g. "right then", "now".	Headings, new chapters, paragraph changes, words like "firstly" and "in conclusion".
7: No direct equivalent.	Capital letters for names and beginning of sentences.
8: Gap fillers, e.g. "You know"	Hesitations not shown in final form of writing.
9: Checks on listener attention and to maintain interaction such as: "Do you know what I mean?"	Perhaps less common but checks on reader involvement employed, e.g. "Try to bear in mind" and "If you have followed my arguments so far".

Spoken language, because it is immediate and often improvised, will typically "chain" ideas together (addition and accretion), whilst writing, which has often been carefully planned, utilises the device of embedding and subordination. Younger writers will typically construct long, rambling sentences held together with the conjunction "and". The National Literacy Strategy outlines a range of strategies to move children on from this tendency, and in Year 6, for example, recommends ways in which sentence construction and cohesion may be improved by the more frequent use of such connectives as "because" and "just then" and the writing of complex sentences.

An exploration of the differences between speech and writing can be particularly productive with older pupils from Year 9 onwards, but we should be careful not to imply that there are rigid divisions between speech and writing. As pupils may quickly point out, it is clear that speech is not always informal; spoken texts such as lectures and presentations may exhibit features that conform more closely to the typical registers of writing with clearly demarcated sentences containing co-ordinated and subordinated clauses. Conversely, e-mails and especially text messages often intentionally convey the casualness of speech.

XI: WIDER PERSPECTIVES

As mentioned earlier, children's first written work is usually based on their speech. In recognising the transition from the mode of talk to that of writing, Vygotsky (1986) provides useful cognitive insights in distinguishing between the two main functions of language: that of *inner speech* for mediating our own thoughts and that of *external speech* for communicating with others. In relation to literacy and the gulf that may exist between these two modes of communication for some children, he commented:

> ..... the difficulties of mastering the mechanics of writing [cannot] account for the tremendous lag between the schoolchild's oral language and written language (Vygotsky, 1986, p. 180).

In writing, he stressed, for reasons of clarity, precise syntax is often demanded in situations where there may be little shared knowledge between communicators, whereas oral communication is often characterised by its improvised and condensed immediacy.

The seminal views of another Russian, Bakhtin (1986), who offers further valuable perspectives regarding analyses of spoken and written language are also worthy of consideration for those concerned with literacy . His insights marked a real advance in terms of our understanding in that he based his analyses on everyday speech and writing on their social context rather than on abstract considerations of linguistic systems. Bakhtin thought Saussure's category of *langue* (the organising framework that native speakers possess to determine a well-formed expression) was simplistic, and contended that language was, like society, characterised by being stratified from the top and in perpetual flux with myriad forms that reflected complex social and cultural realities. For example, speech genres such as social dialects and specific group behaviours as well as what we recognise the language of authority (an important consideration in the classroom) all evolved organically and continue to compete with one another.

These ideas regarding language diversity and change relate to the jargon of OFSTED and the trendy language of subcultures as well as everyday norms of communication. We might consider all of these as separate genres. All these genres, Bahktin asserted, are part of the social and linguistic interplay of everyday life and these utterances reflect the speaker's world-view and particular situation. "The range of these utterances is highly heterogeneous and each one is a product of the sequence of previous or presupposed utterances- a dialogic relationship in which the utterance receives and responds to a singular situation" (Bakhtin, 1986, p. 60).

Another crucial distinction that Bakhtin makes in relation to the primacy debate is to distinguish broadly between primary and secondary genres. Speech is seen as primary and writing as secondary. Language as a whole is an unending dialogic web with endless possibilities; the primary genre is speech with its multiple, continuous interactions and cross-connections. Each utterance is unique and unrepeatable owing to its location in a social dimension that in turn determines the type of communication open to the individual. Teachers will be familiar with the feeling that a particular class or group of pupils is in some way unique. Much of this is invariably due to the social, cultural and linguistic behaviours of groups and individuals as they interact with the speech patterns and rituals of teachers - in the dynamic and distinctive ways that Bakhtin suggests. We need only cast our minds back to the idiosyncrasies of teachers who taught us to remind ourselves of the unique social and linguistic behaviours of these experiences which were so important at the time but which have now long vanished. These ideas also connect usefully with the drivers of language change that may lead to the growth of new local forms which then evolve and decay as the vagaries of linguistic fashion dictate.

Biber (1988) confirms these arguments in that, though speech is often given primacy by linguists, in Western cultures it is writing that is accorded more prestige by adults and that children are required to master the prescriptive rules of writing, not speech. In examining the claims for primacy with respect to both speech and writing, he concludes that it might well be the case that neither speech nor writing should be accorded the status of being "prime". He asserts that the linguistic comparison of both modes is important and that, unlike many past theories about how grammar operates in English, there is not necessarily a significant difference in the grammatical forms present in speech and writing. Spoken and written forms of language do, however, represent separate systems, each with its own logic and, more significantly, different stylistic tendencies. Another key consideration is that writing tends to be more detached and abstract and thus less personally involved than speech. In other words, depending on the communicative *function* of the text and the *context* of the speaker or writer, spoken and written discourse could look very different or similar. Hughes (1996) comments on Biber's contribution: "Biber concludes that the distinction between speech and writing should be redefined in terms of a stylistic continuum, rather than two discrete entities" (Hughes 1996, p. 146).

XII: FUNCTIONAL AND PRIVILEGED PERSPECTIVES

Halliday has made a huge contribution to this field. In 1989 he offered new insights in his lucid analysis of speech itself as opposed to its physical properties - phonetics and phonology. Firstly, he observed that it is a misconception to view spoken language as simple and written language as intricate; both forms are complex in their own ways:

> The complexity of the written language is static and dense. That of the spoken language is dynamic and intricate. Grammatical intricacy takes the place of lexical density (Halliday, 1989, p. 87).

He elaborates by declaring that writing tends to be simple in its grammatical structure but "highly information-packed" and lexically dense. This simplicity relates to the organisation of writing, its clearly defined interdependent clauses, syntax and structure. Conversely, spontaneous, natural speech is looser in terms of its lack of sentences but displays instead a "dynamic complexity" in its intricate flow of expression. For him too, the relationship of speech and writing is essentially complementary as: "alternative 'outputs'- alternative realisations of the meaning potential of language" (Halliday 1989, p. 92). Writing, he continues, cannot embody all the meaning potential of speech, owing to the absence of prosodic and paralinguistic features. Secondly, though there is some overlap in their functions, there is usually a logical "division of labour" in the ways in which speech and writing are deployed according to the demands of the context. These views concur with the organisational perspectives of Bakhtin: "The meanings that are expressed in contexts where writing is used are not normally translated into talk" (Bakhtin, 1981, p. 93).

Perhaps the most profound distinction he proposes is that speech and writing, "impose different grids on experience" (Bakhtin, 1981, p. 93). There is a sense, he suggests, in which they shape different realities. Writing creates a world of things; talking creates a world of happening. The implication seems to be that talk is for Halliday in many senses more "basic", and "nearer to reality". This concept of the structure of language affecting the way in which we perceive the world is reminiscent of the long-standing Sapir-Whorf hypothesis (see Wardhaugh, 1993, pp. 218-225 for a fuller discussion), outlined at the start of this chapter, which postulates close relationships between language forms and perceptions of the world. It is also interesting to make connections here with Bakhtin's view of speech as the primary genre. Thus, we might view the verbal utterance as more vibrant and animate on account of its being steeped in social immediacy, whilst writing often (but not always) remains at one remove from the reality in which it is situated.

Halliday offers pertinent comments on language and learning in this context: "Put from the learner's point of view: reading/writing and listening/speaking are different ways of learning because they are different ways of knowing" (Halliday, 1989, p. 97). He elaborates on these distinctions by suggesting that writing is essentially *synoptic* in that "it defines the universe as product rather than as process" (p. 97). Conversely, the spoken language presents a *dynamic* view. In the spoken language, phenomena do not exist; they happen.

One of the main ways that writing achieves its "high-lexical" density, Halliday argues, is its tendency to contain more grammatical metaphors. Spoken language tends to use verbs, whilst written language is more "highly coded" in that it uses nouns; verbs are, for Halliday, more direct and closer to reality. In writing, the commonplace transfer of meaning into nominalised forms, particularly in textbooks, can be described as grammatical metaphors. One of his examples will suffice to illustrate this; in talk we might say, "She spoke about five points." In writing this might be "translated" as: "Her speech covered five points." (Nominalisation is the process by which nouns are made from a word from another word class e.g. my thinking, redness)

In relation to learning and teaching, we are reminded that young children find grammatical metaphors hard to understand. It is suggested that clauses such as "the new term beckons" or "tradition dictates that we raise our hands" are non-literal and likely to prove difficult for some pupils to comprehend. The tendency of textbooks to be lexically dense and rich in grammatical metaphor may lead to further difficulties for some pupils. Finally, a succinct clarification on how we should perceive the different natures of spoken and written language is also offered:

> It is wrong, therefore, to think of the written language as highly organised, structured and complex while the spoken language is disorganised, fragmentary and simple. The spoken language is every bit as highly organised as the written, and is capable of just as great a degree of complexity. Only, it is complex in a different way (Halliday, 1989, p 87).

Ideas concerning the social status of speech and writing were also discussed in the Language in the

National Curriculum (LINC) materials produced under the editorship of Carter (1992). Here, the higher prestige often accorded to writing is attributed to the fact that until relatively recently only a minority could write well. We are also reminded that Latin was once regarded as the model against which English should be measured; many ill-conceived ideas of linguistic etiquette have their origins in the imposition of this false template for English. In addition, the forms of writing are more fixed and, as we discussed earlier, linguistic changes often first occur in speech. These may be adopted as the norm only after their acceptance gains ground over time.

Maybin and Mercer (1996) build on the work of Halliday and comment on the vocabulary of speech and writing; they point out that the lexis of writing is often polysyllabic and Latinate. In contrast, speech has a higher proportion of Anglo-Saxon words and more repetition of individual words. The concept of modality ("have to", "could" etc) is also usefully highlighted in relation to the immediacy of talk:

> Modal forms express the speaker's attitudes ... and are much more common in spoken English, with its direct, face-to-face interactional purposes, than in the more "distant" medium of formal writing (Maybin and Mercer, 1996, p. 44).

Finally, it is worth bearing in mind the wisdom of T.S.Eliot on the distinctive but complementary characteristics of talk and writing:

> ... an identical spoken and written language would be practically intolerable. If we spoke as we write we should find no one to listen: and if we wrote as we speak we should find no one to read. The spoken and written language must not be too near together, as they must not be too far apart (T.S. Eliot cited in Hughes 1996, p.5).

XIII: ISSUES FOR TEACHERS

Teachers have, of course, always corrected pupils' speech in the classroom but Romaine suggests that these interventions sometimes need to be more judiciously informed in terms of their awareness regarding the grammar and nature of spoken English.

> It is hard to have judgements about speech independently of notions of correctness we are taught in school when we learn to read and write. Studies have shown that teachers routinely correct children in school for using forms that are quite acceptable in speech. Moreover, they use these forms themselves in the classroom. Not surprisingly, the children are confused about what the teacher wants (Romaine, 1994, p. 200).

Such muddled practice is clearly unhelpful in developing pupils' oral fluency and also indicative of some teachers' insecurity about how language operates particularly with respect to spoken English. Perera (1994) argues that teachers need greater explicit grammatical knowledge, not simply so that they can teach this knowledge but so that they possess a more informed understanding of the causes of pupils' errors, which in turn would enable them to respond more constructively to pupils' speech and writing.

In connection with ideas of linguistic rectitude something must be said here about Standard English in relation to spoken and written forms. Firstly, Milroy (1987) has highlighted the problems that stem from an inflexible adherence to the model of written English and reminds us that we should not correct a child's spoken English according to the rules that apply to standard written English.

As we know, OFSTED school inspections in England do make judgements on pupils' talk and their competence in Standard English. A similar situation exists regarding Estyn in Wales. What follows is an extract from recent advice issued to OFSTED inspectors; it seems to presume that firm criteria exist by which pupils' proficiency in spoken Standard English in both formal and informal situations can be measured.

> Formal discussion gives you a chance to see how confidently and appropriately pupils can talk, explain and describe, and how fluent and articulate they are, when talking to a person they do not know, in Standard English. On the other hand, appropriately informal discussions can enable you to make judgements about the achievements of pupils who feel uncomfortable in a formal setting (OFSTED, 2001, p. 13).

To conclude, no matter how complex theories may become regarding the correct approach to language development and literacy, we cannot escape the central role that language plays in our lives. Words are fascinating things and language has enormous power to allow us to be spontaneous, expressive and creative. We are moved by it in various ways on a daily basis, and it gives us the means to communicate at a personal and global level.

4 Educational and Spiritual Development

I: INTRODUCTION

The spiritual aspect of a person is considered to be a key feature of what makes us human. Whilst being natural and integral to a person, it is assumed by those with responsibility for educational policy and practice that this is not something that will necessarily grow and flourish independently of structured guidance and assistance from others. As a consequence the education system of England and Wales has ensured that guidance and support is enshrined in legislation and advice. Inspectors of schools determine the quality of their effectiveness in promoting this dimension of education.

All of the above assumes that there is a shared understanding of the exact meaning of what spirituality and spiritual development are. In recent years there has been no shortage of literature which seeks to clarify this, though with varying degrees of success. Whether or not this literature has filtered through to schools and teachers, already hard pressed to keep abreast of a plethora of educational initiatives and legislation, is a question that needs asking.

Not unreasonably, teachers are expected to have knowledge and understanding of the subjects they teach and the pedagogies which promote effective delivery. When it comes to spirituality and the spiritual development of pupils, how far does teachers' understanding of these terms determine their interpretation and implementation of the statutory requirements to provide opportunities for the children in their charge to develop spiritually? This chapter seeks to explore key issues relating to the meanings of "spiritual" and "spiritual development". We will begin with a brief historical perspective starting with the Education Act of 1944 and then examine the meaning of these terms.

II: HISTORICAL PERSPECTIVES

(a) **The 1944 Education Act:** The horrors of the Second World War proved a serious setback for those who believed in the moral and spiritual progress of mankind, and it was against this backdrop that the 1944 Education Act was framed, partly as "a blueprint for the moral and spiritual rejuvenation of society" (Wright, 2000, p.63). Religious Instruction (RI) and school worship, which were practically universal prior to 1944 (Copley, 2000, p.57), were now compulsory under the Act. Despite the concern of some over the compulsory requirement, a sound grounding in Christian values was considered to be beneficial to the development of children. There was always the so-called "conscience clause" in section 25 of the Act which provided an avenue for withdrawal from both RI and school worship for teachers and children whose parents wished to exercise it.

The requirements of the 1944 Act which incorporated "spiritual development" as a statutory requirement in the education of children remain to this day (e.g. Education Act 2002, sections 78 and 99). The 1944 Act explicitly stated that public education should "contributes towards the spiritual, moral, mental and physical development of the community". Whilst there can be little doubt that the spiritual dimension of education was confined within the narrow parameters of a confessional Christian education (Wright, 2000) and that spirituality was almost exclusively Christian spirituality, it was not without a degree of controversy and debate that its inclusion was secured. Gilliat (1996, p. 162) has pointed out that the "spiritual" did not form part of the original draft of the legislation and it was Viscount Bledisloe, in the House of Lords, during the Bill's Committee Stage, who stated that, along with the Christian ethic, "it is spirituality which we want to advance at every stage of our national education if we want to promote morality as well as the other virtues of our race." This early link between the spiritual and moral (and, in this case, the religious), considered vital by some (Tate, 1996, para. 23) and confused by others (Beck, 1999), is one that persists and is an issue to which we shall return.

Despite the undoubted Christian connotations behind the word "spiritual" in the 1944 Act, it is the inherent ambiguity of the word that has ensured its survival in subsequent education acts. The understanding of the meaning of "spiritual" held by R.A.Butler, the President of the Board of Education who drafted the Act, and by Winston Churchill, the Prime Minister, were not the same. Butler's was a Christian spirituality, whilst for Churchill it was, "a mixture of citizenship, pride in the community and country, and a sort of muscular aestheticism" (Copley, 2000, p.69). Thus, the spiritual, along with the moral and religious requirements of the 1944 Act, were intended to make pupils aware of God (as perceived by Christians) and ensure they became decent subjects (Isherwood, 1999, p 80).

It is interesting to note that Canon Hall, Chief Officer of the National Society, revealed in an interview in 1943 that "spiritual" was introduced into the Act in preference to "religious" because the Archbishop of Canterbury, William Temple, thought that nobody would know what it meant and it could come to permeate the whole educational process (Naylor, 2001, p.8). Given the place of religious instruction and daily acts of worship in the Act and the confessional nature of both, it seems a somewhat pointless reason for the choice of the word "spiritual" in place of "religious". It is far more likely they were seen as complementary to each other rather than part of a subtle conspiracy (Ferguson, 1981) transmuting religion into spirituality. Those who framed the wording of the Act were probably unaware of future debate and controversy over the nature and coherence of "secular spirituality".

(b) **Her Majesty's Inspectorate: *Curriculum 11-16*:** This vagueness surrounding the meaning of the word "spiritual" is something of a double-edged sword that can assist as well as prevent agreement concerning its purpose, value and meaning in the educational system. Is it not enough to believe it is good without having the necessity to define clearly what it means? (Sutherland, 1997, p.19) If it is essentially a benign and harmless requirement, its statutory protection will be widely accepted (Hay and Nye, 1998, p.8).

Accepted it was in 1944, and there it remained, essentially unchallenged, until Her Majesty's Inspectorate (HMI) published their discussion paper *Curriculum 11-16* (DES/HMI, 1977a). This was primarily in response to the Labour Government's Green Paper *Education in Schools: A Consultation Document* (Department of Education and Science [DES], 1977), itself a follow up to James Callaghan's Ruskin College speech in 1976 which came to be widely regarded as asking: "What do the nation's schools exist for?" Influenced by the educational philosopher Paul Hirst (1974), they identified the spiritual as being one of the nine fundamental areas of human knowledge and experience (See chapter 1). In responding to requests to clarify what they meant by "spiritual", they attempted to satisfy all viewpoints by providing both an all-embracing and a religious definition. The first Wright refers to as "broadly anthropological" (Wright, 2000, p.66):

> The spiritual area is concerned with the awareness a person has of those elements in existence and experience which may be defined in terms of inner feelings and beliefs; they affect the way people see themselves and throw light for them on the purpose and meaning of life itself. Often these feelings and beliefs lead people to claim to know God and glimpse the transcendent; sometimes they represent that striving and longing for perfection which characterises human beings but always they are concerned with matters of the heart and root of existence. (DES/HMI, 1977b).

The second, more explicitly religious, definition stated that:

> The spiritual area is concerned with everything in human knowledge or experience that is connected with or derives from a sense of God or of gods. Spirituality is a meaningless adjective for the atheist and of dubious use to the agnostic. Irrespective of personal belief or disbelief, an unaccountable number of people have believed and do believe in the spiritual aspects of human life, and therefore their actions, attitudes and interpretations of events have been influenced accordingly. (DES/HMI, 1977b).

It is possible to appreciate the dilemma of the authors of this document, for, if the term "spiritual" is restricted to a "sense of God", all those who are unable to make this religious commitment are automatically excluded. Within this number there would be a significant proportion of pupils and teachers, for in the intervening years between the 1944 Act and the publication of this discussion paper, Britain had changed. A drop in attendance at places of worship, increasing secularisation, and the influx of those whose religions were not Christian meant that the use of education to reinforce and further the "Christianisation" of the population was considered by many to be inappropriate (Bastide, 1992). The inclusivity of the "anthropological" description was more acceptable to the majority and has paved the way for similar subsequent definitions. This discussion paper encouraged and gave impetus to the trend to separate the spiritual from the religious whilst, at the same time, giving it educational legitimacy.

(c) **The 1988 Education Reform Act:** It was the 1988 Education Reform Act which yet again brought the "spiritual" to the fore and confirmed its educational legitimacy. Once more this was a result of lobbying on the part of the Lords. The early drafts of the Act made no mention of the promotion of the "spiritual, moral, cultural, mental and physical development of pupils" (Alves, 1991), for the then Secretary of State for Education and Science, Kenneth Baker, did not regard the role of the faith communities as paramount in the framing of the Bill (Baker, 1993, p.207). Even the position of RI (though it is now Religious Education [RE]) was at first essentially unchanged and still remains outside the National Curriculum. Baker was soon to learn that it was an area he could not quietly pass over. Once the Bill reached the House of Lords, a group nicknamed "the Tribe" took the opportunity to "re-assert the Christian base for RE and collective worship" (Copley, 2000, p.71). The main thrust of the debate for two of its prominent members, Bishop Leonard and Baroness Cox, was over the place of RE and collective worship, but reference was made to the "spiritual". The ensuing debate raised the "terminological problems" (Copley, 2000, p.74) that still persist. The outcome was that the "spiritual" had its position and, therefore, its status renewed in legislation that has been reaffirmed in subsequent Education Acts, for example, section 351 of the 1996 Education Act and sections 78 and 99 of the Education Act of 2002. Section 1(2) of the 1988 Education Reform Act required a "balanced and broadly based curriculum which promotes the spiritual, moral, cultural, mental and physical development of pupils at the school and of society."

It is open to question whether or not the requirement for schools to promote the spiritual development of those in their charge made any notable impact on those schools and teachers struggling to come to terms with a prescriptive, demanding and somewhat overloaded National Curriculum (NC). In the years immediately following the introduction of the NC there was no real guidance about the ways schools should interpret, let alone implement, this statutory obligation. Was it, as Copley (2000, p. 76) suggests, to be incorporated into RE and daily acts of collective worship (the latter a duty seldom complied with by the majority of secondary schools), or should it permeate the whole curriculum? Or was it merely a sop towards those who questioned the utilitarian, market driven philosophy behind the NC and a means of showing that the legislators really were concerned about the development of the "whole child"?

(d) **Inspection of the Spiritual, Moral, Social and Cultural (SMSC) Aspects of a School:** In effect, the spiritual was a dormant side issue within the mainstream educational debate. There were more important matters for schools than to address explicitly the "how" and "why" of spiritual development and to pay it anything more than lip service. This was to change with the 1992 Education (Schools) Act, which required the "spiritual, moral, social and cultural" (SMSC) dimension to be inspected by the Office for Standards in Education (OFSTED) in England and the Office of Her Majesty's Chief Inspector (OHMCI) (later renamed as Estyn) in Wales. A school's provision for opportunities for the spiritual development of pupils was now to be scrutinised and a judgement concerning the quality of this provision was to be made on a five-point scale. As Wright (2000, p. 68) says, schools would now, need – however half-heartedly – to attend to the issue.

To do this effectively they would need clarification and guidance. The lack of clarity on matters spiritual extended to those who were to inspect as well as those being inspected. It is highly questionable, as research has shown, whether subsequent guidance did meet this objective. What was clear was that the inspectorate moved towards inspecting provision or opportunities for spiritual development rather than the measured performance of pupils. This did not mean that inspectors were to ignore the outcomes of this provision but the difficulties of doing so were recognised. They claimed that "it is not impossible to recognise someone who is spiritually impoverished, morally stunted, socially inadequate or culturally deprived" (OFSTED, 1994). In extreme circumstances this may well be the case, but the difficulties in coming to a judgment on the stage of spiritual development of pupils (or anyone else for that matter) is extremely difficult even for the most perceptive of inspectors. (It is marginally easier to determine the other three – moral, social and cultural - in the SMSC quartet.) Assessment or measurement of spiritual development (a phrase which implies growth) remains a contentious issue.

Guidance was forthcoming in the form of discussion papers from the National Curriculum Council (NCC, 1993), OFSTED (1994) and the School Curriculum and Assessment Authority (SCAA, 1995, 1996b). As Copley succinctly puts it,

> Spiritual development was thus in the hands of unelected quangos, to be implemented by untrained headteachers and assessed by school inspectors whose other work was geared towards scoring performance and measuring progress (Copley, 2000, p 104).

(e) **Discussion Papers:**

(i) *Spiritual and Moral Development (NCC, 1993; SCAA, 1995)*: The NCC discussion paper, *Spiritual and Moral Development*, issued in 1993 and later reissued by SCAA in 1995, set the trend for what was to follow from official sources and acquired what Wright (2000, p. 68) refers to as a quasi-authoritative status. It adopted and further built upon the all inclusive definition and model of spirituality given by the DES and HMI (1977a and 1977b). Whilst RE and collective worship were important vehicles for its delivery, they were certainly not the only ones. Spiritual development applied to "all pupils" and to "every area of the curriculum and all aspects of school life" (SCAA, 1995). Carr (1995, p. 85) argues that this document adopted a "scattershot approach" whereby spiritual education was prised from its exclusive connection with religious education only to be loosely re-attached to almost everything under the curricular sun.

The discussion paper highlighted seven aspects of spiritual development: beliefs; a sense of awe, wonder and mystery; experiencing feelings of transcendence; search for meaning and purpose; self-knowledge; relationships; creativity; and feelings and emotions. Spiritual development becomes a catchall net that encompasses so many aspects of life that they inevitably apply to every thinking and feeling person. The paper acknowledged that most people could relate to these areas but would differ in the interpretations and meanings that they ascribed to them. Here was a suggestion that spiritual development was a subjective response to common experiences. What might be spiritual for one person might not prove to be so for another.

(ii) *Spiritual, Moral, Social and Cultural Development (OFSTED, 1994) and Religious Education and Collective Worship (Department for Education [DFE], 1994)*: Building upon their *Framework for the Inspection of Schools* (OFSTED, 1993b), OFSTED issued a discussion paper, *Spiritual, Moral, Social and Cultural Development* (OFSTED, 1994), intended to assist schools and inspectors. Stewart Sutherland, then Chief Inspector of Schools, believed it was necessary to determine what value a school adds to the personal lives of pupils. The complexity of arriving at a judgment was recognised but not considered an excuse for avoiding making difficult decisions. The Department for Education's advisory circular *Religious Education and Collective Worship* (Circular 1/94 in England and Circular 10/94 in Wales, sections 2-5) drew attention to the concern of the Government that schools were paying insufficient attention to the spiritual, moral and cultural aspects of pupils' development and the need for a set of shared values which a school promotes. With reference to the "spiritual" the OFSTED discussion paper attempted to meet this concern by reiterating the description of spiritual development given in the Framework for Inspection (OFSTED, 1993b). It ran as follows:

> Spiritual development relates to that aspect of inner life through which pupils acquire insights into their personal existence which are of enduring worth. It is characterised by reflection, the attribution of meaning to experience, valuing a non-material dimension to life and intimations of an enduring reality. "Spiritual" is not synonymous with "religious"; all areas of the curriculum may contribute to pupils' spiritual development (OFSTED, 1994, p. 8).

The document once more placed the spiritual firmly in the universal, inclusive camp. Again, it recognised there would be "genuine differences" in approaches to the spiritual. The danger was that something which could mean different things to different people could eventually mean what you wanted it to mean. As Copley (2000, p. 76) asks, "If it is present everywhere, how is this distinguishable from its being nowhere?" Others have called the ubiquitous nature of the spiritual into question. Carr (1995, p. 95) claims it is "misleading to the point of eccentricity for proponents of spiritual education across the curriculum to suggest spiritual education may occur whenever and wherever."

In making their evaluation of schools' provision for spiritual development inspectors were guided to look at:

- the values and attitudes the school identifies, upholds and fosters;
- the contribution made by the whole curriculum;
- religious education, acts of collective worship and other assemblies;
- extra-curricular activity, together with the general ethos and climate of the school (OFSTED, 1994).

Thus whilst religious education and collective worship are specifically mentioned as vehicles for providing opportunities for spiritual development (an undoubted link to the religious basis of spirituality found in the 1944 Act), they are by no means the only subject or area of school life making such a contribution.

(iii) *Education for Adult Life: the Spiritual and Moral Development of Young People (SCAA, 1996b)*: The SCAA discussion paper, *Education for Adult Life: the Spiritual and Moral Development of Young People* (SCAA, 1996b), added little to the debate but mainly reaffirmed the importance and cross-curricular nature of spiritual development. The definition drew on previous ones, encompassing, as did the others, a wide range of human experience and activity. Indeed, the omnipresent nature of the spiritual, for some, extended to all learning. It strengthened the link between the spiritual and the moral, its inclusive nature and position in education becoming essentially value driven.

(iv) *Forum on Values in Education and the Community (Qualifications and Curriculum Authority [QCA], 1998)*: The role of the teacher in all this was unclear. Were they "spiritual directors" (Richardson, 1988) or "nurturers" of spirituality (Erricker and Erricker, 1997)? In other words, in the field of spirituality and values, are they teachers or facilitators or both? Did the requirement to provide opportunities for the spiritual development of pupils apply to all teachers no matter what their own subject discipline and personal views? How were schools to address these questions in a real and practical way? There was still confusion and a lack of consensus about exactly what was meant by "spiritual development" and how it was an integral and important part of a greater shared value system of schools and society. For consistency and some degree of parity of experience it was suggested that there was a need for some common agreement on values (SCAA, 1996b).

This recommendation and the call for coherence in the approach to spiritual, moral, social and cultural development (SCAA, 1996b) paved the way for the Forum on Values in Education and the Community which met in 1997. Its remit was (i) to decide whether there were any shared values in our pluralist society and (ii) to decide how schools might be supported in the promotion of pupils' spiritual, moral, social and cultural development. After extensive debate and consultation, common agreement was reached on shared values that all should promote in a civilised society. There were centred on four areas: the self; relationships; society; and the environment. It was acknowledged that responsibility of instilling these values in young people lay with society at large but schools clearly had an important contribution to make.

The Qualifications and Curriculum Authority (QCA), which had now replaced SCAA, addressed itself to the second part of the remit by producing, after a six month consultation, a pack entitled *The Promotion of Pupils' Spiritual, Moral, Social and Cultural Development – Draft Guidance for Pilot Work* (QCA, 1997). Based on a six-step process to create a whole school approach, the pack offered explicit examples of how each subject of the curriculum might promote the spiritual development of pupils (as well as the moral, social and cultural), along with case studies and an illustrative matrix for schools to use in their planning and a blank matrix for schools to use to construct their policy. In attempting to answer the question, "What is involved in promoting pupils' spiritual development?" the authors argued that the following should be encouraged:

- the growth of pupils' spirit, their understanding of their own strengths and weaknesses, their self-respect, creativity and will to achieve their full potential (for the good of themselves, others and society);

- pupils' ability to ask, and try to find answers to life's major questions, including questions about the purpose of life and the existence and nature of God; and

- pupils' acquisition of the knowledge, understanding, skills, attitudes and qualities they need to foster their own inner lives and non-material well being throughout life.

There is undoubtedly an appeal to this draft material that clearly guides school and exemplifies ideas they may chose to adopt. As Best (2000) says, it gives the impression of being rational, systematic and comprehensive and he refers to this approach as the "Rational Objectivist Model". What it also appeared to do was perpetuate the apparent paradox between an individualist model of spirituality and a quasi-governmental, centralised model. Not all were convinced of the universality and efficacy of the approach proposed. Whilst Talbot and Tate (2000) argue that values, unlike personal preferences, are qualities that are in themselves worthy of esteem, and Tate (1996) states that to be accepted by all they cannot be controversial, others saw them as falling far short of a Christian worldview (Thatcher, 1999, p. 40).

Thatcher (1999) recognises that the values of spiritually developed people will be communal, but argues that the documents produced by the Forum fail to take account of real differences. In doing so they not only separate the past from the present but also facts from values. For many this lies at the heart of the debate concerning the spiritual and spiritual development. Do they retain any coherence outside of a religious (and for some Christian) context? Thatcher's criticisms have some foundation, but they unfairly attack the conclusions of the Forum, for it fully recognised that the values that it promoted were not a definitive statement of all the values that schools should promote but a common consensual framework upon which they might build. Indeed, Thatcher (p. 52) suggests that loving God and loving your neighbour encapsulate what needs to be said about a spiritually developed person. The confessional nature of the first of these requirements results in the same problem that faced the DES and HMI in 1977, namely the exclusion of all those who are unwilling to subscribe to religious beliefs.

(v) *Framework for Personal and Social Education (ACCAC, 2000b)*: Spirituality is also one of the key aspects of the *Framework for Personal and Social Education* which has, from September 2003, formed a compulsory part of the school curriculum in Wales (Qualifications, Curriculum and Assessment Authority for Wales [ACCAC], 2000b). Here the "spiritual" is one of ten aspects of a person in society, and it is worth quoting in full the section on spiritual development, which, we are told:

> has two main dimensions in that it is concerned with developing the inner life and motivates us to look beyond ourselves. The former involves the development of personal insight, beliefs and values and encourages pupils to reflect on their experiences, ponder some of the deeper questions of life and search for meaning and truth. Pupils can also be inspired to express those inner feelings using imagination and creativity. The latter dimension recognises the human experience of transcendence which takes us beyond the mundane and material. This can be evoked by a sense of awe and wonder at the natural world, by the mysteries of life and death, by the limitations of human understanding or by a response to a divine being (ACCAC, 2000b, p. 7).

(vi) *Promoting and Evaluating Pupils' Spiritual, Moral, Social and Cultural Development, (OFSTED, 2004)*: As a consequence of changes to the Framework for the Inspection of Schools in 2004, OFSTED published further guidance in March 2004 in an attempt to clarify meanings and provide practical case studies for inspectors. The publication confirmed the importance and centrality of pupils' SMSC development to the educational process along with an acknowledgement of current confusion. As previous discussion papers had realised, there was a need to come up with a definition which would appeal and be acceptable to as many people as possible. This laudable premise, however, is as fraught with the same difficulties as the previous papers. Nevertheless, if SMSC is to be inspected and its effectiveness judged, there needs to be what OFSTED terms a "working definition". Whilst this is offered on an "advisory basis only" (OFSTED, 2004, p. 4), such a definition inevitably comes to be regarded as authoritative by both teachers and those who inspect them, and schools will address pupils' SMSC development in accordance with this guidance.

The continuing centrality of SMSC in the education of pupils is partly because it is considered to be something of a panacea to the real and perceived problems of society. The OFSTED paper clearly sees SMSC as at least part of the solution to a list of ills ranging from teenage pregnancy to the failure of young people to vote in elections (p.5). The continued cross-curricular nature of SMSC is a positive aspect of the vision of the role of education in promoting social cohesion put forward by a previous Secretary of State for Education (Blunkett, 2001). The interconnectedness of the four areas of SMSC is reiterated, especially in the case of the spiritual. Yet, the paper does provide definitions and examples of what inspectors are to look for in each of these areas. In order to achieve Blunkett's aim of creating an "inclusive society" (Blunkett, 2001) these definitions need to be acceptable to the majority and refrain from any overtly inclusive interpretation. As such, the universal nature of spirituality is reiterated in the tradition of previous discussion papers.

Spirituality is certainly not seen as the preserve of those of a religious persuasion. Apart from the reasoning that gives rise to the universal definition given in the OFSTED document, the pragmatic implications for inspectors are fully recognised:

> The inspection framework must apply to both sets of individuals (those with a strong religious faith and non-believers), and those at all points of the spectrum. It is vital to press towards a common currency of shared understanding (OFSTED, 2004, p. 8).

OFSTED recognised the necessity of a definition that would act as a "common denominator" (p.11) and identified three principal elements of spirituality:

- the development of insights, principles, beliefs, attitudes and values which guide and motivate us. For many pupils, these will have a significant religious basis.

- a developing understanding of feelings and emotions which causes us to reflect and to learn.

- for all pupils, a developing recognition that their insights, principles, beliefs, attitudes and values should influence, inspire or guide them in life (OFSTED, 2004, p. 11).

Here we see the way in which spiritual development is seen as encompassing both the intellectual and emotional development of pupils. It combines the perceived polarisation that currently exists in the debate on spiritual education between the academic study of spiritual traditions on the one hand and guided introspection and the explorations of feelings on the other.

The combination of these three elements of spiritual development in schools results in the following OFSTED definition:

> Spiritual development is the development of the non-material element of a human being which animates and sustains us and, depending on our point of view, either ends or continues in

some form when we die. It is about the development of a sense of identity, self-worth, personal insight, meaning and purpose. It is about the development of a pupil's "spirit". Some people may call it the development of a pupil's "soul"; others as the development of "personality" or "character" (OFSTED, 2004, p. 12).

The above definition practically equates the spiritual with the life force or essence of a person and in doing so employs a degree of tautology. It is not altogether helpful to say that spiritual development is the development of a pupil's spirit. The term "soul" is as unclear as the term "spiritual" when one is required to define exactly what the word means. The usual understanding of the word is within a religious context, and so the statement immediately proceeds to include those who would prefer a more secular meaning. The result implies that "soul", "personality" and "character" are practically synonymous. This is questionable from not only a theological perspective. Whilst it might be argued that there is no such thing as the former no one can deny the existence of the other two aspects of a person. The difficulty for teachers and inspectors is how to promote and measure opportunities for this development and the success of these opportunities.

The paper tells inspectors that they will need to use their professional judgement (p. 12), but it provides them with a catalogue of characteristics pupils are likely to show and a set of activities schools might undertake to encourage this spiritual development (pp. 13-14). These comprehensive lists paint a picture of a reflective, tolerant and caring person with an appreciation of "the intangible – for example, beauty, truth, love, goodness, order – as well as for mystery, paradox and ambiguity" (p.13). The document also states that schools should be "monitoring, in simple, pragmatic ways, the success of what is provided" (p.14). Herein lies the crux of the problem. Do teachers share this broad understanding of spiritual development? Is such a broad understanding really a coherent and accurate description of what is truly meant by spiritual and spiritual development? The whole question of definitions to which all can subscribe is addressed in the next sections.

III: PROBLEMS IN DEFINITIONS

The world of academia has responded to this quasi-official guidance with varying degrees of approval to downright hostility, exposing the pretence that all agree with the current definitions and guidance. The coherence of the "official" guidance has been challenged and in doing so academics have produced their own definitions and theories as to what it is that constitutes the essence of good spiritual education, thus implying that current definitions and guidance fail to correspond to what might be termed "good education". Thus, their definitions tend to be stipulative or programmatic (Scheffler, 1960), reflecting the values and opinions of each individual author. The following section examines some of the problems which are created by this multiplicity of definitions.

(a) **Range of Contemporary Meanings:** When given an exercise in "brainstorming" what they mean by the word "spiritual" (an activity suggested by Hammond *et al.*, 1990 and Wright, 2000, p. 8), students' responses have reflected the wide variety of interpretations currently given to the word, ranging from the religious to the "New Age" and occult; from the mystical to general techniques for self-improvement and self-fulfilment. The emphasis is usually on an inner experience and perception of life. Beck (1999, pp. 163-164) reveals the assortment of meanings and associations carried by the term "spiritual" in everyday usage. This raises the question whether we allow individuals to define the word and interpret experiences for themselves as "spiritual" or whether we assess these experiences and personality traits against given criteria for spirituality and judge them accordingly. The former course runs the risk, according to Thatcher (1991, p. 26), of "rampant epistemological dualism and private individualism", whilst the latter restricts the spiritual to whatever an author's criteria are and thus excludes people who fail to meet these perceived requirements.

(b) **Dictionary Definitions and Origins:** It may be argued that, rather than seeking to find a satisfactory definition by asking people what the term means to them, it is better to refer to a dictionary where a simple account of a word is provided together with a study of its etymology. Some of the definitions offered by the *Concise Oxford Dictionary are*:

(i) concerning the spirit as opposed to matter;

(ii) concerned with sacred or religious things; and

(iii) of a refined and sensitive soul.

An etymological approach, usually starting with the derivation of the word from the Latin *spiritus* (Lewis and Short, 1966), is interesting, but original meanings seldom correspond to current understanding and usage. The Latin *spiritus* meaning "breath" also has a secondary meaning of "inspiration" (Mursell, 2001) and to "enliven" (Hoad, 1989). Carson identifies the emergence of the term "spirituality" in French Catholic thought (Carson, 1996, p. 556). It referred primarily to a discipline which was to be distinguished from dogma by the way in which it concentrated on the reactions to objects in the religious consciousness. However, the term "spiritual" is not exclusive to the Christian tradition and now extends to other faith traditions, atheism and agnosticism.

(c) **Confusion:** The phrases used to emphasise the difficulty and confusion associated with definitions of the "spiritual" and "spiritual development" are both colourful and revealing. It is variously referred to as a "spiritual Esperanto" (Gay, 1998), "a classic case of the Emperor's clothes" (Copley, 2000) and "a weasel word" (Brown, 1997). The consequence of all this is the danger of becoming lost in "a cloud of mutual incomprehension" (Hay and Nye, 1998, p.4) with "much talk of spiritual education liable to be vacuous" (Carr, 1996, p.160) or "psycho-babble and management speak" (Carr and Haldane, 2003, p. 6). As Copley (2000, p. 11) says, exploration in the field can be likened to plaiting fog.

The confusion which surrounds the word should provide us with a word of warning in even attempting to elicit a mutually agreed definition. Indeed, it may be the case that it really does encompass a broad spectrum of meanings with each one being equally acceptable. The result is an over abundance of meanings (Ungoed-Thomas, 1986, p. 7), and there is the danger that the concept becomes meaningless (Markham, 1999, p. 143). Woods *et al.* (1997, p. 25) suggest that any single definition which attempts to incorporate an acceptable meaning in a plural society risks producing a bland notion of spirituality with little substantive meaning. The obvious advantage of this lack of clarity and precision is that the spiritual can become all encompassing and applied to just about every aspect of life. Everything is potentially spiritual. This may well be the case, but it begs the question as to the value such looseness of definition has for pupils, teachers and school inspectors. If the spiritual can be present across the school curriculum, as the guidance documents cited above suggest, it becomes increasingly difficult to pin down precisely what it is we are looking for.

(d) **The Need for Clarity:** Despite these difficulties it is a word all are familiar with, even if they find it difficult to articulate exactly what they mean by it. Carr (1995, p. 85) is nearer the mark when he argues that, whilst precise definitions are well-nigh impossible, we do need to have "a reasonable secure grasp of *meaning* of terms in order that they can be used to any real purpose". The spiritual remains an integral part of the educational system and has been there since 1944. As such it would be a benefit to all concerned in the educational process to arrive at a mutually agreed definition or to find some other way of clarifying the meaning of the concept.

IV: CRITERIA FOR SPIRITUALITY

The difficulties of trying to find a definition of words like "spiritual" are recognised by Scheffler (1960) and Peters (1966). The more modern approach to the clarification of concepts of this type, which has emerged from the works of Wittgenstein and other linguistic philosophers, is to consider the use of criteria which pick out the chief characteristics of a term. In accordance with this approach, the following four criteria are suggested to help teachers and others working in an educational setting to acquire a clearer understand of the term "spiritual".

(a) **Wholeness and Full Humanity:** In recent years the University of Surrey, Roehampton, has hosted an annual international summer conference entitled "Education, Spirituality and the Whole Child". This is also the title of a book edited by Ron Best (1996) who was the originator of these annual conferences. The key word here which links spirituality with education is "wholeness". The implication is that a truly educated person is also a spiritual person; for education is much more than academic learning and the acquisition of knowledge and skills. A number of writers take this view and link spiritual development with a move towards wholeness and being fully human. For Isherwood and McEwan (1993) spiritual development involves "imagining wholeness"; for Priestley it is about human potential and what a person might become (Priestly, 1985, p.115).

What, then, is the essence of "wholeness", being fully human and being an intrinsically spiritual being, all of which are capable of being developed through the educational process? Two things which are frequently identified as quintessential to the spiritual and spiritual development are the human capability of transcendence and the quality of relationships. Both of these profoundly colour the way in which we see life, imbue it with a sense of meaning and assign value. In other words it leads to a way of knowing and experiencing which influences the way we perceive and interpret reality. As Jung said in his letters, "Life that just happens in and for itself is not real life; it is real only when it is *known*" (Jaffe, 1989, p.15). Or, as Socrates said, "To let no day pass without discussing goodness and all the other subjects about which you hear me talking and examining both myself and others is really the very best thing a man can do. Life without this sort of examination is not worth living" (Plato, 1954, pp. 71-72).

Spiritual development is thus transformative. It enables the person to identify what is truly important in life. According to Zohar and Marshall (2000, p. 15), this self-awareness is a test for genuine SQ (spiritual intelligence). They go on to say that this way of knowing is something that "utterly transforms our understanding and our lives" (p. 66). For Myers and Myers (1999, pp. 28-32) it is a quality of being fully human which allows us to transcend the known and contemplate the unknown. How and why does it do this?

(b) **Transcendence:** The spiritual both causes and enables us to transcend the ordinary or perhaps see something special in the ordinary, what Webster (1996, p. 249) refers to as a "freshness of perception" and Lealman (1982, p. 59) as "the strange within the familiar". For McCreery (1996, p. 197) the spiritual is an awareness that there is something other, something greater than the course of everyday events, while Heimbrock (2004, pp. 119-131) links it with what is sacred to children and this tends to be in the personal sphere of their lives whereby they perceive the extraordinary within ordinary life. For Buckley (1987, p. 360) it is when the experience of wonder reaches a deep and profound level. As such, "transcendence is perhaps the most essential quality of the spiritual" (Zohar and Marshall, 2000, p. 68). Du Boulay encapsulates such feelings in her description of the consequences of the experience of Bede Griffiths when, as a schoolboy, he walked through the fields on a summer's day:

> The normal pattern of his thinking was disrupted and now he knew that there was another dimension to existence. He had experienced one of those moments in which people come face to face with reality: "We see our life for a moment in its true perspective in relation to eternity. We are freed from the flux of time and see something of the eternal order which underlies it. We are no longer isolated individuals in conflict with our surroundings; we are part of whole, elements in a universal harmony" (Du Boulay, 1999, pp.16-17; Griffiths, 1954, p.11).

These transformative experiences, which come to most people at some time, may be ascribed to different sources: divine (Bowker, 1995; Hick, 1999); natural (Maslow, 1964; Hamer, 2005); or induced (Huxley, 1971; Wells, 1973, pp.189-212). They may vary in intensity from the mystical experience to the merely "feel good". This transcendental dimension of spirituality is not necessarily exclusive to any belief system, though some tend to associate it with a religious perspective on life (Elton-Chalcroft, 2001, pp. 10-12).

The guidance papers from educational bodies confirm the importance and significance of this dimension (DES/HMI, 1977b; NCC, 1993; SCAA, 1995; ACCAC, 2000b), and "awe" and "wonder" are two terms frequently encountered in school policies for spiritual development. McCreery (2001, p. 19) found that these were by far the most common response from teachers when asked to describe what they understood by "spiritual".

(c) **Relationships:** Few would question the importance of relationships within our lives. Humans are by nature gregarious creatures, and it is our interaction with others and our environment which goes a long way towards forming the persons we are. As Crompton (1998, p. 42) points out, "relatedness" is one of the key words in naming the spiritual life. We also interact with ourselves, but to locate the spiritual principally in inner self reflection as a means to a deeper self understanding and self improvement is to denude the spiritual of a crucial aspect of what it is. This Wright refers to as a kind of "spiritual autism" (Wright, 1999, p. 34). At the same time we need to beware of elevating what many would regard as ordinary interaction to the status of the spiritual where even the sharing of sweets becomes the spirituality of fellowship (Hay and Nye, 1998, p.122). Doubtless, ordinary events can be interpreted in a variety of ways; it is a matter of "seeing as", but once more much rests on the individual's interpretation of these interactions. Moreover, communal spirituality is not always necessarily a positive thing, as some the more extreme groups and movements illustrate.

Williams (1997, p. 2), basing his understanding of "educating the spirit" on scripture, says it involves particular kinds of relationships to others. It is the way in which we relate to others, the environment and to God. Similarly, Fisher (1999, p. 31) identifies four sets of relationships which contribute towards a person's spiritual health. These are: a relationship with oneself; others, the environment; and with a higher order. These four domains he referred to as: personal; communal; environmental; and global. Bradford (1995, p. 35) also stresses the importance of positive relationships with ourselves, our family, with God and our faith community (if we belong to one), and with others and the wider world. Thus, for him spirituality is "a tripartite concept, the three parts of which – human, devotional and practical – fit closely together and complement the whole" (p. 1).

(d) **Ultimate Questions and the Search for Meaning:** Ultimate questions which are questions of universal application and significance but have no easy or mutually agreed answers are seen as indicators of the spiritual and a means of providing opportunities for spiritual development. These questions bring us "face to face with ultimate questions of life and death, beauty and ugliness, good and evil, security and anxiety, meaning and despair" (Wright, 1999, p. 12). This is considered to be a form of intelligence with which we address and solve problems of meaning and value (Zohar and Marshall, 2000, pp.2-3). Indeed, Zohar and Marshall claim that it is this capacity to search for meaning and value which distinguishes us from animals (p. 4).

Of all the questions which focus the mind on purpose, value and meaning, the ultimate is concerned with death. Rinpoche's popular book *The Tibetan Book of Living and Dying* (1992) stresses the importance of contemplating death as a means of spiritual development. In a contribution to a later work he underscores how it is a means to self-understanding and spiritual development when he says "because if we can only learn how to face death, then we'll have learned the most important lesson of life: how to face *ourselves* and so come to terms with ourselves, in the deepest possible sense, as human beings" (Longaker, 1998, p.xi).

Whilst this may appear a maudlin and depressing topic to focus upon in life and especially in schools, it need not be the case. The Isle of Wight Agreed Syllabus for Religious Education incorporates the theme of death in both primary and secondary schools, and death education is to be found in such centres as the Association for Death Education and Counselling and the National Center for Death Education, across the United States. Sutherland (1995, p. 23) argues that "a proper spiritual development will encourage a recognition, then an understanding, then a response to human finitude". Death's finality is necessary for us to take life seriously with its many moral decisions. Life becomes a gift. So paradoxically the very event that robs life of meaning also imparts it.

V: SPIRITUALITY, MORALITY AND RELIGION

(a) **Spirituality and Morality:** The proximity of the spiritual to the moral, social and cultural in both the educational legislation and the guidance partly implies that we are perhaps wrong to try to explore the essence of spirituality independently of, if not the other three, then certainly the moral. There are those who feel that the spiritual is the leading member of the four. Alan Brown (1997) of the National Society claims that, "if the 'spiritual' is properly and fully addressed, the 'moral, social and cultural' will fall into place more easily." Smith (1999, p. i) endorses this view, stating that "it can even be argued that if we deal adequately with the spiritual dimension of education the moral, social and cultural dimensions will be easier to provide for". For Hay morality arises out of spiritual insight and, if schools seriously address their responsibilities of fostering spiritual awareness, then children are more likely to grow up to be morally responsible members of the community (Hay and Nye, 1998, p39).

However, the question must be asked whether a person can be both spiritual and amoral or even immoral at the same time. According to Hull and Williams the answer must be in the negative, but, given the OFSTED and other criteria for clarifying the meaning of "spirituality", it might be argued that Hitler was a spiritual person with his sense of purpose in life that drove and sustained him, his aesthetic appreciation of the music of Wagner, his imagination and his creativity, however perversely applied. Hitler may also be considered to have what some consider spiritual qualities based on his mesmerising affect on others (Gardner, 1999, p. 57). Rabbi Naftali Brawer claims that Hitler had very deep spiritual yearnings and that he was a hypersensitive man incredibly attuned to spiritual and perhaps evil spiritual matters (Portillo, British Broadcasting Corporation [BBC], 2001). If this is the case then clearly spirituality can be separated from morality; for no sensible person would argue that Hitler was a good and moral person. The selection of Hitler as an example of a "spiritual" person may appear shocking when we consider the heinous crimes he sanctioned, but it does serve to illustrate that, like most people, he was not a one-dimensional character, but rather a mixture of traits, capable of acts of both kindness and cruelty. Such an example, however, does lead us to agree with Smith (1999, p. 3) when he says that not all manifestations of spirituality are healthy and that we should be wary of assuming that all that is spiritual is good. It also indicates that spiritual experiences do not necessarily transform all aspects of a person's life for the better. "Inwards" is not necessarily synonymous with "upwards" (Copley, 2000, p. 10). From our "deepest humanity" comes both evil as well as good (Thatcher, 1999, p. 9).

Not all are keen to forge this link between the spiritual and the moral. Just as religion and spirituality are not necessarily connected in the eyes of many people, neither are spirituality and morality. Oscar Wilde recognised this in what came to be known as De Profundis, when he argued that his experience of suffering which he deemed spiritual made him a deeper but not necessarily a better person.

> But while to propose to be a better man is a piece of unscientific cant, to have become a deeper man is the privilege of those who have suffered. And such I think I have become (Wilde, 1997, p. 788).

It was his inner light (the spiritual) which helped him rather than morality or religion (Pearson, 1998, pp. 327-328). Others confirm that a spiritual experience may well be (or even should be) transformative, but not necessarily in terms of the moral betterment of the individual. Gilbert (1998, p. x), in referring to a mystical experience he had, asks whether it made him a better person. In the moral sense, as usually understood, he would answer "No", but he recognised that it did unquestionably change him. What he believed he encountered was the certainty of a Reality beyond the world of the senses, and this heightened his awareness but did not alter his moral sensibilities or the code by which he lived.

If we subscribe to this tenuous and unpredictable connection between the spiritual and the moral, then we are in effect saying that the spiritual is essentially introspective and that spiritual well-being is concerned with our own well-being. The well-being of others becomes secondary and incidental to our own. An agreed moral code may be desirable but not essential for spiritual growth and development. This is perhaps an excessive and unfair interpretation of the views of those who, like Carr, are merely arguing that spiritual truths are often distinguishable from ethical and moral claims inasmuch as they are not essentially prescriptive (Carr and Haldane, 2003, p. 221).

This, I suspect, is an extreme position most would not subscribe to. Should not the moral aspect of a person be used as a criterion for assessing the educational value, if not the efficacy, of spiritual development? Indeed, Erricker (1998, p. 59) argues that the guidance from bodies such as SCAA indicates that the fostering of spiritual development is directed to a moral end. Wright (2000, p. 12) contends that the atrocities of the Twentieth Century, such as Auschwitz, are icons of a spiritual, rather than moral, vacuum, thus implying that the spiritual is an antecedent of the moral. Hick (1999, p. 8) shares the premise that it is the spiritual which leads to a clarity of moral vision. There are, however, those who affirm their moral responsibilities whilst denying their spiritual nature.

We might well reverse the question in our search for the connection (if any) between the spiritual and the moral, and ask: what makes the moral spiritual? Inevitably, our environment, cultural heritage, religious persuasions and even gender and biological makeup impinge upon, and to some extent determine, our experience and interpretation of the spiritual. As far as schools are concerned, we may say "yes" in terms of behaviour, but "no" for private beliefs. The two, however, are interconnected, for our beliefs often determine our behaviour and play a major part in our understanding of right and wrong.

To return to our "chicken and egg" conundrum: in what sense does the spiritual enhance moral views and actions and are the latter necessary for authentic spiritual development? For the likes of McGhee (2003, pp. 26-29), the spiritual involves a higher kind of moral understanding and awareness, and for Jacobs (2003, pp. 55-56) and Sherman (2003, pp. 67-80), basing their views on the Aristotelian conception of virtuous conduct, spirituality completes and perfects virtue. Thus, for some, the spiritual enhances moral action and thinking. Others such as Haldane (2003, p. 14) argue that the spiritual is not primarily concerned with moral actions towards others but rather a person's interpretation of experiences or, as he puts it, "what personal demeanour one develops in the face of reality as one understands it". Here the spiritual is our perception and understanding of life's experiences and is not reducible to ethics (p.19), though it is difficult to say whether it is the experiences which give rise to a spiritual interpretation or an inherent predilection towards the spiritual which causes us to interpret experiences in the way in which we do.

McGhee (2003, p. 28) suggests that there is clearly a connection between the moral and the spiritual, for without the moral the spiritual is enfeebled and attenuated. Indeed, he prefers to place the moral before the spiritual and feels this should be the case in current guidance to schools. Thus, the spiritual adds an extra dimension to the moral. Two people may perform the same action but the intention of one may be "superior and more refined" than that of the other. As an example, he cites the compassion of Christ with our own. To view the action from a spiritual perspective gives a superior vantage point to the person concerned. Morality thus "ascends towards and transforms itself into the 'spiritual' in a single line of development, and so locks them together." Unlike Haldane, who focuses on experience rather than conduct, McGhee sees conduct as a criterion for assessing the spiritual (p.31). In terms of education and the place of both the spiritual and moral in schools this seems the preferred option, but does this mean that the spiritual needs the moral more than vice versa in order to measure the success of the opportunities provided?

(b) **Spirituality and Religion:** If, as we have suggested above, the spiritual in some sense requires the moral as a means of evaluating its authenticity and the moral is in some sense enhanced by the spiritual, can the same be said of religion? We have seen that McGhee is in no doubt that genuine spirituality requires both:

> I suggest that any notion of "spirituality" that is conceived independently both of religion *and* of moral life is enfeebled and attenuated (McGhee, 2003, p. 28).

Not unnaturally, many of those of a religious disposition will tend to identify spirituality with religion. For some the spiritual is the essence of true religion (Leech, 1985; Toon, 1990; Carson, 1996; Sheldrake, 1999) and the spiritual without religion becomes an idiosyncratic self-indulgence. Much of the argument centres on the nature of reality and truth. If we live in a theistic universe, or to put it simply if we are created by God and will return to God, then true spirituality will assist the individual in this journey. If this is the case then spirituality is what Cottingham (2003, p. 47) calls "a *metaphysically freighted* notion". Clearly, our attitude towards religion, whether positive, negative or one of tolerant indifference, has implications for the way in which we view and interpret our spiritual lives and development.

Given the religious history of mankind and more specifically the religious history of Britain, we evidently cannot ignore the role religion has played in forging our understanding of spirituality. As we have seen, when the spiritual was confirmed in educational legislation in 1944 it was coated with Christian connotations. Over time this bond has been weakened but not severed. The question this raises is: do the notions of spirituality and spiritual development retain any coherence independently of religion? Should the spiritual be "tethered" to, or be "untethered" from religion? (Alexander and McLaughlin, 2002, pp. 356-373)

Thatcher (1999, p. 4) claims that it is far from obvious that spirituality without theology is even coherent. Carson takes a similar view when he suggests that any break of the spiritual from its religious roots is detrimental and perilous:

> If spirituality becomes an end in itself, detached from the core, and largely without biblical or theological norms to define it and anchor it in the objective gospel, then pursuit of spirituality, however nebulously defined, will degenerate into nothing more than the pursuit of certain kinds of experience (Carson, 1996, p. 567).

The implication is that, if spirituality has its roots in religion, then the plant of spirituality will die if it is severed from this source of sustenance. Any serious study of spirituality cannot ignore religion. Indeed, despite the cross curricular nature of spirituality, guidance provided by OFSTED and Estyn to those assigned to inspect SMSC in schools explicitly directs them to religious education lessons and acts of collective worship or school assemblies as one of their primary sources of evidence for the provision of opportunities for spiritual development. Thus, any critical study of spirituality must make reference to religion.

Yet, religion and spirituality are not necessarily synonymous, as the guidance constantly reminds us. Much of the debate centres on the problem of definitions. The way in which we interpret the experiences of life, however, is the root of the problem. For one man's religious experience is another's figment of the imagination or profound aesthetic encounter with the marvels of life. What one sees as an encounter with the Divine another sees as an encounter with the mysteries of the Self. Religion then is but one coat spirituality might wear (Copley, 2000, p.139).

There are two fundamental flaws in the argument that spirituality only retains coherence within a religious framework. These are:

- The assumption that there is coherence within and between religions.

- The denial of authentic spiritual experience and development to those who reject the fundamental tenets of all religions.

These two issues will now be explored:

(i) *The assumption that there is coherence within and between religions*: First, it is false to think that placing spirituality in a religious context adds to its coherence. Apart from the obvious differences between religions and the way in which they interpret what they perceive as reality, each religion is far from a monolithic entity. Whilst the origin of the term "spiritual" may have its home in religion and each religion espouses the spiritual path, King (1997, p. 495) rightly points out that "each religious tradition knows many different schools of spirituality, and past and present spirituality are not necessarily the same, not even in the same religion". Chronological and cultural contexts result in a variety of spiritual paths.

There has been a marked decline in church attendance in Britain in recent years. To some extent this decline has been mirrored across Europe and even mainline churches in North America. Using Davie's *Religion in Britain Since 1945: Believing Without Belonging* (1994), Wright (2000, p. 51) notes that at first glance the evidence regarding religious community membership appears to contradict the notion that we live in a predominantly secular and pluralistic society with about seventy-one per cent of the British population claiming membership of a religious community. This apparent religiosity is, however, as Wright points out, somewhat superficial and nominal with only fifteen per cent claiming to practise their religion on a regular basis. A BBC survey on belief in Britain at the turn of the century (BBC, 2000) revealed that traditional religion is in sharper decline than we might have previously thought. Within the last fifty years there has been a marked change in the religious landscape of Britain. Forty-five per cent of the population never go to church and fifty per cent go once a year. Even the sixty-nine per cent, who still use the church for significant turning points in their lives such as weddings, represents a drop of ten per cent in ten years. Despite this, only eight per cent regard themselves as atheists. Streib, (2005, p. 134) using the Shell surveys (1985, 1992, 2000) and other research databases, (Schmidtchen, 1997; Pollack, 1996) documents a decline of church membership in Germany and shows how the German churches have reason to be concerned about membership among the younger generation, especially in the East. Again, there has been a marked decline in church attendance by adolescents from fifty-nine percent in 1953 to sixteen per cent by the end of the Twentieth Century (Streib, 2005, p.134).

Across the Atlantic the seeming religious fervour of the Americans is mainly confined to the charismatic and Pentecostal churches. There has been a noticeable drop in church membership of the so-called mainline churches in the United States (Naisbitt and Aburdene, 1999), and Bibby (2002) has recorded parallel trends in Canada. These writers and surveys also note that this waning of traditional and recognisable expressions of religiosity has not been mirrored in the search for the spiritual. In 1990 fifty-six per cent of the population in Britain called themselves religious, and, whilst this fell to twenty-seven per cent in 2000, in the same year thirty-one per cent referred to themselves as spiritual (BBC, 2000). Thatcher asks whether there is an inverse relation between increased secularisation and increased attention to spirituality (Thatcher, 1999, p. 1).

Streib shows how religiosity amongst adolescents is not necessarily diminishing but merely changing. Forty-five per cent think Britain would be a worse place without traditional religion (BBC, 2000). There is a transformation in the ways in which religion is expressed. Essentially, there is a greater emphasis on individual practice and preferences, one of the corollaries of which is that religious expression becomes more invisible and difficult to quantify. Streib (2005, p. 139) asks how we can characterise the new way of searching for religion or of being religious. There appears to have been a paradigm shift in the search for the sacred and for meaning in life from the religious to the spiritual. The search is still there but the labels have changed.

This new generation of "spiritual seekers" has been characterised by Beaudoin (1998) as Generation X. He shows how this Generation X adopts an *a la carte* approach to religion and spirituality, forever recombining and forming new spiritualities (Beaudoin, 1998, p.178). This he identifies as irreverent "bricolating" (from the word *bricolage* which means making do with materials at hand to solve particular problems and questions, in this case religious). Roof (1993 and 1999) has also shown how the baby-boom generation remain deeply interested in spirituality despite dropping out of organised religion. An example of this consumerist approach to religion and spirituality was epitomised in the Channel 4 television series *Spirituality Shopper*, where three non-believers were allowed to try out various religious practices for a month to see if they would help to solve their modern-day problems. This "designer spirituality" was seen by many traditionalists as a trivialisation of faith, but was defended by its presenter, the athlete Jonathan Edwards (himself a committed Christian), as providing an opportunity to take "non-religious people who think there is something missing in their lives and trying to find ways to live better" (Petre, 2005, p. 8).

Within this shifting religious and spiritual landscape Gollnick (2003, p. 156) detects the emergence of the concept of *implicit religion*, which refers to whatever functions like a religion, even though it does not appear to be a religion as conventionally understood. Baily (2002, p. 67) shows how such a broad and encompassing definition, with its emphasis on commitment, can embrace "secular faith and spirituality". Gollnick notes that implicit religion has much in common with certain forms of spirituality such as the way in which they both address questions of identity, values, worldview and meaning without necessarily referring to organised religion.

Religion then may be seen by some as a dimension of spirituality but not a necessary one, whilst to others spirituality is but one of the many dimensions of religion and not always the most important.

(ii) *spirituality and the rejection of religion*: Human beings can live quite well without recourse to religious faith, but can they live without a healthy spiritual aspect to their lives? If we assume, as many do, that such experiences are an integral part of being human, then clearly they are "an aspect of a person in society" (ACCAC, 2000b) irrespective of a person's religious persuasions (or lack of them). This brings us back to what we considered the second fundamental flaw in tethering spirituality to religion. This is the denial of authentic spiritual experience and development to those who reject the fundamental tenets of all religions and thus impose limitations on the numbers of those capable of attaining spiritual awareness.

There is a mix of views in our schools, and to reject a spiritual aspect to a person who is not religious is, I suspect, to disenfranchise a significant number of pupils who hold no religious beliefs and may well have no desire to acquire any. This is not the same as saying that children do not need to be acquainted with religious traditions as part of their education. Indeed, for an understanding and exploration of the spiritual, the place of spirituality in religious traditions must be incorporated. It does assume, despite the objections of some, that there can be a non-religious spirituality and that schools can offer opportunities for spiritual development to take place.

VI: TRIGGERS OR CAUSES OF SPIRITUAL EXPERIENCES

The findings of psychology, neuropshychology and neurobiology give us an insight into spiritual experiences as much as the disciplines of philosophy and theology. Some even refer to these areas of research as *neurotheology* (Keating, 2001, p.1). Neuroscience or brain science has been able to indicate that certain parts of the brain are active during religious and spiritual experiences. Indeed, it is practically impossible to distinguish between the two in terms of brain activity. Some have used this to imply that both religion and spirituality are part and product of the evolutionary process and hard-wired into the brain and our genes (Zohar and Marshall, 2000; D'Aquili and Newberg, 2001; Heffern,

2001; Hamer, 2005; Olkowski, 2006). The parts of the brain which are stimulated during these experiences are the temporal lobes. In fact, Persinger was able to induce a religious/spiritual experience by artificially stimulating this part of the brain (Zohar and Marshall, 2000, pp. 92-93).

The brain can also be stimulated artificially by drugs (Jackson, 1997, p. 228), and again anyone reading accounts of the drug induced visions and experiences of the likes of Huxley (mescalin) and Leary (LSD – lysergic acid diethylaminde) have little option other than to agree with Stace who says of the drug experience: "It's not a matter of it being similar to mystical experience; it is mystical experience" (Zaehner, 1972, p. 79; See also Huxley, 1971; Gilbert, 1998, pp. 72-76; Murray 2002, pp.398-409). Clearly mental illness and drug induced experiences are not something schools need unduly concern themselves with, other than possibly studying the causes, effects and implications associated with these areas.

Some of the other triggers or causes which have been recognised are more likely to be encountered by schools. Hardy (1979, pp. 28-29) lists twenty triggers which I have listed below in order of occurrence:

1. Depression and despair
2. Prayer and meditation
3. Natural beauty
4. Participation in religious worship
5. Literature, drama and film
6. Illness
7. Music
8. Crisis in personal relationships
9. The death of others
10. Sacred places
11. Visual art
12. Creative work
13. Relaxation
14. Silence, solitude
15. The prospect of death (*this scored the same as the previous trigger*)
16. Drugs: anaesthetic
17. Physical activity
18. Childbirth
19. Happiness
20. Drugs: psychedelic

Moreover, Hay suggests that the most commonly reported context for a contemporary spiritual experience is some form of crisis (Hay, 1987; Jackson, 1997, p. 248).

Just as the definitions for the spiritual encompass the many areas and experiences of life, so too the triggers for spiritual experiences can come from a multitude of sources, both positive and negative. From the above lists we can see at a glance those which might be applicable to the work of schools and those which might be less suitable. Added to this we need to question whether it is the role of schools to plan to give spiritual experiences to pupils or to provide opportunities for spiritual development to take place. Should they enable pupils to refine their awareness of the wonder, mystery and value of life or is this better left to individual pupils, some of whom may be more predisposed to these "spiritual reactions" than others? This is associated with the question whether spiritual experiences are spontaneous or worked for and whether the experiences are sufficient in themselves or part of a process of linear development and growth towards some kind of goal.

VII: SPIRITUALITY AND TRUTH

Education is, at least in part, a disinterested search for the truth, though not all people fully utilise this capacity, for they are capable of believing as true the most ridiculous things often in the face of evidence to the contrary (Russell, 1992, pp.73-99; Shermer, 2000). Is this the case with spiritual experience and, if so, does it really matter? Are we to agree with Kierkegaard when he said that truth is subjectivity? Or are we to subject experiences and feelings to some kind of "truth test" in order to be sure of their validity and accuracy?

According to Carr (1994, pp. 221-138; 1995, p. 94) spiritual enquiry qualifies as a truth-seeking enterprise. Truth seeking and truth finding are not, however, necessarily synonymous. As there is no overriding unity of expression or goal to spiritual experiences, are we now to define the truth of the experience as relative to the person having the experience? Wright (1999, p. 30) argues that in a climate of post-modern spirituality the "truth" is that there is no truth. This is based on the view that there is no possible way of knowing if the spiritual insights of individuals give an accurate and truthful account of reality. If we accept this post-modernist premise, then it follows that in the context of spiritual development and spirituality truth is not important.

If, as we have suggested earlier, spirituality and spiritual experiences are in the main life enhancing and transformative in that they give meaning and value to life does it in some way undermine their efficacy if they are based on false premises and illusions? We have seen that there is great variety regarding these experiences and what is considered spiritual development within and between religions, and between religious and secular interpretations of experiences. Can all be right? Wright (p. 35) raises pertinent questions when he says that the atheist and the theist cannot both be right; therefore the spirituality of one must be flawed and, if Islam is true, then only Moslems have authentic spirituality.

In trying to respond to these concerns we lead ourselves on something of a wild goose chase, for the question of authentic and ultimate truth is beyond our grasp. The ultimate explanation of reality is not accessible to us and it is presumptuous to assume that it should be despite our inner desire for knowledge and understanding. Yet, in order to safeguard against a worrying escalation of pseudo-truths associated with rampant individualism we need to temper our evaluations of the spiritual with reference to reason, shared objective reality and morality. This involves a combination of aspects of the coherence, correspondence and pragmatic theories of truth (For a summary of these see *Concise*

Routledge Encyclopaedia of Philosophy, 2000, pp. 899-900; Honderich, 1995, pp.140; 166-167; 709-710; 881-882). It is desirable for the experiences and views of the individual to agree or cohere with other beliefs they (and others) hold (coherence theory). The insights gained from these experiences should correspond to the world as we know it, in other words the facts (correspondence theory). The insights and experiences should prove to be beneficial not only to the individual but also to others and the wider community, thus assigning them a pragmatic value (pragmatic theory). Each of these truth theories is not without criticisms, but it is not necessary within the confines of this discussion to engage in a detailed philosophical analysis of these.

Wright (1999, p. 45) properly contends that the appraisal of individual spirituality and world views should be made against two clusters of questions:

- Are their views internally coherent? Do their stories make sense?

- How do they relate to alternative world views – both the world view of the school within which they are being nurtured, and the world views on offer within broader society?

This means a critical study of at least some of the spiritual paths and histories along with the provision for opportunities to explore and discuss one's own "spiritual" thoughts and feelings. Thus, in subjects such as religious education this would involve, as Radford (1999, p. 166) suggests, the process of exploring spiritual experience through conceptual frameworks provided by religious texts relevant to the spiritual interests of the pupils. This includes an acceptance of the possibility that we may be wrong or misguided. Much of this comes through asking questions. Education for spiritual development should be what a person must become in order to gain access to the truth and how access to the truth so gained has the power to transform elements of the subject (Cottingham, 2003, p. 46). New insights into reality undoubtedly come through education. This is a two way process as the external world both informs and moulds us, but we also see and experience it from our own perspectives with its limitations. As Kant showed, the innate structure of being human (minds and bodies) determines what we can know. This is a constantly unfolding dynamic with the mind imposing its own imperative categories. As with a work of art, our experience of it is part a product of the work and part a product of our own construction (Radford, 1999, p.170). They can be differing levels of interpretation and explanation, which are not necessarily contradictory. There are different ways of classifying and interpreting our experiences (Ayer, 1971, p. 244). When we describe a mental event it can be described subjectively and, in theory, neurobiologically. It would "represent equivalent statements in different universes of discourse, and can be translated one into the other" (Rose, 1976, p. 29). As such, a spiritual experience or insight is not necessarily wrong because it is not subject to the usual rules of verification. A logical positivist position is not an appropriate stance to take. There will always remain a subjective and personal element whereby the spiritual occurrence is "true" for the recipient, but for this truth to be assimilated and accepted by the wider community, and to some extent by the recipient, it should be measured against the criteria listed above.

Given what we have argued above, the implications for education are twofold:

(i) The school can provide a curriculum and experiences which may precipitate a spontaneous reaction that can be described as a spiritual experience. This is similar to the argument for the statutory retention of acts of collective worship whereby pupils are led to the "threshold of worship" but may or may not be induced actually to worship with its accompanying experiences.

(ii) Schools can design a programme of activities with the explicit intention of stirring up specific experiences and emotions which may be regarded as spiritual. These might include meditative practices (Erricker and Erricker, 2001) or "creative visualisations" and "guided fantasies" (Hammond *et al.*, 1990; Stone, 1992). Both approaches imply that there is benefit and value to pupils in exploring this aspect of their nature. The question is how then do we translate all of this into the practical day-to-day life of schools?

VIII: SPIRITULITY AND EDUCATION

(a) **Spirituality and Schools:** Few would argue that a spiritual education should provide a healthy environment for individual growth and place emphasis on the value of each person as he or she grows into maturity (Bowness and Carter, 1999, p. 233). This involves not just thinking about spirituality but also thinking about education. Spiritual education is apparently not limited to named subjects of the curriculum and is much more than a subject in its own right. It is meant to be cross curricular and all pervasive across the life of the school. According to Rodger (1996, p. 60) it is a different way of *knowing*, *doing* and *being*. It has to do with the way in which institutions structure themselves that goes beyond the "drivelling uplift" of mission statements (Williams, 1997, p. 6).

There are those, however, who take issue with the supposed cross curricular nature of spiritual education, regarding it as misleading to the point of eccentricity and wrongheaded to suggest that it "may occur whenever and wherever" (Carr, 1995, p. 95; 1996, p. 162). To do so is a recipe for confusion and miscommunication (Beck, 1999, p.165). It is, they claim, clearly more evident and accessible in certain subjects such as religious education, arts, literature and music than in others such as mathematics. McCreery (2001, p. 12) found that amongst primary school teachers the three most popular subject areas in relation to the spiritual were science, art and personal, social and health education (PSHE) and the least popular were drama, mathematics and physical education.

(b) **Spirituality and Philosophies which Have Shaped Education:** We cannot ignore the philosophies which have had an impact on the way in which education is understood. I have implied throughout this chapter that our current education system in state schools is essentially liberal and secular whilst still retaining a statutory obligation to the place and value of religious education and acts of collective worship. This is perhaps an over simplification and what we observe happening in schools is a blend of a number of philosophies which have helped to form the way in which spirituality is understood. Wright gives a comprehensive summary of these influences in his book *Spirituality and Education* (2000). What we find is a curious mixture of materialism, empiricism, romanticism, existentialism, post-modernism and critical realism. For a concise summary of these philosophies the reader is referred to Bullock and Trombley (1999) and Stewart (1997).

Materialism and empiricism with their emphasis on concrete experience, objective reality and the need for verification are to be found primarily in the sciences and technologies of the curriculum. Here one might perhaps expect a tolerant but not altogether sympathetic view of the responsibility of schools to stimulate spiritual development. Romanticism provides a balance to this and to rationalism, with its emphasis on the importance of feeling, emotions and the subjective imagination. Here the emphasis is on the primacy of the perceiver on the world he/she perceives. Many of the notions of romanticism remain central to the modern mind and thus to education and find expression in the arts, literature and music.

Existentialism with its reaction against idealism has been embraced more readily on the continent than in Britain. It explores and investigates the peculiarities of human existence, the loss of certainties and ways of living authentically. Wright's ultimate questions and concerns and Sutherland's focus on the awareness of our finitude as a means of spiritual development incorporate and embrace this movement. Post-modernism, like existentialism, sees a move towards individualism with its rejection of grand narratives and totalistic explanations. There is less confidence in the old certainties. Its effect on spiritual development has been to encourage individualism and, as we have discussed above, the idiosyncratic truth of experiences and world views.

Finally, critical realism takes a more sophisticated view of reason and experience. It accepts that there is an independent reality which we can experience and from which we can derive knowledge. This is the approach favoured by Wright (2000, p. 25) who says that "critical realism treads a path between absolute certainty and absolute relativism: we can obtain knowledge of reality, but such knowledge will always be contingent, always engaged in the process of striving for deeper understanding, always open to new insight". Here we see the need to balance experience and feeling against knowledge of the world. The spiritual is to be evaluated and assessed against objective reality – or at least what we know of it.

If we consider all the above, we can see how schools have incorporated elements of each in the way in which they educate children. Ideally, schools advance evidence based approaches to leaning, they encourage creativity and mutual respect for differences within loosely defined parameters, and they promote critical reflection, shared values and positive attitudes and skills.

(c) **Spiritual Literacy:** Tests and examinations assess the academic progress and development of pupils. We have a fair understanding of what a literate and numerate person should be and schools use a range of methods to advance children towards these goals. What methods, however, do schools employ to create a spiritually literate person, assuming they know what one is?

Many have contributed to the debate, both to suggest and to provide the means to promote spiritual development. Some have been more successful in advancing their ideas than others. Success however is not the sole criterion for judging the coherence and validity of an approach. We have already touched upon some of the ideas schools are advised to adopt in order to provide opportunities for spiritual development. Wright suggests that pupils should wrestle with ultimate questions, meaning and truth, a view shared by Zohar and Marshall. As such, it is a search for knowledge and wisdom. Wright would agree with Carr who believes this involves the study of a range of spiritual traditions and spiritual truths. Some, such as Keating, specifically recommend using texts of the Wisdom literature as a means of raising these issues and considering the insights of at least some of the great traditions. Students, he contends, in their early years of schooling need to be more outwardly directed and receive their guidance from external sources of authority. But, at the end of their schooling, they need to begin a process of inwardly evaluating what they have learnt, of constructing their own meaning, of making it their own, if they wish to enter adulthood (Keating, 2001, p.1). This is sound advice for all aspects of education and not just the spiritual. Critical reflection on learning is one of the indicators of an educated person.

(d) **Spirituality and Teachers:** If, as is supposed, teachers are sources of authority who are required to introduce children to additional sources of authority on matters spiritual, then it presupposes they have a knowledge and understanding of these matters. This is an assumption which is not necessarily borne out by the facts. Do teachers have a clear understanding of what is expected of them in terms of the spiritual development of the pupils in their charge? McCreery (2001) found that amongst the teachers she questioned there was a perceived absence of help in this area and that most were left to their own resources. Not only this, but teachers themselves were involved in a personal search regarding their own spiritual development. As a result, their own perceived spirituality and stage of spiritual development based on their life experiences impacted on the way they approached the topic in schools. Not surprisingly, those with a specific religious commitment were more likely to be able to identify the spiritual in their work while those who were hostile to the statutory requirement for schools to teach religious education were more unreceptive to the notion of spirituality in schools. More mature teachers - aged forty or above - with years of experience and those holding positions of seniority in the school were more positive and confident in their views of the spiritual. This results, as McCreery says, in diverse and unpredictable approaches to dealing with the spiritual in schools. This diversity of interpretation, which we have already touched upon, is confirmed by Watson (2000, pp. 91-101).

This lack of confidence and diversity of approach are partly due to lack of initial and subsequent training for teachers (McCreery, 2001, p.14). Eaude (2001, p. 1) found that practically all the teachers he spoke to said they had received no training at all. Lecturers at universities and colleges clearly feel that they have more pressing priorities than to spend valuable time training teachers in this "marginal" area. This may partly explain the OFSTED review of 1998, which judged nearly half the secondary schools as "poor" at fostering spiritual development (Gay, 2000, p.63). This lack of explicit training is not necessarily the result of indifference towards the "spiritual" on the part of students. Tacey (2002, pp. 171-182) found that students at his university were deeply interested in spirituality and their own spiritual development, but university teachers were reluctant to engage with this interest as a result of its questionable academic credentials. Pupils also believe that schools should be involved in their spiritual development (Watson, 2001, p.10), since most seek some kind of spiritual fulfilment (Zohar and Marshall, 2000, p.8), and schools can make a contribution towards this.

Given that the spiritual has been an integral part of education in this country from 1944 and before, this lack of explicit training should not be the case with those on initial teacher training courses.

However, when one takes into account the number of standards which have to be met in order to achieve qualified teacher status and the time in which training institutions have to address each of these, it is not surprising that the spiritual, if not neglected, is only give cursory attention.

Whether intentionally or not, teachers play a significant part in the formation of the spiritual development of the pupils in their charge. Indoctrination is not to be condoned or encouraged, but neutrality is difficult, if not impossible, to sustain. As Wright (2000, p. 16) says, "those who acknowledge their prior philosophical commitments are likely to be better educators than those who fail to do so". No longer is it the case that teachers are expected to hide their views and beliefs as long as they balance these and allow pupils to explore a range of perspectives. The liberal education found in schools, as Beck (1999, p. 174) says, is neither intended to make pupils religious nor to prevent them from being religious, but to bring them to understanding. Children invariably ask questions and search for meaning and thus, according to some, have a natural spirituality (Coles, 1992; Zohar and Marshall, 2000). What strategies do and should teachers use to satisfy these needs and actively promote spiritual development?

(e) **Methods Used to Promote and Address the Spiritual Development of Children:** In recent years there has been no shortage of advice on how schools might promote the spiritual development of pupils. The bulk of this is based on a given view of what we mean by spirituality and spiritual development. This is essentially inclusive and an exploration of inner experiences (Hammond, et al., 1990; Stone, 1992).

This position is primarily based on the work and standpoint of the likes of Hay and Erricker who are not without their critics. Hay worked with Hammond and others on the publication of *New Methods in Religious Education: An Experiential Approach* (1990), which quickly became a formative text and source of guidance for teachers. Despite the guidance coming from the various educational bodies stressing the whole school and cross curricular nature of the "spiritual", it was usually assigned to the religious education specialist to interpret and deliver this component of education. Uncertainty, however, was not the prerogative of the non-specialist, and teachers of religious education also welcomed help and direction on these matters. It was *New Methods in Religious Education: An Experiential Approach* (1990) which came to their rescue and gave direction to the debate on "spiritual development". The essence of the work was to suggest strategies which encouraged pupils to explore their inner experiences, enabling them to become aware of the way in which they see the world and to understand how theirs is only one of many perspectives (Hammond *et al.*, 1990, p. 6). It "would help pupils to open their personal awareness to those aspects of ordinary experience which religious people take particularly seriously" (Hammond et al., 1990, p.11). Part of the justification for this approach was based on the findings of research mentioned earlier that "religious/spiritual experience" is widespread and that a proportion of members of every class from about year 9 will believe that they have had such experiences (Hammond *et al.*, 1990, p.15).

Hay, agreeing with Hardy, accepted that the notion of spirituality is biologically built into the human species (Hay and Nye, 1998, p. 16). To avoid the risk of at best ignoring, and at worst stifling these important experiences, the authors came up with classroom based activities which were designed to make children "aware of and to take seriously their own inner experience and their potential to be aware" (Hammond et al.,1990, p. 17). In engaging in these activities, designed to provide opportunities for spiritual development, pupils would become "aware of the power of language and intention to structure our experience" and "demonstrate that there is more than one perspective to reality" (Hammond et al., 1990, pp. 15-17). All are capable of exploring their inner experiences, whether or not they have any religious convictions, for all children have an innate capacity for spiritual awareness, what Hay and Nye identified as a "relational consciousness" based on a sense of mystery and meaning in life, a sense of their own identity and place in the world. This approach is thus both inclusive and personal.

This approach is also found in the work of Erricker et al. (1997) and The Children and Worldviews Project. Erricker adopts an even more radical approach towards the ever changing nature of spirituality and rules out the possibility of identifying an immutable biological essence of children's spirituality. What he does is to allow children to say what they consider to be important and meaningful to them and thus identify their individual subjective spirituality (Erricker et al., 1997, p. 34). As such, he adopts a position which is not only "inclusivist" but also "relativist". The research identified recurring themes based on children's hopes and fears and uncovered a rich vein of imagination in the search for identity and meaning. The recurring themes which children return to are: belonging and identity; violence and conflict; death, loss and family separation; God, heaven and hell; dens and special places; relationships with others; and the natural world. These contribute to the building of children's sense of identity, in other words, a spiritual self. Erricker found that children display a far greater moral, emotional and spiritual maturity that many give them credit for. Indeed, adults often avoid the issues children wish to talk about through inexperience, reluctance or discomfort. He concludes that adults, and this clearly includes teachers, can and should play an important role in supporting children with these matters.

Is this exploration of inner experiences really the way forward in providing opportunities for the spiritual development of children? Thatcher (1991, pp. 22-27) is of the opinion that this fashionable experiential approach is deeply flawed. To identify a person primarily with his/her inner self is a misleading and philosophically spurious view of a human being. This individualism with its implied dualism is "a crippling price to pay for this misidentification of spirituality with inwardness" (p.23). Thatcher's vitriolic attack on this approach is somewhat unfair as the proponents of it do not espouse a radical dualism but rather wish to illustrate the importance of experience and inner feelings in the search for the spiritual. In a response to Thatcher they categorically deny that their approach is "a withdrawal into a private space which neglects community and cosmos" (Hay and Hammond, 1992, p. 45). The activities in New Methods in Religious Education: An Experiential Approach not only encourage children to become aware of their thoughts and feelings but also their bodies, senses and the environment around them (Hay and Hammond, 1992, pp.146-147). This "inner" approach and methodology is also central to most, if not all, religious traditions which emphasise prayer and meditation as a means of spiritual growth. "Inwardness" as a metaphor points to depth rather than superficiality and it encourages us to focus on intention and meaning. By adopting these classroom strategies teachers can encourage children to engage in the four main tasks which help develop spirituality:

- helping them to keep an open mind;

- enabling them to explore different ways of seeing;

- fostering personal awareness; and

- nurturing their awareness of the social and political dimensions of spirituality (Hay and Nye, 1998, pp. 163-172).

What is questionable is whether the activities suggested by Hammond *et al.* and Erricker's conversations with children designed to explore their "micro-narratives" of everyday life (Taggart, 2002, p. 62) provide opportunities to develop the spiritual as well as the emotional and moral side of their lives. Perhaps this is an unfair question, for as we have seen, it is extremely difficult to differentiate clearly between the three and there is clearly an overlap between them. The self-knowledge, self-criticism and increased empathy which are claimed to be the by-products of this guided introspection are not necessarily "spiritual" qualities. Indeed, much of what passes for "spiritual" development may be better described as emotional and moral development. If we leave it to the individual to decide for himself/herself, we once more run the risk of fostering a personal and possibly eccentric spirituality and of being accused of advancing the "scourge of relativism" (Taggart, 2002, p. 61). As a means of countering this it is important to retain what Taggart (2002, p.61) and others refer to as a "relational quality" whereby we measure and qualify our experiences against those of others both present and past. Erricker is not unaware of the inherent dangers of his approach and rejects "an anything goes" relativism in favour of a philosophical relativism which appreciates and respects the divergence of views.

Whereas it is necessary to take into account the reservations we raised in the section *Spirituality and Morality*, the important binding and qualifying factors of "good" spiritual development are shared values and moral outcomes, and a spirituality which in some way changes lives. It is noteworthy that the Errickers regard spiritual education as a means to spiritual activism against capitalist globalising economic practices. Spiritual education involves encouraging the sense of fairness and justice which young people have. Again, critics may well say that this is more akin to socialist moralising than spiritual development.

Other reservations can be levelled at this approach of encouraging children to embark on mental or spiritual journeys through "guided fantasies", "creative visualisations" (Hammond *et al.*, 1990; Stone, 1992) or classroom meditation (Erricker and Erricker, 2001). One of these is the concern about the unpredictable outcomes of such activities and the possible "demons" which might be activated and released. As Miller (2002, p. 74) contends, teachers are not trained therapists and should be cautious about blurring the boundaries of their different roles. What is required is a clear context and framework within which these activities are to take place.

Spiritual development implies some kind of progress. Just as pupils progress through the levels of the National Curriculum so, it is to be assumed, they may progress upwards in spirituality. At least this appears to be what is implied in the term "spiritual development". Yet, whilst spiritual progress or development is desirable, it may well be a wrongheaded way of looking at it in a school context. Linear development in matters spiritual, like matters religious, is by no means a guaranteed certainty and is notoriously difficult to ascertain. For example, is the religiously mature person one who has a good academic knowledge and understanding of a wide range of religions but does not believe in God or one who accepts and believes all that his religion tells him? Indeed, some are of the opinion that our current education system actively stifles the natural spirituality of children (Hay and Nye, 1998 p. 18). Unlike other areas of the curriculum, there is no universally accepted test for the spiritual level of the child; nor should there be. All schools can do is encourage a process which makes room and space for spiritual growth to happen.

How are they to do this? In order to answer this question we need to pull together all the disparate yet interconnected strands of this chapter.

IX: CONCLUSIONS

In view of what has been said of spirituality and spirituality in schools we are left in little doubt that it is a complex and controversial subject which gives rise to strong views and heated debate. At the outset we aimed, as far as is possible, to arrive at a comprehensive and convincing picture of "spirituality" and "spiritual development". Assuming we have arrived at some kind of acceptable picture of what it is, we also want to consider how we might translate and apply these findings into the most appropriate methods, processes and content of what may be regarded as good spiritual education. The conclusions we have arrived at may be summarised as follows:

(a) A precise definition is well nigh impossible and runs the risk of controlling and restricting "spirituality" and "spiritual development" within narrow and exclusive parameters. It is better and more acceptable to identify criteria or the principal characteristics of these concepts.

(b) These criteria incorporate transcendence, positive relationships, and a search for meaning and truth. Moreover, the experience of the "spiritual" is widespread and can make a positive contribution to "wholeness" and well being. Schools can address these by inspiring and stimulating pupils through the curriculum, by promoting a positive school ethos which is one of mutual care, respect and a recognition of the intrinsic value of the individual and the wider community; and by allowing and encouraging pupils to ask questions and explore complex issues of meaning and values.

(c) Whilst spirituality may often find expression through religion, it is not synonymous with it. Spiritual experiences and development can and do form a part of the experiences of those subscribing to a wide range of life styles and world views, both secular and religious. Thus, an inclusive approach to spirituality and spiritual development by schools is both rationally sound and desirable.

(d) "Spirituality" and "spiritual development" are not the same as morality and moral development, but the moral is a legitimate means of assessing the efficacy and value of the former. In all probability teachers are more comfortable with their understanding of moral development than they are with spiritual development.

(e) Looking "inwards" and "outwards" provides a balance and counters the charge of idiosyncratic spiritual indulgence on the one hand and censorious evaluation of what constitutes the "spiritual" against set criteria on the other.

(f) "Spirituality" and "spiritual development" in schools ideally balance process and content. They encourage critical reflection of "inner" feelings and experiences – one's own and those of others. Those of others include not just one's own contemporaries within the educational establishment and the immediate community but also the teachings and insights of the great traditions and teachers (both religious and secular) on matters "spiritual", both past and present.

(g) Addressing matters "spiritual" means not shying away from sensitive and difficult issues and topics such as loss and death. Insights into meaning and values come through a range of human emotions.

(h) Teachers and pupils are both on a journey of exploration, and schools should focus on creating the circumstances in which "spiritual development" may take place and restrain themselves from attempting to force and "level" the spiritual progress of pupils. Success criteria can be based only upon pupils' knowledge and understanding of "spiritual" traditions and the skill of critical reflection. Much of what is seen as spiritual development may well take place in the private sphere of a person's life, and children, as much as adults, have a right to privacy in this domain and should not be forced to reveal their innermost thoughts and feelings. Nonetheless, schools should still provide an appropriate context in which they are able to talk about issues and matters which are important to them.

The essence of the above summary may be usefully encapsulated in what has become the key feature of "good" religious education, namely "learning about" and "learning from" religion. Hence, "good" spiritual education would involve the school in planning opportunities for "spiritual development" to take place and providing an environment which is conducive to "learning about" and "learning from" spirituality. This combines the academic and the experiential and can take place across a range of subjects and aspects of school life and ethos, though opportunities are more readily available in some subjects and some areas than others.

Even when schools take their responsibility to provide opportunities for spiritual development seriously, the nature of the task will always remain something of an enigma given the differing views on the topic. We should have some sympathy for those who consider the requirement an unnecessary burden on schools. Is it not enough to deliver and keep up-to-date with the ever changing curriculum? Is it not enough to expect schools to provide a place when pupils' moral, social and cultural attitudes and skills are developed and enriched without the encumbrance of the mysteries of the spiritual? Is it not the principal wish of parents that schools provide expertise and guidance for their offspring in the subjects they study, create an ethos of fairness and respect and leave matters spiritual to them? Is not our spiritual development the way in which we react and respond to what life throws at us?

The answer to all of the above questions is a qualified "yes". But, as school is a part of life and a very important and formative part, we are bound to encounter the "spiritual" there, whether it is planned or not. How much better it would be for all concerned that this is recognised, understood and not left to chance. As Heimbrock (2004, p. 131) argues, "multicultural society needs people who are informed and can choose with regard to ultimate questions by applying knowledge insight and argument. Civilised society needs individuals who have developed ways of expressing and communicating their emotions ... who have language for their deepest longings and anxieties and for encounters with the beautiful and uncanny in their lives".

5 Assessment for Learning

I: INTRODUCTION

The term "assessment" is familiar to most people both within and outside educational circles. It is a term that conjures up a variety of memories, emotions and ideas. All too often the perception of assessment in schools is that of tests and examinations, usually instilling feelings of unhappiness and fear of failure within the student. In fact, a recent publication by the Assessment Reform Group (ARG) (2002b) examines pupil motivation, and one of the main findings which emerges is that testing has a negative impact upon students' motivation for learning. However, Conner (1991) traces the roots of the noun *assessment* to the Latin verb *assidere*, which means "to sit beside". He then suggests that, if it is linked to another Latin verb, *educere* ("to lead out"), educational assessment can be seen as a two way process which brings out children's potential by allowing them opportunities to demonstrate understanding. This chapter will explore various aspects of assessment within the contemporary educational system and will focus upon recent developments, especially *assessment for learning* (AfL).

Knight (1995) describes assessment as a moral activity. He states that what we value in our society or culture is reflected in what we choose to assess and how we undertake the process. Arends (1998) sees it as the gathering of information about pupils and students through formal testing or informally through observation or interaction, while Harding and Beech (1991) state that assessment is usually employed to make judgements about an individual in relation to a large group of people. The emphasis in recent years is very much on the formative aspect of assessment and ways in which this can enhance the pupil's learning. Assessment becomes formative when the evidence gained from evaluating a pupil's work is used to adopt the teaching so that it meets the needs of the learner (Black *et al.*, 2003). Gipps, McCallum and Hargreaves (2000) support this view and assert that assessment is formative when pupils compare their work with the standards implied within reference levels provided by the teacher. The information acquired from this process is then used to narrow the gap between actual achievement and the requirements of these reference levels (Sadler, 1989).

Although there is debate over the exact meanings of certain terms associated with assessment, the following definitions will be used within this chapter:

- **Assessment** is used of the work of a pupil or a student.

- **Evaluation** is directed at a system, such as a lesson or a curriculum or even the educational provisions of a local authority.

- **Appraisal** is made of the deliverer of the educational process who may be a school teacher or a university tutor.

Three important types of assessment which require definition are:

- **Summative Assessment**, which is seen as a summing up of an individual's achievement over a period of learning. This could be an end of term test or a recognised qualification such as an Advanced level within the General Certificate of Education (GCE). Summative assessment occurs at the end of a learning period, and, although it can provide useful information, it is deemed to be of less importance than formative assessment as its potential to make an impact upon future learning is limited.

- **Formative Assessment**, which is recognised as a very useful tool to move learning forward. This mode of assessment is an on-going process, which provides information to the teacher who can then offer suitable learning opportunities. It should also empower the pupil or student by providing a way to narrow the gap between where he is now and where he wishes to be in the future. The teacher is in a position to recognise what is needed and the learner then uses this in order to close the gap.

- **Diagnostic Assessment**, which is applied to a specific difficulty in learning. The teacher is able to pinpoint the problem and provide appropriately adjusted work to help overcome the difficulty. It may, for example, occur if a learner is experiencing problems with a mathematical concept. A diagnostic test can then highlight the exact level at which the pupil or student is failing. Diagnostic assessment can also provide information if a learner has language difficulties, for example, phonetics.

II: HISTORICAL PERSPECTIVE

(a) **Traditional Assessment Practice:** It is not the intention of this chapter to delve into the educational philosophy of the Ancient World or Medieval Europe to report upon the origins and reasons for assessment within schooling. However, it is worth noting that in the past memory played a significant role in what was seen as learning, for example, the mastery of Latin grammar by Medieval monks in order to learn off by heart Latin texts. Assessment, under such circumstances, was merely asking the students to regurgitate information by answering questions about the grammar which they had learnt.

What is relevant within our educational systems in developed countries is that pupils and students alike are assessed to a large degree by questioning and their ability to provide "the right answer." As Wilbrink asserts,

> The difference between modern and Medieval testing seems to be mainly that not the salvation of one's soul but that of one's career depends on producing the right answer (Wilbrink, 1997, p. 33).

The historical perspective for the purpose of this chapter will begin with the final report of the National

Curriculum Task Group on Assessment and Testing (TGAT) which was published in 1988 and subsequent developments which have helped shape the current assessment regime.

(b) **Assessment Under the National Curriculum:** It is difficult to discuss education over the past few decades without recognising that it has been driven by the political motivation to make teachers more accountable to central government (See chapter 6). This is certainly true of the assessment regime established in England and Wales from 1989 as the National Curriculum was gradually introduced in the wake of the Education Reform Act of 1988. The responsibility of determining the system of assessment under this newly created statutory curriculum was allocated to the TGAT which was appointed under the chairmanship of Professor Paul Black by the Conservative government in 1987. The group's principal brief was to devise an assessment system which could be used to chart the progress of pupils studying the various subjects within the mandatory curriculum. Even the layout and old style type used in the group's final report in 1988 seemed a significant indicator of the way in which the government of that period wished the assessment regime to develop. The publication of the report caused much concern amongst teachers, as the government's proposals included testing children at the ages of seven, eleven, fourteen and sixteen in all the disciplines which constituted the National Curriculum. However, as Conner (1991) observes,

> Much to the surprise of many, the report was considerably more ambitious and much more forward-thinking than was anticipated, and included suggestions with potential for the improvement of children's learning experiences and more successful monitoring of their progress (Conner, 1991, p.15).

In fact one of the central thrusts of the report was to make assessment more formative in its nature, thus providing useful information to teachers in order to move the learning forward.

> Promoting children's learning is the principal aim of school. Assessment lies at the heart of this process. It can provide a framework in which educational objectives may be set and pupils' progress charted and expressed. It can yield a basis for planning the next educational steps in response to children's needs (National Curriculum Task Group on Assessment and Testing, 1988, paragraph 3).

This, in the light of today's approach to assessment, is an example of how the TGAT report was indeed forward thinking in its recommended approach to assessment in schools. This is an area that will be investigated in much greater detail later in this chapter.

The initial aim of the proposals by the TGAT was formally to assess all subjects based upon teacher assessment (TA) and Standard Assessment Tasks (SATs). The level of achievement was to be measured against "Attainment Targets" prescribed by the various working groups for each subject within the National Curriculum. These SATs involved written and practical activities of the type familiar to pupils from their normal lessons, and the TGAT envisaged that a choice of activities would be offered, for example, open-ended writing, multiple choice questions, oral response, practical work and computer input. Thus, in the 1991 SATs at Key Stage 3 in English pupils began by reading Coleridge's *Ancient Mariner*, discussed the distinctiveness of ballads and wrote and performed their own poetry. One hour a week was to be allocated over nine weeks to this project. However, the volume of work involved in the marking of these SATs was considerable, and teachers in 1993 boycotted the whole assessment mechanism imposed by the Conservative government. This led the government to appoint Sir Ron Dearing to review the curriculum and its assessment arrangements, and his report advocated a much-slimmed down National Curriculum with testing only in the core subjects (Dearing, 1993). It is also significant to note that the *Standard Assessment Tasks* now became paper and pencil *National Curriculum tests* in accordance with the wishes of the then Prime Minister, John Major.

Another contentious area for teachers was the establishment by the Conservative government of "league tables" of schools' results in these tests as a means of allowing parents to form an opinion of their academic achievements and thus to make a more informed choice of the school their child attended. Clearly, the whole purpose of the league tables was to make schools more accountable to parents, local authorities and government ministers through the production of statistical evidence. However, the argument put by teachers was that league tables dependent upon National Curriculum test and GCSE results were based mainly on formal testing which was isolated from the teaching and learning that took place in the classroom. It was also felt that a school could and should offer an education which included more than just academic success.

(c) **Developments in Wales:** Over the past few years the Welsh Assembly Government has been shaping its own policy for assessment within schools in Wales. Jane Davidson, Minister for Education, Lifelong Learning and Skills, announced in 2001 plans to abolish National Curriculum tests. She has emphasised that, although this might end formal testing, it would certainly not be the end of assessment: "We will have formal and reported teacher assessment. But it will be integral, not peripheral, to teaching and learning" (Gold, 2004).

However, the phasing out of the tests has created the problem of ensuring consistency in formal assessment by teachers. How can the results of different schools, for example, the isolated rural village school and the inner city school, be meaningfully compared? Davidson believes that moderation is the key:

> Moderation is the big difficulty still to overcome…People need to have confidence in it, but it needs not to be too complicated and not to put unreasonable demands on teachers. If it works, then we will have information which is focused on the child, expanding their learning horizons, rather than just recording a point in history (Gold, 2004).

This approach mirrors that of the Assessment Reform Group, which sees assessment as a major tool for learning rather than the mere recording of a particular milestone in a child's learning.

III: ASSESSMENT FOR LEARNING (AfL)

In 1989 the British Educational Research Association (BERA) set up the Policy Task Group on Assessment, which in 1996 became the Assessment Reform Group (ARG). The aim of the group was to study assessment practices and policies and to disseminate findings through a variety of routes such as publications, conferences and courses.

A significant piece of research was undertaken by Black and Wiliam in 1998. They looked at the available studies concerned with formative assessment across all educational sectors and published their findings in the pamphlet *Inside the Black Box: Raising Standards Through Classroom Assessment*. The resultant analysis highlighted the positive benefits of formative assessment for learning and achievement at all levels of education (Juwah *et al.*, 2004). Black and Wiliam (1998) set out to investigate three key questions regarding formative assessment:

- Is there evidence that improving formative assessment raises standards?

- Is there evidence that there is room for improvement?

- Is there evidence about ways of improving formative assessment?

Conclusions based on their findings indicated a positive response to each question.

The Assessment Reform Group defines assessment for learning as:

the process of seeking and interpreting evidence for use by learners and their teachers to decide where the learners are in their learning, where they need to go, and how best to get there (Assessment Reform Group, 2002a, p.2).

Torrance and Pryor (1998) conceptualise formative assessment as convergent and divergent. Convergent formative assessment is pertinent to a behaviourist view of learning. They believe that it is accomplished by the teacher and tends to be a repeated form of summative or continuous assessment rather than true formative assessment. This is what Black *et al.* (2003) describe as "micro-summative assessment". Divergent assessment, however, is located firmly within a constructivist view of learning in which both teacher and learner have a joint understanding of what assessment is taking place and it thus accords more closely with contemporary theories of learning. The pupil can initiate assessment as well as be a recipient of it. The General Teaching Council for Wales (GTCW) shows that the dominant purpose of assessment in the view of teachers in schools has been formal and summative as a consequence of the government's pre-occupation with "leagues tables". This, it believes, "has many negative consequences", one of which is that teaching becomes distorted (GTCW, 2004, p.2).

Assessment for learning changes the focus from assessments which are carried out on particular occasions and can be infrequent and formal to an informal approach which is designed to promote the students' learning. It is "embedded in all aspects of teaching and learning" (Black *et al.*, 2003). An activity that incorporates assessment for learning not only provides feedback for the teacher; it can also aid students in assessing themselves and each other. This can then have an impact upon the teaching and learning activities.The Assessment Reform Group has produced ten principles for successful formative assessment (Assessment Reform Group, 2002a). The view that assessment feedback should provide information only for teachers is challenged as the Group views feedback as both "the evoking of evidence and a response to that evidence by using it in some way to improve the learning" (Black *et al.*, 2003).

IV: A RATIONALE FOR ASSESSMENT FOR LEARNING

The following rationale is suggested for the adoption of assessment for learning at all stages of education.

(a) **Constructivism:** The constructivist model of learning is a key element of assessment for learning. The traditional model of teaching and learning is very much concerned with the transfer of information to the learner, while assessment merely checks whether that body of information has been duly absorbed. The constructivist model tends to shift the emphasis from the teacher to the learner. The teacher should not be the font of all knowledge, transmitting information to passive learners. Assessment for learning encourages pupils to be active in their own learning. Hence, a teacher should prompt, mediate, coach and assist the learner to assess his or her own understanding. Brooks and Brooks (1993) believe that as long as we have pupils and teachers asking each other questions in order to make sense of the world then we have a constructivist classroom.

Driver and Bell (1986) offer a useful summary of the constuctivist approach: "As learning is influenced by prior knowledge and attitudes, individuals construct meaning through experience." Contructivism sets out to place emphasis on the meaning of what a child learns, and also the strategies by which he takes an active part in constructing new meaning. Learning is so much easier when it makes sense to the child.

Every theory has its critics, and can be disproved by finding a single observation which is inconsistent with the tenets of that theory (Hawking, 1988). Indeed, critics of constructivism have put forward a number of objections to its acceptance:

(i) It is successful only with children from privileged backgrounds who have an environment conducive to learning and committed teachers.

(ii) The positivist approach emphasises an independent external word, which can be known objectively in a realist or true sense. The constructivists' view of keen observation and motivation is seen as an obstruction (Littledyke and Huxford, 1998).

(iii) There will not be full coverage of the contents of the National Curriculum if learners are allowed to drive their own learning.

(iv) The School Council Humanities Project argued cogently that the constructivist approach reflected in "New Maths" had adversely affected a generation of pupils who did not know their times tables and could not divide a number without using a calculator.

However, research from the Science Process and Concept Exploration (SPACE) project, which explored the understanding of children aged between five and eleven of science within a constructivist framework, did show that there was a potential gain for learners when teaching methods were adopted which were based upon constructivist principles. The assertion is that constructivism develops the necessary thinking skills, an aim very much in vogue in the present educational climate, together with communication and social skills. It also allows a wider range of assessment procedures which are linked closely with learning and the student's needs. Consequently, it can promote intrinsic motivation to learn. Wheatly (1991) believes that there should be a definite shift towards creating "learning environments" which would help children construct their own learning.

(b) **Thinking Skills:** Assessment for learning is concerned to enable pupils and students to become independent learners. Hence, they require opportunities to develop thinking skills, and the adoption of assessment for learning allows for an open and stimulating environment in which these skills can flourish.

Developing children as thinkers has been a goal for some time in education, leading figures in this field being such researchers as Reuven Feuerstein and Matthew Lipman. The argument is that children are not being taught the thinking skills needed to deal with real-life situations. The International Assessment of Educational Progress (in Costa, 1991) and the Third International Maths and Science Study (1997) both paint a similar picture of the declining use of higher-order thinking in all areas of the curriculum. Although the need for direct teaching of thinking skills would seem to be there, the current assessment system within our educational system is ill equipped to meet that end.

Fisher (1990) discusses the use of non-verbal testing as an indicator of intelligence and feels that it has little predictive power outside the school context. He does not believe that it measures important skills in the real world such as assimilating information or solving problems. This is a view which has been widely held and has driven educators to seek more appropriate measures and methodologies for enhancing children's thinking skills.

Matthew Lipman's *Philosophy for Children* stemmed from a belief that his university students' inability to think effectively began in school, where they learned facts and were trained to accept authoritative opinions, but were not taught to think for themselves. Consequently, he left his post as a university philosophy professor and set up the Institute for the Advancement of Philosophy for Children (I.A.P.C.) at Montclair State College, New Jersey, creating the programme *Philosophy for Children* (Lipman, Sharp and Oscanyan, 1980). He believed that children are natural philosophers since they are fascinated by the world around them and view it with curiosity and wonder. His educational programmes are based upon novels, the actions and dilemmas of whose characters provide the teacher with opportunities for discussion. These debates are open and designed to encourage and promote children's questioning of the situations in which the characters find themselves throughout the novels. One of Lipman's key beliefs is that children's sophistication in thinking is not determined by age but by practising the appropriate skills which will enhance their ability to become independent thinkers. He feels that children use reasoning as soon as they learn how to speak. Therefore, age is not a barrier to developing thinking skills as would seem to be suggested by the work of Piaget.

Reuven Feuerstein's educational philosophy stemmed from his work with highly traumatised children after the Second World War. Their upbringing and experiences during the war had significant ramifications for their education. In fact, these children measured by the conventional approach of intelligence testing were deemed to be ineducable (Feuerstein, *et al.*, 1980). The complex instrument devised by Feuerstein and his team identified deficiencies in cognitive functions and provided strategies of intervention which helped the children's learning and thinking skills. It developed into a programme termed *Instrumental Enrichment* (IE) over forty years ago which provided opportunities for discussion and allowed children to gain from understanding the learning processes of others. Much later work on the development of thinking skills was based on Feuerstein's findings. Although initially designed for remedial work with adolescents, it is now used widely with various age groups and abilities.

Another relevant programme is ACTS, designed to **A**ctivate **C**hildren's **T**hinking **S**kills. It provides a framework for enhancing thinking across curriculum areas. There are several core concepts involved in ACTS and it is argued that thinking should be:

(i) *Explicit*: If we are to make learning meaningful and help children to make judgements derived from reason, then it is vital that it is made clear to them what we mean by these types of thinking. This principle involves: cognitive education; cognitive coaching; cognitive instruction; and cognitive intervention.

(ii) *Active*: The learner should be what McGuiness (1999) calls an "active creator". Learning is about searching for meaning and finding structure, being able to think flexibly, developing a critical approach to new information and being able to communicate thoughts effectively.

(iii) *Challenging*: Critical and challenging thinking is required in a number of contexts and at all ages. It is required for reading comprehension, problem solving, thinking in science, interpreting historical materials and aesthetic appreciation. It is the sort of thinking that cannot be described as routine. It is more complex, offering multiple rather than single solutions. It requires the individual to interpret, impose meaning, discover structure and make judgements.

(iv) *Metacognitive*: Talking about the thinking process itself is important for children. They need to be able to make their own thinking more explicit and thus be able to reflect upon the cognitive strategies they actually employ. Becoming reflective thinkers has been identified as a significant tool in promoting what McGuiness (1999) describes as "a thinking skills curriculum".

In order to develop these skills the ACTS programme advocates:

(i) *Dialogue*: The design of activities which promote reflection and dialogue with peers and teachers is a core concept in developing thinking skills in children. When designing activities it is important to recognise that children bring their own conceptions and misconceptions to the classroom. Teachers use their knowledge about children's thinking process, pedagogy and content to devise such socially mediated activities.

(ii) *Disposition*: The ACTS programme considers that "developing thinking may have as much to do with creating a disposition to be a good thinker as it has to do with acquiring specific skills and strategies". The classroom needs to encourage an atmosphere where talking about thinking, contradicting, questioning, predicting and doubting constitute the norm.

(*Adapted from* ACTS II *Sustainable Thinking Classrooms – A Handbook or Teachers of Key Stage 2 Pupils*)

Carol McGuiness (1999) and others, for example, Adams and Wallace (1991), provide a wide range of programmes for schools to use. Most accept the importance of the use of discussion to enhance language skills and improve pupils' ability to articulate their opinions clearly, promoting what Fisher terms a "community of enquiry". Research by Karin Murris and the work of the Society for the Advancement of Philosophical Enquiry in Education (SAPERE) based upon Lipman's *Philosophy for Children* also reinforces the concept of a learning community. It is widely used in the UK, and Fisher has written extensively about teaching thinking in the primary classroom (Fisher, 1998). In addition, Edward De Bono (1986) has examined the working of the brain and shown how this can be used to help children become better thinkers, while Smith (2000) and Buzan (2000) amongst others through the Accelerated Learning in Primary Schools (ALPS) approach and the accelerated learning cycle have promoted the use of brain compatible learning as a means of developing children's thinking skills.

(c) **Good Practice in the Classroom:** The Assessment Reform Group (2002a) has produced ten research-based principles of assessment for learning which are meant to inform and guide classroom practice. They claim that assessment for learning should:

- be part of effective planning for teaching and learning;
- focus on how pupils and students learn;
- be recognised as central to classroom practice;
- be regarded as a key professional skill for teachers;
- be sensitive and constructive because any assessment has an emotional impact;
- take account of the importance of learner motivation;
- promote commitment to learning goals and a shared understanding of the criteria by which they are assessed;
- allow learners to receive constructive guidance about how to improve;
- develop learners' capacity for self-assessment so that they can become reflective and self-managing;
- recognise the full range of achievements of all learners.

Each of these principles will be examined in greater detail.

(i) *Effective planning of teaching and learning*: Assessment for learning is embedded in teaching and learning, and the planning undertaken by teachers needs to reflect ways in which both the teacher and pupil can move the learning forward by measuring information about progress against the chosen learning goals. In order to make valid judgements they must both be fully aware of the criteria that will be used to make an assessment of the learner's performance. The planning process can also provide a structure for feedback and further progress.

(ii) *Focus on how pupils and students learn*: Research into this area has been extensive over the last ten to fifteen years (Lazear, 2000; Wolfe, 2001; Smith, 2002). It is linked closely to what neuroscientists can now tell us about the human brain through the use of scanners. The implications for those in education are significant, and, as Shaw and Hawse assert, "in many ways the findings of neuroscientists support what is commonly understood to be effective teaching methods" (Shaw and Hawse, 1998, p.1). For the purposes of this topic several learning theories will be adumbrated.

(1) THEORY OF THE TRIUNE BRAIN: MacLean's (1990) theory of the triune brain has been popular amongst educationalists for some years now for understanding the way in which we assess children and their response to certain types of assessment, although this approach, is seen by some to be rather dated (Smith, 2002). The neurologist Paul MacLean proposed that we have not one human brain but three, which he referred to as the "triune brain". He saw the three brains working as "three interconnected biological computers, [each] with its own special intelligence, its own subjectivity, its own sense of time and space and its own memory". The model developed by MacLean relates to the historical development of the human brain, and it is suggested that each layer of the brain has developed in response to the evolutionary needs of humans. The three brains are:

■ *THE REPTILIAN BRAIN OR R-COMPLEX:* This is the primitive brain which is similar to that found in lower animals. It is the oldest part of our brain, its name being derived from the fact that the brain stem and cerebellum dominate in animals such as reptiles. It is rigid and ritualistic and survives by routine. Another characteristic of the reptilian brain or the archipallium is that behaviours are automatic and highly resistant to change. We are all aware of the "blood-rush" or "the adrenaline burst" when a threat is perceived. Our heart beats faster and blood pounds in our ears. Under these circumstances the other parts of the brain cannot function until the problem has been resolved or the threat has subsided.

■ *THE LIMBIC SYSTEM OR PALEOMAMMALIAN BRAIN:* In 1952 MacLean used the term "limbic system" for what he thought was the middle area of the brain. This, he believes, evolved when mammals appeared. It provides personal identity and houses our emotional makeup. The limbic system, according to this theory, converts information into long term memory and recall. It is similar to that found in most mammals, especially the earliest ones. This is where the decision is taken whether to fight or flee. It also controls our feeding and sexual behaviour. MacLean suggests that this part of the brain can be a great danger to us. He considers that our value judgements are located here rather than in the more advanced neocortex. It is also interesting to note that some neuroscientists believe that a selection process goes on in this part of the brain which determines the memories that are stored. This is achieved by the attachment of an emotional marker to a particular event that has taken place so that it can be recalled at a later date. In order to survive we must be able to avoid pain and repeat pleasurable experiences. MacLean thinks that our very survival is governed by our emotional response and determination whether something is "agreeable" or "disagreeable".

■ *THE NEOCORTEX OR CEREBRAL CORTEX:* This is the largest part of the human brain and is sometimes called the "thinking cap" as it facilitates such processes as written and spoken language. Other names for it are the *superior* or *rational* or *neomammalian* brain. It is what MacLean describes as "the mother of invention and the father of abstract thought". Other animals have a neocortex, but it is usually relatively small with few, if any folds. Folds within the brain mean greater surface area and permit more complex functions. The neocortex is the most recently evolved part of our brain. We use it to solve problems and ascertain patterns of meaning. It is like a crumpled newspaper, which, if unfolded, would occupy several square metres. A less complex animal than a human being, for example a mouse, could function in a way that would look reasonably normal without a cortex. On the other hand, a human without a cortex would be a vegetable and incapable of functioning.

The neocortex has two hemispheres: the left and the right. The *corpus callosum* acts like a go-between sending messages back and forth. Hart (2000) believes that "humans never really cognitively understand or learn something... until they can create a personal metaphor or model". The brain needs to make connections and patterns and create mental models. It is within this area of the brain that we do this.

These layers of the brain are connected, although the full extent of this is unknown. It would be wrong to think that whilst one part of the brain is working the other two are not. It may be reasonable to propose that at certain times and under certain conditions one part is dominant and the other parts of the brain act in support.

The significance for assessment is the role of the reptilian brain and the extent to which the pupil feels sufficiently relaxed and ready to display understanding. The likelihood of a pupil's being in a relaxed state under examination or test conditions is highly debatable.

As has been noted, it is the view of Smith (2002) that this theory is long out of date and the only reason that it has endured so long is that "it has a powerful, easily understood metaphorical value". He states that "the three brain theory is not wrong; it is out of date".

(2) THEORY OF MULTIPLE INTELLIGENCES: Howard Gardner's more modern theory is having an impact upon teachers' perceptions of intelligence (Gardner, 1993). Traditional thinking in this area has been based upon intelligence quotient testing devised by the French psychologist Alfred Binet. Gardner's theory proposes that there is a range of intelligences, each of which relates to important aspects of human capability. Initially, Gardner identified seven intelligences; at a later stage he extended the list to eight:

- linguistic intelligence;

- logical-mathematical intelligence;

- spatial intelligence;

- kinaesthetic intelligence;

- musical intelligence;

- interpersonal intelligence;

- intrapersonal intelligence;

- naturalist intelligence.

The implications for assessment are significant. The culture of our schools and the nature of the National Curriculum are strongly rooted in the two intelligences of linguistic and logical-mathematical. Gardner believes that many children may not be able to display understanding through these two media as successfully as they may through their preferred intelligences. Hence, current practice can lead to a flawed picture of children's abilities and to an undervaluing of their potential for learning. Gardner recognises that these intelligences develop at different times and to varying degrees in each individual. Therefore, the suggestion is that children should be provided with full opportunities to explore and exercise all their intelligences. In the opinion of Whitaker (1997) this is highly significant since it offers an explanation for the differences that occur in pupils and also indicates why some pupils lack interest and motivation in class. He believes that learning is at best a haphazard construction, and any theories which can throw light upon a more effective approach to teaching need to be embraced.

(3) THE TRIARCHIC MODEL: Sternberg (1985, 1996) shares Gardner's dislike for the standard definition of intelligence and proposes a "triarchic model" consisting of three intelligences: analytical; creative; and practical. However, he finds Gardner's criteria for defining intelligence as suspect and argues in favour of using the word "talents" rather than "intelligences" in recounting Gardner's theory.

(4) ACCELERATED LEARNING IN PRIMARY SCHOOLS (ALPS): Alistair Smith's approach to Accelerated Learning in Primary Schools taps into current thinking by offering an accelerated learning cycle. The basis of the cycle is the provision of frequent, structured opportunities to demonstrate understanding.

Originally the Accelerated Learning Cycle had seven phases. However, in order to emphasise the importance of the learner in this cycle and to make it more accessible to the learner and the teacher, the model has now been redesigned with four areas.

- *CONNECT PHASE:* This phase includes the old headings of *connect*, *big picture* and *described outcomes*, which are basically designed to direct the pupil to the learning. They connect him/her with any previous learning and establish the learning outcomes for the forthcoming activity.

- *ACTIVATE PHASE:* In the original seven stages two of them, *input* and *activate*, were intended to help the learner make sense of the topic being introduced. These now come under the *activate phase* where the learners face problems posed by the teacher, who designs them in such a way as to encourage a multi-sensory approach to learning.

- *DEMONSTRATE PHASE:* This phase in the original cycle was where the learner displayed understanding of the work being undertaken. In the revised model it remains unchanged.

- *CONSOLIDATE PHASE:* This phase also remains the same as it was in the earlier seven phase cycle, in that it is the stage where learners can measure their own understanding through a meaningful review of their work.

This revision has been in response to three major arguments. First, there was the feeling that the work had, in some cases, been hijacked and was seen as merely teaching performance, whereas the emphasis had always been upon the learner and the learning. Secondly, ease of access to a four stage cycle with generic headings makes it easier for the learner and the teacher to share ideas about the learning, and, finally, many current learning initiatives and the thinking behind them can be conveniently accommodated within a four part cycle (www.Alite).

These are, of course, just a few of the researchers and educationalists who promote the idea that understanding of ways in which children learn will help promote their achievement and enable them to become active within their own learning.

(iii) *Recognised as being central to classroom practice*: It would be difficult to define good teaching without including the assessment strategies which take place in the classroom. Setting tasks and asking questions which require pupils to display understanding and specific skills are integral to the art of teaching. Observation of pupils' actions and words is used to provide further challenges, and judgements are made about the best approaches to improve learning. Conner talks of the importance of looking "at the way pupils go about their work and not just at the products, that is, an emphasis on the process of learning" (Conner, 1991, p.51). All these forms of assessment are essential elements of classroom practice. The constant dialogue between pupil and teacher leads to reflection on learning for both parties.

(iv) *To be regarded as a key professional skill for teachers*: The skills required by teachers to plan for assessment, the use of feedback from pupils to enhance learning and the ability to support pupils with self-assessment and peer assessment need to be developed through initial and continuing professional development.

(v) *The need to be sensitive and constructive because any assessment has an emotional impact*: A study undertaken by the Assessment Reform Group into testing and pupil and student motivation provides strong evidence to show that testing can have a negative impact upon pupils' motivation. The Group claims that:

> Many aspects of the impact have significant consequences for pupils' future learning, and thus are causes for concern. At the same time the findings indicate ways to increase the positive impact and to decrease the negative impact on pupils' motivation for learning (Assessment and Reform Group, 2002b, p. 2).

The findings support the contention that teachers need to be aware of the consequences of giving learners grades and marks. The importance of constructive feedback in order to make improvements cannot be overstated. The focus when marking needs to be on the work itself and not the pupil in order to maximise the learning and motivation.

(vi) *To recognise the importance of learner motivation*: In the same report the Assessment Reform Group observes that, even at primary school level, pupils are aware of the restrictive nature of testing. The marks or grades they obtain are frequently thought to be more important than the actual content and process of the learning.

> When tests become the main criteria by which pupils are judged, and by which they judge themselves, those whose strengths lie outside the subjects tested have a low opinion of their capabilities (Assessment Reform Group, 2002b, p. 4).

Comparison with other pupils' achievements is also highly unlikely to motivate children; it is much more likely to have the opposite effect. Assessment methods should provide constructive feedback which allows pupils a way forward and also an element of autonomy in determining the direction to be taken.

(vii) *To promote a commitment to sharing learning goals and understanding the criteria by which the assessment is made*: Learners need a clear understanding of what it is they are trying to achieve and the yardstick which will be used to identify the degree of success they attain. Sharing the learning outcomes and discussing with learners how to achieve them are activities central to assessment for learning. This argument will be developed further in later sections.

(viii) *To receive constructive guidance on the ways to improve*: In order to improve learners require clear guidance on their strengths and areas for improvement. This will also be developed further in the section relating to feedback.

(ix) *To promote self-assessment skills in order to develop independent, self-managing learners*: Providing pupils with the tools which enable them to seek out new skills and knowledge changes the whole process of education from one in which the teacher drives the learning to one in which the student decides upon the next stage to be undertaken. Consequently, learners need to be equipped with the skills of self-reflection.

(x) *To acknowledge the full range of achievements of all learners*: The recognition that education should be about more than just linguistic and mathematical ability is important if pupils are to be offered the opportunity to develop in all areas of learning.

(d) **Teaching and Learning Practices:** Black and Wiliam (1998) suggest four main teaching and learning practices: questioning; feedback; sharing criteria; and self-assessment.

(i) *Questioning*: Cotton (2003) describes a question as any sentence which has an interrogative form or function. He cites research which indicates that questioning is second only to lecturing in popularity as a teaching method and that teachers can spend between thirty-five to fifty per cent of their teaching time questioning pupils. One of the main reasons for asking questions should be to inform the future planning of the next step in a pupil's learning. Teachers therefore need an arsenal of questions to use with children and an understanding of the various forms of questions available to them.

Black *et al.* (2003) recognise that for teachers "questioning is an essential part of their practice" (p.32), while Wyse (2002) believes that the type of question used allows teachers to address the aims of the teaching and learning. Pollard (1997) identifies two main types of questions employed within the classroom, the first being the *pyscho-social* question which is concerned with relationships between the teacher and pupil or pupil and pupil. The second form is described as the *pedagogical* question, which has as its objective subject-related concepts. These two forms of questioning allow teachers not only to identify knowledge and understanding but also to address attitudes and feelings, thereby paying attention to the affective as well as the cognitive domain.

Wragg and Brown (1993 and 2001) categorise questions into three main forms. The type used depends upon the information required by the teacher.

(1) CONCEPTUAL QUESTIONS are concerned with a pupil's reasoning and ideas about a topic or subject.

(2) EMPIRICAL QUESTIONS require factually based responses.

(3) VALUE QUESTIONS allow teachers to explore pupils' attitudes, opinions and moral judgements.

It is important to find a balance between the various forms of questioning, not only for the purposes of assessment but also in order to stimulate different forms of thinking from the pupil. A child searching for a factual answer is very different from one who is offering a personal viewpoint or value judgement.

Another valid point is raised by Fleer (1992), who discusses the importance of interaction between children and their teacher. The assertion is that, since language facilitates most learning, verbal questioning between the pupil and the teacher is essential. One conclusion drawn from Fleer's study is that "the ultimate success and the depth of learning was the quality of the teacher's interaction" (p. 394). A skill that teachers need to nurture is that of "wait time". This is central to assessment for learning, and Black *et al.* (2003) describe the difficulty some teachers have in adjusting this time and illustrate the argument with an example derived from their research:

> Increasing wait time after asking questions proved difficult to start with due to my habitual desire to "add" something almost immediately after asking the original question (Black *et al.*, 2003, p.33).

This tendency to add a supplementary question if the original is met with silence is almost irresistible for some teachers. Indeed, research by Rowe (1974) suggested that teachers' wait time between questions was as little as 0.9 seconds. The short time allowed gives pupils little opportunity, if any, to formulate an answer to the question. Rowe (1996) subsequently undertook further research into "wait time" and discovered that, if teachers were to pause between three to ten seconds, significant improvements occurred. It was noted that:

- Students' responses were longer and more frequent.

- The unsolicited pupil responses increased.

- There was a decrease in the "I don't know" answer.

- Pupils appeared more confident when answering.

- There was an increase in the number of speculative responses.

- There was an increase in the interaction between pupils.

- Inferences based on evidence increased.

- Pupils asked more questions.

- There was an increase in responses by pupils described by their teachers as "less able".

Interestingly, this last point about the so called "less able" child reflects the findings of Black and

Wiliam (1998) that the benefits of assessment for learning are proportionately greater for children in this category.

Smith and Call (1999) refer to the concept of *processing time*. They suggest that teachers should use processing cues which will "defer an immediate response in favour of a delayed response" (p.132). Examples of this form of cue would be:

> "Martin, in a few minute I'm going to ask you about….. but first of all let me……"

> "During our last Science lesson we looked at…….Can you all think of three words that we learned linked to that topic? I'll give you a minute or two to think. In the meantime I'll….."

These researchers also believe that embedding questions at the beginning of a lesson or teaching episode can be of benefit to the learner. The assertion is that the processes our brain uses for memory work unconsciously - what they term "the tip of the tongue" phenomenon. Sometimes we search hard for a fact or to put a name to a face, but in an unrelated activity we can recall the name or remember the fact. Embedding, according to Smith and Call, utilises that self-same phenomenon during a learning experience.

(ii) *Feedback*: Clarke (2003) asserts that the provision of marks and other forms of classroom feedback to pupils can promote self-esteem, motivate and positively enhance children's learning. However, it can also demoralise and alienate pupils just as easily. Black and Wiliam (1998), therefore, advocate careful reflection concerning the responses we make to pupils' assignments. They suggest that feedback should be designed to stimulate a thoughtful response, focus upon specific errors and weaknesses and advise on ways in which improvements can be made, related specifically to the task at hand.

Smith and Call (1999) also support the need for clear feedback; otherwise, "progress will be slow and the learner may stray from the path. Children need feedback that provides a clear idea of progress made towards targets" (p.136). This philosophy is reflected in precepts given to teachers by the former Welsh advisory body on the curriculum, assessment and examinations, ACCAC. It is argued that comments should:

- offer a clear way forward;
- identify strengths and weaknesses;
- make comments individualised and subject specific.

Similarly, Kluger and DeNisi (1996) accept that for feedback to be successful, especially written comments, teachers have to be thoughtful and careful about what is written. This, they assert, requires much time and effort.

It is important that the learner receives constructive criticism rather than smiley faces or a comment such as "good". In these cases he or she has been given no indication of the reasons why the piece of work was successful or of strategies by which it can be made even better. Gipps (1997) agrees that unfounded and constant praise can become meaningless. Most learners gain from praise and encouragement. However, this should be offered only when a piece of work genuinely deserves commendation. There is a danger that constant approbation for less meritorious efforts will devalue that praise in the eyes of the learner. A valuable approach is to sandwich advice on areas for improvement between feedback on positive aspects of the work.

Oral feedback is the most common form used in schools and provides opportunities for constructive interaction between teacher and learner. It can be directed at individuals, small groups or the whole class. When comments are provided to individuals or small groups, other pupils, by listening in, may indirectly benefit. The creation of a fruitful learning environment where learners do not feel threatened by oral feedback can, of course, take time. The results of the survey conducted by Kluger and DeNisi (1996), based on 3,000 reports involving 13,000 students, showed that oral feedback raised achievement in sixty per cent of cases. The obvious question raised, therefore, is how teachers can help the other forty per cent. The identification of those elements which make up effective oral feedback is a challenge for educationalists.

As for written feedback, assessment for learning promotes the practice that it should focus on particular qualities of a learner's work and should avoid making comparisons with the work of other pupils. It should offer high quality, informative comments on selected aspects of the work rather than a blanket marking of everything. This would mean a significant change for many educators (DFES, 2004a).

Black *et al.* (2003) cite an interesting piece of research conducted by Butler in 1988. She employed three different strategies of giving feedback to learners: marks; comments; and a combination of both mark and comments. As Black and his collaborators state, "the last is the method by which most teachers provide feedback to their learners in the UK". The unexpected results showed that the greatest learning gains were made when the students received comments only. Black *et al.* go on to list the arguments offered by teachers justifying the provision of comment rather than numerical marks or grades:

(1) Students rarely read the comments, preferring to compare the marks with those of their peers as a first reaction when they receive work assessed by their teachers.

(2) Teachers do not often give students time in class to read the comments which are written on their assignments, and few pupils, if any, scrutinise these comments at home.

(3) In most cases the comments are brief and/or not specific.

(4) The same written comments frequently recur in pupils' books, implying that they do not take note of or act upon the advice they receive.

(iii) *Sharing the criteria for successful learning*: It is important to be clear about the terminology used in educational establishments to indicate the expectations made of pupils in undertaking assignments. The DFES (2004a) provides the following useful definitions:

(1) TEACHING OBJECTIVES are written by teachers and can be found in schemes or units of work.

(2) LEARNING OBJECTIVES are derived directly from teaching objectives and may be relevant for a given lesson or series of lessons.

(3) LEARNING OUTCOMES refer to the achievement by pupils of the learning objectives. Learning outcomes inform future teaching and future learning objectives.

The terms SUCCESS CRITERIA and ASSESSMENT CRITERIA are also commonly used with reference to the standards students are expected to achieve in order to be awarded a certain mark or grade. The words LEARNING OUTCOMES are adopted here to define the translation of these criteria into pupil-friendly language to enable them to know what they have to do in order to demonstrate achievement in a particular context.

Within the primary school strategies for sharing learning objectives and outcomes are becoming more prevalent. Examples are: WILF ("What I'm looking for"); and TIB ("This is because"). These and other similar expressions are shared with pupils at the beginning of a learning episode and written in such a way that children can understand and act upon them. According to Clarke (2003) the provision of a clear focus along these lines is the best way to proceed. Expectations need to be shared with learners so that they are aware of the standards which they are meant to achieve. She further develops the point that it is a right of learners to be aware of what is being looked for by the teacher so that they can work towards these aspirations. She offers the following examples:

(1) TEACHER'S LEARNING OBJECTIVE: To begin to use letter sounds as an aid to decoding unfamiliar words.

WORDS USED WITH PUPILS: "What I want to know is: if you can't read a word, can you say the beginning sound? This will help you guess or find the word."

(2) TEACHER'S LEARNING OBJECTIVE: To ascertain the role played by different parts of the digestive system.

WORDS USED WITH PUPILS: "What I am looking for is whether you can explain the journey of food from entry to exit using the names for each body bit. This will help you understand how your body works."

Target setting with learners, according to Smith and Call (1999), "properly done, can be the main lifelong learning skill that will accelerate the performance of all the children".

(iv) *Self-assessment and peer assessment*: Black *et al.* (2003) believe that the most difficult step for learners to take on the road to successful self-assessment is seeing their work as a set of goals. "Insofar as they do, students begin to develop an overview of that work so that it becomes possible for them to manage and control it for themselves" (p.49). It is suggested that peer assessment may even be a prior requirement for self-assessment. The link between assessment, planning and the teaching and learning process is inextricable. Gipps, McCallum and Brown (1996) claim that the practice of self-assessment rarely extends beyond "lip-service" and that its full potential is rarely realised in schools.

Success depends upon the pupils' having ownership of their learning so that motivation will develop when they are aware of the goals to which they need to aspire. It is also necessary that they understand the value of peer and self-assessment and do not view them negatively as a technique to enable the teacher to avoid marking their work. Done successfully, self and peer assessments become integral parts of the learning process. They are not easy skills to develop and Headington (2000) believes that pupils may have grown dependent upon assessments by others and are therefore reluctant to make judgements themselves.

Black *et al.* (2003) outline a number of advantages for peer assessment. It may motivate learners to work more carefully and enable them to discuss their work in a language they naturally use. It is also possible that they will accept criticism more readily from a peer than from a teacher. A further advantage is that it can be a vehicle for conveying meaning to those who are struggling with a particular concept. Such research studies assert that peer assessment aids pupils in recognising their learning needs and provides teachers with information related to those needs, whilst allowing them freedom to observe and reflect on what learning is taking place.

V: APPLICATIONS

(a) **Adopting the Principles and Practices of Assessment for Learning in a Higher Education Context:** As was mentioned earlier in this chapter, *Inside The Black Box* (Black and Wiliam, 1998) is a significant publication. In it the authors begin with the premise that teaching and learning have to be interactive. The main focus of the research undertaken by the Assessment Reform Group was upon the impact of formative assessment strategies upon the learning and attainment of children in schools. Good assessment practices in primary and secondary schools have, of course, been the topic of research for a number of years, and the messages and lessons learnt can be transferred to other sectors of the educational system (Gipps, McCallum and Hargreaves, 2000).

Assessment for learning is currently used in schools, and there is a movement towards exploring and implementing its practices within higher educational institutions, the aim being to help them use formative assessment "more effectively to promote student learning" (Juwah *et al.*, 2004). It is true that research into assessment for learning in post-compulsory education is less well developed than it is in schools. In fact, some findings actually highlight the dearth of evidence in the post-sixteen sector, and it has been recommended that more should be done to "explore how assessment policies which underpin rather than undermine lifelong learning ambitions can be developed" (Torrance, 2004). Within the higher education context, an increasingly diverse student body and the creation of larger teaching groups frequently mean that only higher degree students now receive the luxury of one-to-one tutorials and individual formative feedback on their work (Hill, 1995).

Nonetheless, the movement over the last ten to fifteen years has been to encourage the participation of higher education students within the assessment process (Nicol, 1997; Black and William, 1998; Clarke, 1998). Sadler (1989) believes that the transfer of the necessary skills of the teacher to students is the key to successful formative assessment, and this view is supported by Yorke (2003) and Boud (2000) who contend that in order to make sense of the feedback provided the students must possess the same skills as the teacher. Sadler's work has been the catalyst for a great deal of the recent research into self-assessment. Self and peer assessment are now recognised as cornerstones of effective learning (McDonald and Boud, 2003) and are embedded deeply in the assessment for learning philosophy discussed earlier. Sadler (1989) recognises that it is extremely difficult for the learner to achieve a learning objective successfully unless that objective is fully understood and the student is able to assess what needs to be done in order to achieve it.

Sutton (1995) believes that a systematic approach needs to be followed by a teacher who understands that self-assessment can be an aid to learning. This understanding must be shared by both teacher and learner. There is a strong belief that students need guidance and support in learning how to assess themselves and others successfully, and Clarke (1998) suggests focused training in self-assessment. Black *et al.* (2003) find that the skills required to make judgements about particular problems are lacking in students and also that they are not always able to decide on realistic targets needed to remedy situations within a specific time frame. In order to address this it is advocated that lecturers should aim to create an environment in which feedback by means of the provision of comments is the norm and where students work together in understanding and using these comments constructively. This, it is believed, will produce improvements in learning, as too often the abstract nature of assessment criteria and the feedback given by some tutors do not offer a clear overview of the objectives of the assignment and the steps which have to be taken in order to complete it successfully.

Based upon the principles of assessment for learning advocated by the Assessment Reform Group, Juwah *et al.* (2004) provide a conceptual model for Higher Education in order to enhance student learning through effective formative feedback. The seven principles are:

    (i) *facilitating the development of self- assessment in learning;*

    (ii) *encouraging tutor and peer dialogue within the process of assessment;*

    (iii) *helping to clarify the assessment criteria and expected standards;*

    (iv) *providing opportunities to close the gap between current and desired performance;*

    (v) *delivering high quality information to students about their learning;*

    (vi) *encouraging positive motivational beliefs and self-esteem;*

    (vii) *providing information to tutors which can be used to help shape the teaching.*

An interesting piece of research, which is again published by the Assessment Reform Group (2002b), looked at the impact of summative testing on pupils' motivation for learning. What emerged from the work was strong evidence to suggest that this form of assessment had a negative impact upon motivation. As higher education is dependent upon summative forms of assessment for degree classifications, the possible impact upon students' motivation and self-esteem could influence their learning during this stage and beyond. An important aim within courses of initial teacher education and training, with which the author is primarily concerned, is to produce reflective thinkers. However, within the assessment structure associated with higher education, the use of summative assessment continually stresses the importance of marks and grades. This in turn leads to the adoption of test-taking strategies which are likely to reduce such higher order thinking skills as analysis, synthesis and evaluation (Paris *et al.*, 1991). This judgement is supported by the General Teaching Council for Wales when it asserts that as early as year 6 the curriculum narrows to those subjects which are formally assessed and that teachers have become "adept at preparing their pupils to succeed in the tests, but this tends to work against the wider aim of developing pupils as learners" (GTCW, 2004, p.2).

(b) A Case Study:

(i) *The Background*: A project involving the use of assessment for learning was undertaken within the School of Education of the University of Wales Institute, Cardiff (UWIC) from 2003 onwards. It began with a module delivered at level 5 of the National Qualifications Framework as part of the three-year full time BA (Hons) Primary Education course. The module was compulsory for all students in the second year cohort and linked closely with their experiences during their school placement. The content addressed many of the key professional and pedagogical skills of teachers, for example, planning, classroom organisation, pupil management and discipline, learning theories, teaching methods and the assessment of pupils' learning. The principles of assessment for learning formed part of this module's content, and, as the team of tutors responsible for its construction and delivery believed that it was important to model the best practice in their own pedagogy, assessment for learning practices were built into the teaching, learning and assessment of the module. During the academic year 2003 – 2004, the module coursework assignment for students was changed from one reflective report to three shorter reports which would enable the tutors to provide formative feedback and the students to use these comments to improve their performance. The feedback given by the tutors identified areas for improvement but no specific marks were actually shared with the students.

(ii) *Assessment for Learning Strategies Included Within the Module*: When modifying the learning, teaching and assessment strategies employed in the delivery of the module, the project team drew from the considerable research base which already exists on assessment for learning, though, as we have seen in this chapter, much of this research centres upon learning in schools rather than higher education (Assessment Reform Group 2002a). Particular emphasis was placed on the following practices which have been identified in research as essential to assessment for learning (James, 2003):

(1) Helping learners to understand what counts as quality in learning by explicit reference to clear assessment criteria and the use of exemplars of good practice.

(2) Providing appropriate feedback with an emphasis on ways of improving. Comments rather than marks were offered.

(3) Timing the submission of assignments in such a way that the students were able to re-draft their work in the light of formative feedback received in relation to previous assignments.

(4) Engaging learners to participate in peer and self-assessment.

All these strategies were introduced into the module. Students were able to choose a specific topic for each report from a list relating to the contents of the module which were addressed in group taught sessions during the three preceding weeks. They were informed that the emphasis was on "linking theory and practice" and were given three specific criteria for the assignment:

- the depth of reflective thought and analysis of the topics;

- the amount of research undertaken by them, including publications as well as electronic references;

- the ability to link theory and personal experience.

They were also reminded of the normal practice on the course: that the UWIC general assessment criteria available in the student handbook would also be used in marking their work. It was explained that, whereas their tutors would provide and record marks, the first two reports would be returned with formative comments only.

During the first taught session students were shown an exemplar piece of work from the previous cohort which had been awarded a first class honours classification. They were asked to analyse this piece of work using both the general and specific criteria for the assignment so that they came to recognise what counted as quality and what made this a first class piece of work.

(iii) *Engaging Learners in Self and Peer Assessment*: As the aim of the project was to utilise assessment for learning in this undergraduate programme, it was decided to include a stronger element of self-assessment into the module. As Juwah *et al.* (2004, p. 6) state, " over the last decade there has been an increasing interest in strategies that encourage students to take a more active role in the management of their own learning".

The first reflective reports were submitted in November 2004. The usual practice in the School of Education was for students to submit with all coursework assignments a form which includes a section inviting them to complete a self-assessment of their work against the relevant criteria. Across all courses, the quality of these self-assessments has been highly variable with some students offering brief comments which pay little heed to the specific assessment criteria for the assignment. Each second year student duly completed one of these forms and submitted it with his or her first report. Before the second report was submitted, it was decided to devise a new self-assessment form which would encourage them to highlight their strengths in the light of their first formative feedback. These forms also asked them to identify areas which they felt still needed improvement. They were given guidance on the completion of these forms, again using the criteria which had been explained in the taught sessions. It is perhaps noteworthy that, whilst using the assessment criteria to evaluate the work of peers during one of the taught sessions, several students requested a copy of the general criteria to keep as they found them "really useful". It was pointed out that they were published every year in the student handbook!

The final report was submitted along with all other reports and feedback forms. The students completed a School of Education assignment assessment sheet with the third reflective report, as this was the final submission. They were asked to decide, based upon the degree classification criteria, which category best reflected their final reflective report. "Research shows that direct involvement by students in assessing their own work, and frequent opportunities to reflect on goals, strategies and outcomes are highly effective in enhancing learning and achievement" (McDonald and Boud, 2003).

(iv) *Providing appropriate feedback*: The reports were assessed by tutors, who then recorded the marks but did not convey them to students. Module staff placed the emphasis upon providing students with structured feedback, not only identifying strengths but also setting specific targets for improvement. Many of these targets referred to generic skills, such as use of texts, accurate referencing, and the ability to analyse and use examples from practice to engage in critical reflection. Thus, it was hoped that by addressing these targets the students would show improvement in the next report, even though it was concerned with a different topic.

(v) *Outcomes*: There were definite indications of improvements, as there was a significant difference between the first and second mark. Over the whole cohort a mean improvement of eight marks was discovered. This mode of assessment was repeated over the following two years and similar results were noted.

These outcomes also reflected a major conclusion reached by the Assessment Reform Group that the gains are greater for the less able student. During the academic session 2003 - 2004 it was observed that those who received a third class honours mark in their first report made an average improvement of 10.3 marks by the end of the module. Students whose initial assignments fell within the category of a lower second class honours improved by 5.4 marks, while a gain of only 1.5 was observed in the case of students whose initial mark was in the upper second class honours classification. Since only three students received first class marks in their initial report the number was too small to be a useful indicator. The results obtained in 2003 - 2004 were repeated in 2005 - 2006 and again in 2006 - 2007. Consequently, it may be claimed from this case study and others (Juwah *et al.*, 2004) that elements of assessment for learning can be implemented into university degree courses to the advantage of students.

6 Trends in the Educational System of England and Wales

I: INTRODUCTION

The Education system of England and Wales has undergone constant change in recent years with a spate of legislation on the part of both Conservative and Labour governments. Important Acts of Parliament on education since 1988 have been:

- the Education Reform Act (1988);

- the Education (Schools) Act 1992;

- the Further and Higher Education Act 1992;

- the Education Act 1993;

- the Education Act 1994;

- the Education Act 1996 (This is a consolidating Act which covers in one document relevant legislation on education set out in previous Acts of Parliament);

- the Schools Inspections Act 1996;

- the Education Act 1997;

- the Education (Schools) Act 1997;

- the School Standards and Framework Act 1998;

- the Teaching and Higher Education Act 1998;

- the Learning and Skills Act 2000;

- the Education Act of 2002;

- the Education Act 2005;

- the Education and Inspections Act 2006.

It is possible to contrast the system which emerged after the Second World War in the wake of the Education Act of 1944 with the structure which has developed from the time of the Conservatives' Education Reform Act of 1988. Most of the innovations introduced by the Conservatives have been retained and extended by the Labour government which was first elected to power in May 1997. In this chapter it is intended initially to present a brief survey of the educational system established under the

1944 Education Act. Subsequently, an account will be given of the major trends which have shaped the organisation of educational provision in England and Wales since 1988.

II: THE 1944 EDUCATION ACT

(a) **The Philosophy of the Education Act 1944:** Writing about the educational system in the period before 1988, such commentators as Sir William Alexander (1954), H.C. Dent (1961) and W.O. Lester Smith (1965) argued that the 1944 Education Act created a *partnership* between:

- central government;
- the local education authorities (LEAs);
- teachers.

It was the role of government to establish overall policy, but much freedom was accorded to the LEAs, which had responsibility for organising primary, secondary and further education in their areas. It was also customary for government to consult the teachers' organisations on educational policy. The immediate post-war period has often been referred to as an "era of consensus", that is to say, government, LEAs and teachers shared the same goals and worked towards a common purpose. Education was seen by central government to be a public service like the National Health Service. In the later 1940s and throughout the 1950s both major political parties were concerned primarily with the building of new schools to cater for an expanding child population.

(b) **Powers of the Minister of Education:** The 1994 Education Act established the role of the MINISTER OF EDUCATION with the responsibility of promoting the education of the people of England and Wales. At that time Members of Parliament were reluctant to give the Minister too many powers for fear that this could lead to a totalitarian system and damage the power of the democratically elected LEAs. Hence, the 1944 Act gave the minister no power to:

- determine the school curriculum;
- decide the contents of examination syllabuses;
- run schools directly or employ teachers.

Important powers of the Minister included the right to:

(i) reverse the decisions of an LEA or the governors of a school if they were acting or were proposing to act unreasonably (1994 Act, section 68);

(ii) give specific directions to any authority which was failing to carry out its duties under existing legislation (1944 Act, section 99);

(iii) approve, disapprove or amend LEAs' plans for opening new schools, closing existing schools or changing the character of a school, for example, changing a selective school to a comprehensive school (1944 Act, section 13).

It should be noted, that sections 68 and 99 of the Education Act of 1944 were not employed very often and that at least one LEA – Tameside - successfully appealed to the High Courts in 1976 against a judgement by the Secretary of State under section 68 of the 1994 Act.

(c) **Advisory Bodies:** Section 4 of the Act established the Central Advisory Councils for Education - one for England and one for Wales. Their role was to "advise the Minister upon such matters connected with educational theory and practice, as they think fit, and upon any question referred to them by him". The chairman and other members were appointed by the Minster of Education and served for a period of three years, though their tenure could be extended. The Councils usually consisted of university and college lecturers, teachers, headteachers, local education authority officials, parents and other interested parties. The purpose of this legislation was to ensure that the Minister received advice from a body independent of central government and politicians, which contained people with expertise in education and representatives of different interests (Kogan and Packwood, 1974).

The first chairman of the English Council was Sir Fred Clarke, Director of the Institute of Education of London University. Others included Sir Samuel Gurney-Dixon, chairman of a local authority, Sir Geoffrey Crowther, an economist, and Sir John Newsom, Joint Managing Director of Longmans Green and formerly Director of Education for Hertfordshire. Among the chairmen of the Welsh Council were professors of education - R.I. Aaron and C.E. Gittins - and a professor of physics - F. Llewllyn-Jones.

In the period from 1944 to 1968 the Councils produced a number of major reports, for example, the Gurney-Dixon Report (*Early Leaving*, 1954), the Crowther Report (*Fifteen to Nineteen*, 1959), the Newsom Report (*Half Our Future*, 1963), the Llewellyn-Jones Report (*Science in Education in Wales Today*, 1965), the Plowden Report (*Children and Their Primary Schools*, 1967) and the Gittins Report (*Primary Education in Wales*, 1968).

There were several other councils which provided government with advice during these years, for example, the Secondary School Examinations Council, the National Council for Educational Technology, and the National Advisory Council on the Training and Supply of Teachers.

(d) **Local Education Authorities (LEAs):** These were the locally elected councils for each area in England and Wales, for example, Cardiff City Council. Under the 1944 Education Act they had to employ a staff of professional education officers headed by a Director of Education or Chief Education Officer.

Under Part II of Schedule I of the Act each LEA had to establish an *Education Committee* consisting of members of the authority, that is to say, elected councillors, together with people co-opted by them who had a special interest and expertise in education, for example, local denominations, members of teachers' unions, and representatives of further education. A third of each Education Committee consisted of co-opted members. This Committee would discuss issues appertaining to education in its area, pass resolutions and then report its recommendations to the full Council where a final decision would be taken.

The 1944 Act required LEAs to provide: primary and secondary schools (section 8 [1]); further education (section 41); education for pupils with special educational needs (section 8[2][c]); and a range of services, for example, the provision of milk and meals (section 49), home-school transport (section 55) and medical inspections (section 48). Staff at schools and colleges were employees of the LEA. Universities, however, remained independent of control by local authorities.

In the period from 1944 until about the mid-1960s LEAs were very much the centre of educational decision making in England and Wales, and the Minister of Education was reluctant to intervene in their affairs. This may be illustrated with reference to the Cardiff LEA in the years 1944 to 1950. During this period the authority failed entirely to comply with section 7 of the 1944 Education Act which stated that "the statutory system of public education shall be organised in three progressive stages to be known as primary education, secondary education and further education". It still maintained elementary schools catering for pupils from five to fifteen, and by the late 1940s no plans had been drawn up for the reorganisation of these "all-age" establishments into separate primary and secondary modern schools in the foreseeable future, as was required under the Act. At the request of Cardiff teachers the Member of Parliament for Cardiff Central, after putting a series of questions to the Minister of Education over several years, brought about a debate in the House of Commons in July 1949, during which he asked the Minister to use his powers under section 68 of the Act to compel Cardiff to undertake the changes required by law. Although the Minister was in complete agreement with the Member of Parliament about the appalling state of education in Cardiff, he replied that he hoped never "to use the threat of section 68 … in respect of any authority". The preferred policy was to "persuade" authorities to act upon the law rather than to coerce them to meet the requirements of current legislation (Geen, 1986). The conclusion may be drawn that in the immediate post-war era it was possible for an education authority to ignore the law and to defy central government policy. As the Director of Education for Cardiff in the period from 1949 to 1968 recalled, "Our attitude in those days was: 'This is our decision which we will take in Cardiff. We will consult with you in London after we have made it'."

(e) **Teachers:** In the period from 1944 the government stressed that it wanted a close working relationship with teachers. In the report *Education 1900-1950* the Minister of Education, George Tomlinson, stated that education in the UK was a partnership "between the Central Department, the local education authorities and the teachers" (Ministry of Education, 1951, p. 1). In subsequent years teachers were regularly consulted about developments shaping the educational system.

A good example of this co-operation is the case of comprehensive schooling. In the autumn of 1964 a Labour government came to power with a commitment to comprehensive education. Realising that many Conservative controlled authorities would be hostile to the demise of their grammar schools and not wishing to adopt too confrontational an attitude, the government resolved to issue a circular, which had no legal force, to persuade LEAs to draw up and submit to the Department of Education and Science (DES) plans for comprehensive reorganistion within one year. In drafting this important circular, the Secretary of State, Anthony Crosland, spent some six months discussing its exact contents and wording with the teachers' organisations before the final version was completed (Kogan, Boyle and Crosland, 1971; Fenwick, 1976). Again, during this period of partnership bodies such as the Schools Council, created in 1964 to undertake research into the school curriculum and examinations, were well represented with members of the teaching profession (Kogan, 1978).

It is also interesting to observe the type of teacher which the governments of this period wanted to produce, as the system of initial teacher education and training (ITET) was designed to promote a wide education and to encourage critical reflection about educational issues through the application of the disciplines of philosophy, sociology, psychology and history. The aim of the initiatives ushered in by the Robbins report of 1963 (Committee on Higher Education, 1963) was the creation of a generation of teachers who would be informed thinkers, well equipped to put forward constructive ideas for an improved educational system (Tibble, 1966). In the 1972 White Paper *Education: A Framework for Expansion* (DES, 1972, p. 21) the Conservative government announced its policy of establishing an all-graduate teaching profession.

(f) **Parents:** Under section 76 of the 1944 Act the general principle was established that pupils were to be educated in accordance with the wishes of their parents. In practice, this did not mean that children could be admitted to the school of their parents' choice in defiance of policy determined by the local authority. Catchment areas for schools were defined by LEAs, and parents had no statutory right to send their child to a school outside that area. Consequently, in 1970, when parents in the Hackerford Road area of Cyncoed, Cardiff, protested to the Secretary of State, Edward Short, concerning the Cardiff LEA's policy for their children to attend the new Llanederyn High School rather than the well established and highly regarded Cardiff High School, he affirmed the right of the LEA to decide the issue of school placements and over-ruled the parents' wishes (Geen, 1986).

III: CHANGING PHILOSOPHIES OF EDUCATION

(a) **Changes from 1976:** In the period from 1976 the concept of "partnership" came under attack and there was a greater demand for accountability in the educational system. Reasons for this include:

(i) *complaints from various quarters that educational standards were in decline as the result of poor and incompetent teaching.* For example, Rhodes Boyson, a Conservative MP, argued in 1975 that standards were deteriorating as a result of progressive teaching methods and the poor calibre of entrants to the teaching profession. Teacher training colleges were especially singled out for criticism, and it was alleged that, far from producing competent reflective practitioners, they had "simply become vehicles for the propaganda of 'progressive' education methods which are ineffective in the schools". In some colleges, Boyson continued, booklists consisted of little but Marxist texts (Boyson, 1975, p. 115). The following year Sir Arnold Weinstock (1976) stated that many engineering employers failed to recruit the number of apprentices they needed because, though applicants performed well in examinations, their standards in literacy and numeracy were found to be unsatisfactory in the workplace.

(ii) *the concern of many parents over teaching strategies:* The parents' pressure group, the National Education Association, from 1971 expressed its concern about "recent curriculum changes, doubtful methods of teaching and the excessive freedoms thrust upon the immature" (Locke, 1974, p. 47).

(iii) *awareness of the difficulties involved in dismissing incompetent teachers:* This became clear in the inquiry into the affairs of the William Tyndale Primary School in London in 1976. Parents had been removing their children at an alarming rate as they were dissatisfied with educational standards at the school and were concerned at the attempts of certain of its teachers to indoctrinate pupils in Marxist political theory. A lengthy and very expensive court case was heard before the headteacher and his supporters could be removed from their posts (Jackson and Gretton, 1976).

(iv) *the desire of many teachers to have public recognition that teaching is a profession*: From the mid-1970s some of the professional bodies representing teachers voiced their concern about the need to rid schools of incompetent teachers. In 1975 at the Annual Conference of the British Educational Management and Administration Society Anita Ellis argued that: "The poor self-image and low level of real professionalism which has persisted amongst teachers since the last century has allowed them to defend themselves within a fortress of multi-union armour, whereby the incompetent, the idle and the inadequate who do not break the criminal law have an almost solid security of tenure, regardless of the fact that generations of pupils and colleagues have a 'raw deal' in being obliged to work with them. This is the antithesis of professionalism, and ultimately blocks the righteous demands for accountability from the government, the LEA, parents, pupils, governors and colleagues alike."

(v) *the increasing cost of education at a time of financial stringency in the Western World*: This led many people to demand "value for money" in the educational system.

The change in the official attitude began in 1976 with the call by the Prime Minister, James Callaghan, at Ruskin College, Oxford, for a "great debate" on education. He stressed that "teachers must satisfy parents and industry" that what they were "doing meets their requirements and the needs of their children" (Beecher and Maclure, 1978, p. 11). In July 1977 the Education Secretary, Shirley Williams, issued a Green Paper, *Education in Schools: A Consultative Document*, which argued the need for schools to become more accountable to parents and the public. It stated: "Growing recognition of the need for schools to demonstrate their accountability to the society which they serve requires a coherent and soundly based means of assessment for the educational system as a whole, for schools and for individual pupils". Parents, it added, had a right to know how well their children were doing in different aspects of their school work (DES, 1977, p. 38).

In the 1980s the Conservative government expressed much concern about the need to improve educational standards and it took a renewed interest in many areas of education which had been hitherto left to the discretion of teachers, for example, examinations, the curriculum and the government of schools. During this decade it was frequently argued that teachers should be more accountable to the users of the educational system. Thus, the 1985 White Paper *Better Schools* commented that "the duty of government is to ensure, as far as it can that, through the efforts of all who are involved with our schools, the education of the pupils serves their own and the country's needs and provides a fair return to those who pay for it" (DES, 1985, p. 4).

(b) **The Concept of Accountability:**

(i) *The Meaning of "Accountability"*:

(1) According to the *Oxford Concise Dictionary* "accountability" implies "responsibility to others for action taken".

(2) Writing in the context of education, Maurice Kogan (1986, p. 25) suggests that "accountability" is: "a condition in which individual role holders are liable to review and the application of sanctions if their actions fail to satisfy those with whom they are in an accountability relationship".

(3) Hugh Sockett (1980) argues that the term involves the following criteria:

- An agent is not merely *able* to deliver an account of his actions to another; he is *obliged* to do so. This may be the result of a legal contract or some unwritten agreement without the force of law.

- The agent has the right to use resources which are not his own for purposes which are negotiated between him and the provider to whom he is accountable.

- The agent is held accountable for the outcomes or results of his work or to codes of practice. For example, doctors are accountable to the British Medical Association and barristers to the Bar Council.

(ii) *Positive Aspects of Accountability*: Barton, Beecher, Canning, Eraut and Knight (1980, pp. 98ff.) point to the following positive aspects of accountability and stress that it should not be seen as just meeting external obligations:

(1) It can provide safeguards for members of the profession against various forms of attack. If schools can show satisfactorily that they are performing their obligations, they have some protection against criticism. "If properly designed and implemented, an accountability policy can also provide a defence against attempts to limit autonomy and the enjoyment of legitimate rights and powers" (Barton, Beecher, Canning, Eraut and Knight, 1980, p. 110). In this way schools have some protection against encroachments on their freedom. They are also in a stronger position if they are assailed in the media.

(2) Accountability is a two way process. If teachers are answerable to the LEA, the authority must in turn strive actively to maintain a supportive relationship with them.

(3) Accountability may be seen as a "process of mutual negotiation, in which something is conceded - say, some professional prerogative which contemporary values call into question - and something gained - perhaps a firm declaration of public trust, a renewed guarantee of essential autonomies, or an insurance against future encroachment" (p. 110).

(c) **The Political Philosophy of the New Right:** Under the Conservative governments of Margaret Thatcher and John Major (1979 - 1997) educational policy was dominated by what Demaine (2002) calls the ideas of the New Right. Many of the tenets of this philosophy were written into the Education Reform Act of 1988, the Education (Schools) Act of 1992, the Education Act of 1993, the Education Act of 1994 and the Education Act of 1996. Key tenets were:

(i) *centralisation*: the belief that central government should determine educational policy and impose it - sometimes in a confrontational manner - on local authorities and schools. The notion of partnership in which local authorities and teachers would help decide policy became outdated from this period.

(ii) *the desire to remove all organisations and structures which were intermediate between the individual and central government*. The policy of government from 1988 was to weaken the powers of local authorities. Examples are given in subsequent paragraphs.

(iii) *faith in market forces to drive up standards*. Within the philosophy of the free market parents are viewed as consumers who are encouraged to choose the "best" school for their child. The "best" school is usually defined as the one where the greatest proportion of pupils achieves the highest examination grades in the area. To help consumers make an informed choice schools are required to publish their National Curriculum test and examination results in "league tables" and parents use this information to decide the school their child should attend. Funding is linked to the number of children a school recruits. Under this regime standards are driven up, since successful (and hence popular) schools expand, whilst poorly performing schools have to improve their academic results in order to compete. Schools which consistently fail to attract pupils lose funding and eventually have to close or be "taken over" by their successful competitors. In this way the best schools thrive and the weakest are removed from the educational system.

(iv) *making the providers of educational services accountable to the users of these services*: For example, from the time of the Education Reform Act of 1988 schools have been required to keep parents informed of the results they obtain. Again, from 1992 school inspection has become more frequent and more stringent.

(d) **The Third Way:** Tony Blair, Leader of the Labour Party, which won the general elections in May 1997, June 2001 and May 2005, has frequently referred to the philosophy of "the Third Way", though it has not always been clear what this actually entails. It is usually taken to mean an approach which is distinctive from socialism on the one hand and capitalism on the other. Key aspects of Labour's philosophy are summarised under the following four propositions:

(i) *The state should set a framework of regulations and encourage spontaneous efforts from non-governmental agencies to achieve high standards within that framework*. On coming to power Labour established its policy of raising standards (DFEE, 1997a), and it is significant that its first piece of educational legislation was entitled the *School Standards and Framework Act 1998*. Government's role is seen to be one of introducing legislation and tight regulations concerning education to drive up standards. Nonetheless, it encourages the private sector to play a large role in running the education service within this framework, especially where existing services are deemed to be unsatisfactory. Competition is encouraged among private bodies, and companies which provide the "best value" are given contracts to operate educational services. Where public sector bodies like local authorities are judged to have failed to achieve adequate standards, their duties are taken over by the private sector.

(ii) *Government is committed to employment-centred social policy*: Education is seen to have a key role in enhancing the capability of disadvantaged workers. Hence, vocational education, training for the workforce and lifelong learning are Labour government priorities (Pring, 2005).

(iii) *There should be "zero-tolerance" of failure*. This phrase, borrowed from American politics, has often been used by Labour government ministers. Since 1997 government has set out targets for staff working within the educational system and has taken a stern view if they do not meet them. Accountability and responsibility are important elements within the Third Way.

(iv) *Rather than prescribe any specific over-arching policies, government prefers an approach which is essentially pragmatic.* Consequently, policies which are judged to be successful in practice are allowed to continue.

Chitty and Dunford (1999) note that the Third Way contains most of the policies of the former Conservative government, especially the market forces philosophy, while Sir Michael Barber, head of the Standards and Effectiveness Unit from 1997 until 2001 and of Tony Blair's Delivery Unit from 2001 until 2005, has praised Labour's market-based education system, telling the American website *Education Sector* that "one of the best things Blair did was ... to build on the important Conservative reforms" (Shaw and Mansell, 2006). Specific legislation based upon this philosophy is recounted in the following paragraphs.

IV: CENTRALISATION

Centralisation has been a marked trend under both Conservative and Labour party control since 1988. The government has granted itself extensive powers over virtually every aspect of education, the powers of local authorities have been eroded and it is difficult to describe the relationship between the Department for Education and Skills, local authorities and teachers as a "partnership".

(a) **Powers of the Secretary of State for Children, Schools and Families:** Under the Conservatives the Secretary of State acquired considerable control over the educational system. Powers were granted by Parliament which were never envisaged in 1944, for example, the power to:

- determine the school curriculum and arrangements for testing pupils at the ages of seven, eleven, fourteen and sixteen;

- decide which courses leading to external qualifications can be offered in schools (e.g. GCSE subjects, vocational qualifications);

- require school governors to set and publish performance targets and the results obtained by them;

- publish proposals to rationalise school places and close schools to remove surplus places from the system.

Under Labour the same trend has continued. The School Standards and Framework Act of 1998, the Teaching and Higher Education Act of 1998, the Education Act of 2002, the Education Act of 2005 and the Education and Inspections Act of 2006 have all given the Secretary of State even greater control over the functioning of local authorities and schools, for instance, the ability to:

- suspend the powers of local authorities if (s)he is dissatisfied with their performance;

- direct a local authority to work with an external partner to improve a school at which standards are not acceptable;

- order a local authority to close a school requiring special measures;

- create education action zones;

- impose a compulsory qualification for all new headteachers - the National Professional Qualification for Headteachers.

It has been estimated that under Labour's School Standards and Framework Act of 1998 the Education Secretary was granted an additional seventy powers (Rafferty, 1998). Further powers conferred under subsequent legislation allow him/her to impose changes upon sectors of the educational system, for example, the constitution and role of school governors, by the issue of statutory regulations.

(b) Advisory Bodies:

Since the late 1960s neither Conservative nor Labour governments have welcomed the principle of independent advisory councils and committees of the type described in section II(c) above. Consequently, the Central Advisory Council for England and its Welsh counterpart were disbanded under section 59 of the Education (No. 2) Act 1986 and no such independent body exists today.

Many commentators on the educational system under the Conservatives expressed their concern that government ministers refused to listen to advice from anyone other than their own supporters. In June 1992 Professor Eric Bolton, formerly Chief Inspector of Schools in England, complained in *The Times Educational Supplement* that ministers were "not prepared to listen to heads and teachers or education researchers" but that they did take notice of people representing groups such as the Centre for Policy Studies and the Adam Smith Institute, both of which were associated with the Conservative Party. Professor Bolton concluded: "There is no crime in listening to your political friends. But a wise government listens more widely than that, and especially to those with no political axe to grind".

It is also significant that, when Labour's Education Secretary, David Blunkett, set up various "task forces", for example, the Standards and Effectiveness Unit, the National Task Force On Standards, the Literacy Task Force and the Numeracy Task Force, the people serving on these bodies were chosen directly by him. Professor Michael Barber, who was selected to head the Standards and Effectiveness Unit, had for some time acted as an adviser to the Labour Party on education.

In December 2003 the National Commission on Education, an independent body, in its report *Learning to Succeed: The Next Decade*, criticised the desire of government ministers to control every aspect of the educational system. Sir John Cassells, Director of the Commission, stated that: "If there is one over-arching message that keeps coming through, it is this: the concentration of educational decision-making at the centre has led to a situation where 'command and control' dominates, and this has now reached a point where it is seriously counter-productive" (Cassells, 2003, p.21).

Although the first fifteen sections of the Labour government's Teaching and Higher Education Act of 1998 established a General Teaching Council (GTC) for England and another for Wales, these bodies are primarily concerned with the creation of a code of ethics for the teaching profession, the registration of all qualified teachers and disciplinary action against teachers charged with incompetence or misconduct. They have no power with respect to major issues of educational policy such as the organisation of education or the curriculum.

(c) **Relationship of Central Government and Teachers:**

(i) *Lack of Consultation with the Teachers' Unions*: During the 1980s any consensus between government and teachers broke down in acrimonious disputes concerning pay and working conditions. By the 1990s the teachers' organisations no longer felt that their views were heeded by the Conservative government, and Rafferty, writing in *The Times Educational Supplement* on 14 April 1992, commented that in the early 1990s the teachers' unions were "forced to accept the futility of their role as King Canute on the beaches of Blackpool and Scarborough attempting to stem the tide of Tory reform".

Many instances can be noted when the opinions of the teachers' organisations were ignored by government. For example, most of the teachers' unions expressed total opposition to the recommendations contained in the White Paper *Choice and Diversity: A New Framework for Schools* (DFE, 1992), but their opinions were utterly disregarded and the proposals of the White Paper served as the basis of the Education Act of 1993.

Nor have relations between Labour and teachers' organisations been more cordial, and Martin Lawn, writing in *State Schools, New Labour and the Conservative Legacy*, argues that Labour wants only "efficient employees" (Chitty and Dunford, 1999). Consequently, at its annual conference in 1998 the National Association of Headteachers (NAHT) attacked legislation on target setting. The General Secretary, David Hart, stated that: "We have written to all our secondary members advising them not to agree their targets with local authorities. We regard that as bureaucracy gone mad - it's quite inappropriate" (Thornton, 1998). Again, at the annual conference of the National Union of Teachers (NUT) in April 2001, amid complaints about teachers' workloads, the General Secretary reviewed the period from 1997 to 2001 and concluded that "there has been no attempt at partnership with the unions, and teachers feel they have been vilified" (Barnard and Dean, 2001).

More recently, teachers' unions have expressed their discontent with several aspects of government policy. For example, in March 2005 Steve Sinnott, General Secretary of the NUT described the programme of academies as "immoral" and stated that the union would oppose every new school of this type (Mansell, 2005). Similarly, Chris Keates, General Secretary of the National Association of Schoolmasters Union of Women Teachers (NASUWT), denounced the pay and conditions expected of teachers working in academies (Wilce, 2005), while Mary Bousted, General Secretary of the Association of Teachers and Lecturers (ATL), voiced concern at reports that academies had not met all the government's expectations. She commented that "if there is a directive from No 10, then evidence-based policy goes out the window" (Stewart, 2005b). At the ATL annual conference in 2006 she returned to the attack on academies, alleging that their creation would result in a system whereby other schools would cater for "the underclass" (Slater, 2006). That same year other aspects of government policy were criticised at the NAHT conference: the workload of headteachers; Key Stage 2 tests in England; and the concept of extended schools where there was insufficient funding. Mike Welsh, headteacher of Goddard Park Primary School in Swindon demanded that the government listen to headteachers (Shaw, 2006). "If not," he continued, "the fight starts here and it starts now!"

(ii) *Exclusion of Teachers from Policy Making Bodies*: Bodies such as the Schools Council were terminated in the 1980s, and the teachers' organisations were excluded from the quangos set up by the Conservative and Labour governments, notably the National Curriculum Council, the School Curriculum and Assessment Authority and the Qualifications and Curriculum Authority.

(iii) *Initial Teacher Education and Training*: Under the Conservatives many changes took place in initial teacher education and training. The governments of Margaret Thatcher and John Major sought to break the power of higher education institutions in this field and to reduce the preparation of teachers to a technical-rational approach whereby students were equipped with basic skills to deliver a government-controlled National Curriculum (Leaton Gray, 2006). The 1994 Education Act made it possible for students to acquire qualified teacher status by following courses of training which were located entirely in schools with no involvement on the part of universities or institutes of higher education. To superintend the development of this innovation the Act created the Teacher Training Agency (now the Training and Development Agency for Schools).

Labour has maintained these trends with such initiatives as the Graduate Teacher and the Registered Teacher Programmes. These changes have led many commentators to conclude that government no longer wishes to receive constructive ideas from a teaching profession which may be critical of its policies. Thus, Carr and Hartnett (1996) contend that the "utterly philistine Teacher Training Agency" has done all it can to render teachers compliant, exhausted, always under threat of surveillance and afraid. Similarly, Price, writing of the 1994 Education Act, argues that government no longer wishes initial teacher education and training to involve the type of critical thinking which was encouraged thirty years earlier. The Act, he feels, is "directed to the cultural control of the hearts and minds of the young". Politicians, having identified the educational system as a potential threat to people's acceptance of their plans, have sought to control "the culture of teacher training ... to return the teachers to the task of technical instruction and to leave the promotion of ideology to the government" (Price, 1994, p. 19). Bottery and Wright (2000) agree with these judgements, noting that government does not want a teaching profession which possesses an understanding of what they call the "ecological" areas of ITET, that is to say, influences on children outside the classroom. Furthermore, research by Leaton Gray (2006) shows how teachers trained before the Education Reform Act of 1988 value professional autonomy, while those who have embarked upon a career in teaching after that time assume that the current regime of accountability is a natural part of their environment.

V: WEAKENING THE POWERS OF LOCAL AUTHORITIES

(a) **Devolution of Funding to School Governors:** Under the 1944 Education Act schools and further education colleges were directly funded by LEAs which had full autonomy over educational spending in their areas. The Conservative government's 1988 Education Reform Act introduced the system known as local *management of schools*, which Labour replaced with *fair funding*. Currently, local authorities can retain funding for four purposes only: strategic management; access (e.g. home-school transport); school improvement; and meeting special educational needs. The remainder, known as the *individual schools budget*, must be devolved to the governors of each school. The actual amount each school receives depends primarily on pupil numbers weighted for age together with other factors such as social deprivation. The governors – not the local authority - then have total control over the school budget. The local authority can regain control of a school's budget only where the governors do not manage the finances efficiently or where the standard of education provided is found to be unsatisfactory during inspection.

(b) **Relationship of Local Authorities and Schools:**

(i) *Grant Maintained Schools*: Under the Conservatives' 1988 and 1993 Acts school governors had the right to initiate a ballot among parents on the question of the school's leaving LEA control and becoming a *Grant Maintained School*. Such schools were managed by their governors, who employed the staff and owned the site and premises. There were no LEA representatives on the governing body of these schools.

Resources for grant maintained schools were provided by the Funding Council for Schools in England and the Schools Funding Council for Wales. In some cases the sums received were extremely generous, for which the Conservative government was criticised in Parliament. By the time that the Conservative government went out of power there were 1,199 grant maintained schools in England and Wales, of which 668 were secondary.

(ii) *Foundation Schools*: Labour's School Standards and Framework Act of 1998 abolished grant maintained schools as such. A new category was created in September 1999, and many former grant maintained schools assumed the status of foundation school whereby the governors employ the staff and decide admissions policy. The site and buildings are owned by the foundation, or, if there is no foundation, by the governors. Funding is provided by the local authority and the Funding Councils appointed by the Conservatives have been scrapped. The School Standards and Framework Act stated that foundation schools must have at least two local authority representatives on their governing body.

Over the period it has been in office the Labour government has constantly modified its policy on foundation schools. Initially, the governors of community schools, maintained by local authorities, could choose to assume foundation status. They had to consult interested parties and publish their plans. Objections to the proposed change could be lodged with the local School Organisation Committee within a period of two months and this committee had to reach a decision. However, in 2004 the Department for Education and Skills (DFES) considerably simplified this process by allowing schools to change their status by means of a vote on the part of the governing body, following a brief period of consultation (DFES, 2004b).

Further changes were announced in the White Paper *Higher Standards, Better Schools for All: More Choice for Parents and Pupils* (DFES, 2005b) and enacted in the Education and Inspections Act of 2006, section 33 of which permits foundations or trusts (non-profit making, charitable organisations) controlled by businesses, religious groups, parents, universities, independent schools or charities to appoint a *majority* of the governors to certain foundation schools. In such cases local authority governors cannot have more than twenty per cent of the voting rights and the governors must establish a council consisting of parents of registered pupils at the school to advise them on matters relating to the conduct of the school. Since the governors of trust schools can decide the curriculum they offer and determine staff pay and conditions, these are in effect state-funded independent schools.

(c) **Further and Higher Education:** Under the 1988 Education Reform Act and Further and Higher Education Act of 1992 the following changes were initiated:

(i) The polytechnics and larger colleges of higher education left LEA control to become independent bodies. They were given the opportunity to acquire university status and, like the traditional universities, are now funded by the *Higher Education Funding Council for England* or the *Higher Education Funding Council for Wales*.

(ii) Sixth form, tertiary and further education colleges were removed from LEA control in April 1993 and become independent bodies funded by the *Further Education Funding Council for England* and the *Further Education Funding Council for Wales*. Subsequently, Labour's Learning and Skills Act of 2000 abolished these councils and established in England from April 2001 a new fifteen-member body known as the *Learning and Skills Council for England* to oversee all post-sixteen education and training in England outside the universities. The members of the body include employers, local government, the voluntary sector and trade unions. Forty-seven regional Learning and Skills Councils (LSCs) were appointed under the direction of the national Council with the power to determine what happens in their locality, though at the time of writing (March 2007) plans are at hand to replace them with nine regional councils consisting of between twelve and sixteen members each. Arrangement in Wales are described in section IX.

(d) **Reorganisation of the Council System:** Because of the weakening of the powers of local authorities, section 296 of the Conservatives' 1993 Education Act rescinded the requirement for them to appoint an Education Committee. In addition, the Labour government has made it possible for local authorities to end the traditional system whereby decisions have been taken by committees and ratified by the full council. Instead, councils can choose one of three types of arrangement: a directly elected mayor with an executive of two or more members; a cabinet with a leader; or a directly elected mayor and council manager. Councils still have to approve major decisions and there are committees to scrutinise the resolutions of mayors and cabinets. Thus, in Cardiff the post of Director of Education was abolished in 1999 with the appointment of five "corporate managers" to run the city's services, none of whom had educational experience. The post of Chief Schools Officer became a second rung managerial position.

The Children Act of 2004 again altered the traditional system of local government by establishing a more integrated approach to children's services; each area must establish a *Local Safeguarding Children Board* (LSCB), including the local authority, police, strategic health authority and children and family court advisory and support service. It must also appoint a Director of Children's Services. Consequently, the term "local education authority" has now been dropped under section 162 of the Education and Inspection Act of 2006 in favour of "local authority".

VI: RAISING STANDARDS

(a) **Target Setting:** National targets have been established in terms of the educational qualifications expected of pupils at different ages in both England and Wales (Geen, 2005, pp. 191-210). For example, by 2008 at least fifty per cent of pupils in England are to reach level 5 or above in the National Curriculum level descriptions in each of the core subjects of English, mathematics and science by the end of Key Stage 3.

Sections 6-7 of Labour's School Standards and Framework Act of 1998 required each local authority to set out an *education development plan* (EDP) with targets for its area expressed in terms of the percentage of pupils achieving specified National Curriculum levels, GCSE grades and AS/A level passes. EDPs had to be approved by the Secretary of State, and the governors of each school had to establish targets which conformed with their LEA's development plan. Schools' targets and the actual results obtained were regularly published. Under the Children Act 2004 EDPs are no longer required, as local authorities are now expected to formulate *children and young people's plans* for their area to reflect the more integrated approach to children's services demanded under the Act. Nonetheless, the Secretary of State is empowered under section 102 of the 2005 Education Act to issue regulations by virtue of which local authorities in England must set annual targets in respect of their pupils' performance. Target setting in Wales is the responsibility of the Welsh Assembly Government.

Local authorities must monitor results and issue formal warnings to any of their schools where the standard falls to a level below that which pupils have attained in the past or below that achieved in other comparable schools. In the case of these and other categories of schools causing concern the Education and Inspections Act of 2006 grants extensive powers of intervention to the local authority and Secretary of State.

(b) **Performance Management:** Within the system of performance management, which was introduced to schools in England in September 2000 and to schools in Wales two years later, all teachers are appraised annually. This appraisal is based upon their job description and focuses upon the extent to which they achieve set targets. Thus, objectives are agreed for the school year together with their success criteria. The outcomes of appraisal are important in deciding teachers' progression along the pay scale. The current system is defined in the Education (School Teacher Performance Management) (England) Regulations 2006 and the School Teacher Appraisal (Wales) Regulations 2002.

(c) **Beacon and Leading Edge Schools:** In 1998 central government launched the "beacon school" initiative, under which nursery, primary, secondary and special schools in England which were identified in inspection as being particularly successful could bid for between £20,000 and £50,000 each to undertake activities designed to raise standards in other schools. Seventy-five such schools began operation in September 1998; another 125 joined the scheme in September 1999 and a further fifty in January 2000. By 2003 the total stood at 1,150. The money could be used in a variety of ways, for example, to purchase supply cover for staff visiting other schools and disseminating good practice, to finance open-distance learning packages and to train students and new teachers. It was government policy for a quarter of beacon schools to be in or serving city areas. All beacon schools outside city areas had to have inner city school partners. Some worked with failing schools in an endeavour to improve their standards. For example, St Peter's Collegiate School in Wolverhampton worked with Regis School in the same town.

In 2005 the secondary beacon school programme was replaced with the "leading edge" schools initiative. Specific criteria are established for schools wishing to acquire this status, notably performance, innovation and collaboration with other institutions. Schools in England which achieve "leading edge" status receive £60,000 a year for three years through the Standards Fund. By 2007 there were 205 leading edge schools.

(d) **Zero Tolerance of Failure:** Examples of this aspect of Labour policy are:

(i) *Fast Track Dismissal of Teachers*: In the late 1990s much publicity was given to the alleged 15,000 incompetent teachers estimated by the then Chief Inspector for Schools (England), Chris Woodhead. Consequently, the Labour government in November 1997 announced new measures by which the period in which an unsatisfactory teacher had to show improvement or face dismissal was reduced to six months or, in extreme cases, where the education of pupils was in serious jeopardy, to one month. These procedures, however, begin only after under-performing teachers have been given counselling and/or further training.

(ii) *Schools Requiring Special Measures*: Section 44 of the Education Act of 2005 describes schools requiring special measures as institutions which are "failing to give [their] pupils an acceptable standard of education and the persons responsible for leading, managing or governing the school are not demonstrating the capacity to secure the necessary improvement in the school". Under section 68 of the Education and Inspections Act of 2006, the Secretary of State may require a local authority to *close* any school identified as requiring special measures at a date specified by him/her.

The Labour government's changing policies on schools which are eligible for intervention exemplify its pragmatic approach, as different strategies have been implemented and modified in the light of experience. Initially, it favoured the *Fresh Start Initiative* whereby a failing school was closed and a new one with a different headteacher opened on the site. Existing staff had to re-apply for posts at the new school. In accordance with this policy Hatcham Wood School in Lewisham was re-opened as Telegraph Hill School and only fourteen of the forty-one members of staff from the former establishment were re-employed. Fresh Start was not notoriously successful as some schools failed to make any marked progress. For example, Marina High School in Brighton re-opened in September 1999 as East Brighton College of Media Arts, but in 2003 only twelve per cent of pupils obtained five top grade passes at GCSE, and in 2004 the local authority resolved to close it entirely. More recently, the government has favoured the system of federated schools made possible under sections 24 and 25 of the Education Act of 2002 whereby a successful and a struggling school are twinned under one governing body so that the high achieving school can help the weaker institution to improve. Hence, the Unity Academy in Middlesbrough, which was placed in special measures for unsatisfactory standards, poor leadership and low staff morale, formed a federation with the nearby Macmillan City Technology College in September 2005. Since that time the two schools have been managed by a joint board of governors and a federation director (Shaw, 2005).

Other policies have been introduced to deal with poor performing schools. The Education Act of 2002 and the Education and Inspections Act of 2006 empower both a local authority and the Secretary of State for Education to replace such a school's governing body with an "interim executive board". If this board is successful in bringing about improvement, it is disbanded and a new governing body formed. In accordance with this strategy an interim executive board was appointed by Ruth Kelly, the Education Secretary, in December 2005 to take control of New Monument Primary School in Woking, Surrey, where the percentage of children achieving level 4 in the core subjects had slipped in recent years (e.g. from sixty-five per cent in mathematics to thirty-eight per cent) (Hilbourne, 2005).

The Labour government has also adopted the policy of re-opening failing schools as "academies". This category of school is described in more detail in the section below on the role of the private sector in education. In 2005 the White Paper *Higher Standards, Better Schools for All: More Choice for Parents and Pupils* (DFES, 2005b) announced that schools in England which received a notice to improve from the Office for Standards in Education (OFSTED) would enter special measures if they did not make sufficient progress within one year. Any school in the special measures category where standards did not rise within twelve months would be closed and a competition held for providers to open a new school in its premises. These providers could be parents, private firms or faith groups.

(iii) *Inspection of Local Authorities*: Not only are schools inspected; the same has been true since the late 1990s of local authorities. Currently, major changes are taking place with respect to the inspection of councils. As a result of the Children Act of 2004 inspection from September 2005 has focused upon a range of services - education, probation, health and social services for young people, and section 113 of the Education and Inspections Act of 2006 has created the role of a Chief Inspector of Education, Children's Services and Skills, who is empowered to bring about overall inspections of local authorities in England. Further details of the inspection of local authorities are given below in the context of the role of the private sector in education.

VII: THE OPERATION OF MARKET FORCES

In accordance with the philosophies of both the Conservative and Labour parties parents have been regarded as customers in a free market system. Under the School Standards and Framework Act of 1998 and the Education Act of 2002 local authorities must give parents the right to express in writing a preference for the school they wish their child to attend. To help them to make a rational choice, these parents receive information concerning local schools, for example, National Curriculum test results, the percentages of pupils obtaining the various grades at GCSE, AS and A level and the proportion gaining vocational qualifications. In England schools' results are published as "league tables" in annual school achievement and attainment booklets. After consulting these documents, it is believed, parents are in a strong position to choose the "best" school for their child.

Local authorities must agree to the parents' choice, provided that it is not in opposition to entry arrangements agreed with selective schools and the school has not yet reached its "admission number". Nor do parents have the right of choice if their child has been excluded from two or more schools within a period of two years. In the case of over-subscribed schools admission authorities must publish in order of priority the criteria which are used for deciding admissions, for example, sibling links, catchment area or entry from feeder primary schools. Where catchment area is a criterion, parents who reside in the area and express a preference for the school in writing have priority. Parents living outside the area who state a preference take precedence over those dwelling within the area who do not indicate their wish for their child to attend the school in question. A Code of Practice on admissions has been drawn up by the DFES. Parents whose choice is not met can appeal to a panel independent of the local authority and governors of the school involved.

Under Labour the system of "league tables" has been modified and a measure of "value added" introduced. This means that results are published in such a way that parents can see the progress pupils have made at the school from one key stage to another. The social background and context of the institution are also taken into account.

The philosophy of market forces received a further boost in August 2003 when the DFES instructed local authorities to approve the expansion of popular schools. The following year the government reiterated its policy that *all* schools would be able to expand, provided that they were successful in terms of their results and were consistently popular with parents irrespective of any surplus places in neighbouring schools. They are required to publish their plans for expansion and to consult with interested parties over a period of between four and six weeks. Capital expenditure grants are available.

VIII: THE ROLE OF THE PRIVATE SECTOR IN EDUCATION

Conservative and Labour governments have been very keen for private business enterprises and educational companies like Nord Anglia, Cambridge Education Associates, Capita and the Centre for British Teachers to play a substantial role in running the educational system in order to promote high standards. Specific examples are:

(a) **Local Authorities and Private Enterprise:** Sections 38-41 of the Education Act of 1997 made provision for the inspection of LEAs every five years. Section 8 of the School Standards and Framework Act of 1998 gave the Secretary of State the power to issue specific directions to an LEA if (s)he were dissatisfied with its performance, for example, if it did not set challenging targets or failed to identify schools which were underachieving. In several instances of this type private enterprise was invited to take over the running of local authority services, the DFES retaining a list of approved companies invited to submit bids.

By 2001 government ministers had called for intervention on the part of outside consultants in the case of twenty local authorities. For example, Islington's education service was taken over by the private contractors Cambridge Education Associates on a seven-year contract, while WS Atkins won a five-year contract to run almost all school support services in Southwark. In June 2001 Serco-QAA was given a seven-year contract to run a number of educational services in Bradford. In 2002 similar developments took place in Essex and Surrey, while Bedfordshire, Lincolnshire and Middlesborough went into partnership with HBS, a support service company founded by Welsh Water.

However, by 2003 it appeared that this policy of privatisation was not always successful. Of nine authorities whose services were taken over by private contractors, five were rated as poor, three as unsatisfactory and only one as satisfactory when they were re-inspected. Indeed, Cambridge Education Associates which ran services in Islington was fined a significant percentage of its management fee after failing to meet examination targets. Nord Anglia, which was given control of Hackney's services, was replaced with a not-for-profit trust after it failed to make any significant impact. Similarly, Education Bradford, the trading name of Serco-QAA in that city, met just five of its fifty targets and earned only £8,450 in performance-related bonuses out of a possible total of £870,000. On the other hand, headteachers in Lincolnshire have been pleased with the performance of CfBT, a non-profit making organisation (Stewart, 2006a).

Another policy has been "twinning" by which a successful authority supports and helps a weak one. Under this system Doncaster was twinned with Warwickshire.

(b) **The Private Finance Initiative (PFI):** Under the PFI private sector companies pay the upfront costs for building work on schools and in return receive an annual fee from the local authority for the management and upkeep of these buildings, usually for a period of twenty-five years, after which time they are returned to the local authority. Projects have ranged from new and replacement schools to the provision of ICT equipment. By 2005 there were forty-eight PFI deals covering 378 newly built or refurbished schools, and another 337 schools were under construction (Abrams, 2005). In some instances headteachers and staff have not been very pleased with the outcomes. Rebridge School in Southampton, for example, moved to new premises constructed under PFI where staff and pupils found small classrooms, long narrow corridors which quickly became congested, inadequate sound insulation and lack of ventilation. The headteacher commented that "a PFI is a partnership between a public provider of education and a private funder of buildings and services. The two are not compatible. One is trying to satisfy its shareholders; the other to meet the needs of the students without a profit motive" (Milne, 2006). The DFES (2004b) has undertaken to refurbish or rebuild every secondary school in England and half of all primary schools by 2022, though it does not intend to use the PFI within its plans for primary schools (Stewart, 2006b).

(c) **Compulsory Competitive Tendering and Best Value:** From January 1992 as the result of the Local Government Act of 1988 all local authorities had to put out to compulsory competitive tendering a range of their services. From 1993 this also applied to the careers service.

The Labour government subsequently introduced the system of *Best Value*, under which local authorities have from April 2000 been obliged to review their services and expose them to competitive pressure on a cyclical basis. Instead of providing services to schools themselves, the fundamental role of the local authority is to act as the procurer of services, awarding contracts to companies and monitoring their performance. In October 2000 a paper published by the DFEE, *The Role of the LEA in School Education*, stated that local authorities should "promote a more open market in school services and take steps to ensure that all schools have the knowledge and skills they need to be better purchasers".

(d) **Education Action Zones:** Sections 10-14 of the School Standards and Framework Act dealt with Education Action Zones. Each zone consisted of about twenty primary and secondary schools working under the control of a forum or partnership of people, for example, representatives of local business, parents, voluntary bodies and local authorities with one member appointed by the Secretary of State. Each forum had to raise £250,000 in cash or kind and submit a bid to the Secretary of State. If the bid was accepted, it received £750,000 a year for three years, which could be extended to five.

Each forum had to set demanding targets for its schools and plan educational innovations to achieve these targets. In the zones the National Curriculum could be relaxed to allow for experimentation and the national pay scales and conditions of service could be modified.

Under Labour's *Excellence in Cities* initiative announced in April 1999, up to fifty of the worst performing inner-city schools and their feeder primary schools were allowed to become Education Action Zones. During the school year 1998-99 the first twenty-five zones were created and by the school year 2000-2001 this number had risen to seventy-three. In January 2001 the DFES decided to limit the number of zones to this total and no more were created. The provisions for action zones applied only to England.

In practice, OFSTED found in 2003 that the impact of the action zones upon educational standards had been "variable". Whereas they helped teachers to meet the needs of some disaffected pupils, attendance in most instances either remained static or else it deteriorated. Of twenty-five zones surveyed by OFSTED, only two saw improvements in the Key Stage 2 tests, whilst the achievements of pupils at Key Stage 3 gave cause for concern. The proportion of pupils gaining five GCSE grades A*-C rose in one zone only, declined in two and remained unchanged in the others (OFSTED, 2003b).

(e) **Sponsor Governors:** Sponsors who have contributed substantial financial assistance or services to a school can be co-opted by the other governors to become members of the governing body of that school. Only one or two sponsor governors may be appointed.

(f) **Specialist Schools:** From 1993 the Conservative government allowed schools to make an application to the Education Secretary to assume the status of "specialist school". Areas of specialisation at that time included technology and modern languages. These schools received £100,000 from central government for capital funding together with an annual bonus of £100 per pupil, provided that they could match the initial £100,000 by means of private sponsorship. Each school also had to produce a three-year curriculum development plan showing how it would improve standards through a commitment to the specialisation. These schools could select ten per cent of their intake on aptitude for the specialist subject. By the time the Conservatives left office there were 181 specialist schools in operation. Among the sponsors were the Hong Kong and Shanghai Bank, British and American Tobacco and GEC.

Under Labour the system of specialist schools has been retained and considerably expanded. Secondary schools now have to raise only £50,000 in sponsorship, while schools with fewer than 500 pupils can bid for specialist status provided that they raise £20,000. In November 2002 the Education Secretary announced that *all* secondary schools would be permitted to attain specialist status and a fund would be set up to help any schools which were struggling to raise the necessary sponsorship money. To qualify they would have to show that they had made every effort to find sponsors. All applicants must prepare a four year development plan, setting targets to improve teaching and learning in the specialist subject, and they have to involve other schools in the area, for example, providing inservice training for their staff, setting up homework clubs and making software for numeracy and literacy schemes available to primary-age pupils. If the application is successful, schools receive a £100,000 capital grant and £129 per pupil per year, initially for four year. They are still allowed to select pupils on the basis of aptitude for the specialist subject(s). Current DFES policy (2004b and 2005b) is for all secondary schools in England either to assume specialist status or to become academies.

(g) **The Control of Schools by Private Companies:** The first school to be run by a private company was King's College in Guildford which opened in September 2000. Originally it was King's Manor School which had been identified in inspection in 1998 as a failing institution. The Conservative controlled authority decided to invite private bidders to take over the school under the Fresh Start initiative rather than to close it. Bids were received from several educational companies and the winner was 3Es Ltd, a company run by Stanley Goodchild, formerly Director of Education for Berkshire. The status of the school is voluntary aided with foundation governors appointed by 3Es. The Surrey local authority has since "privatised" two other schools - France Hill (now known as Kings' International) and Abbeylands school. Abbeylands is run by Nord Anglia, a profit-making education company. Moreover, section 7 of the Education and Inspections Act of 2006 has made it possible for private groups such as firms, parents and religious bodies to set up *new* schools with state funding.

(h) **Academies:** The Learning and Skills Act of 2000 and the Education Act of 2002 have made possible the creation of *academies* in England. These are existing schools whose standards are judged to be low in inspection. The Secretary of State is empowered to transfer the school buildings and land to partnerships which then own and run the schools. Subsequently, criteria were established for the eligibility of schools to become academies. These include: being in an area of social disadvantage; buildings in a poor state of repair, low performance compared with other similar schools; under-performance with respect to attendance; and a high proportion of exclusions. Partnerships may include businesses, individuals, churches and voluntary bodies, and they contribute some ten per cent of the building costs. The remaining ninety per cent is provided by central government.

Each academy has its own board of governors which can set the pay and conditions for staff. The governors may vary the school day and year, pay special incentives to teachers and modify the National Curriculum. Local authorities may be represented on the governing body, but the status of the schools is *independent*, and they have the freedom to specialise in *any* subject, devising a curriculum suited to the needs of their pupils. Ten per cent of the intake may be selected by aptitude for the specialist area or areas. Academies are not under any legal obligation to draw pupils from the immediate locality and many have recruited from very wide areas. Any disputes over admissions policy are heard by the Secretary of State. These schools are funded by the government at the same level as specialist schools, provided that agreed targets are achieved. Unlike other independent schools, their pupils have to take the Key Stage 3 National Curriculum tests, GCSE and other approved qualifications, and the staff must have qualified teacher status.

Government policy for the establishment of at least fifty-three academies by 2007 and two hundred by 2010 (DFES, 2004b) was modified in November 2006 when the Prime Minister stated that this number would be doubled to four hundred. The first three opened in September 2002: the Bexley Business Academy in Kent; Greig Academy in Haringey; and Unity Academy in Middlesbrough East. Nine more were opened in 2003, for example, City Academy in Bristol, and another five received their first intake in 2004, for example, London Academy, Brent. By the school year 2006-2007 sixty-nine academies had either been opened or were in the planning stage. Among the sponsors are finance companies, religious groups, football clubs (West Bromwich Albion), the chairman of the Saga Group, property developers, a coat hanger manufacturer, a car dealer and a textiles tycoon. Two of them - Frank Lowe who has funded a sports academy in Brent and Peter Vardy, sponsor of a business and enterprise academy in South Middlesbrough – have received knighthoods from the Blair government. One of the biggest sponsors has been the United Learning Trust chaired by Lord Carey, the former Archbishop of Canterbury, which has founded academies with financial backing from Honda and Vodafone.

Whereas the DFES has expressed the hope that academies can be created in co-operation with local authorities, it has nonetheless affirmed that it "will not stand by and allow local authorities to sustain failure by refusing to engage with academies where they can meet parental demand for school places" (DFES, 2004b, p. 43). To facilitate the development of academies the government in July 2004 set up the *Academy Sponsors Trust* to act as a "matchmaker" between potential sponsors and schools.

(i) **Schools As Companies:** Under the Education Act of 2002 the governors of schools can provide or enter into contracts with other parties to provide a range of services and facilities to benefit pupils, their families and other people in the local community. These services include childcare, adult and family learning, co-located healthcare and social services, for example, onsite clinics funded by local primary care trusts, and such wider community services as internet cafes, shops, advice bureaux and credit unions. They cannot use their delegated budget on initiatives of this nature and any surplus income derived from these activities must be reinvested in the service or the school.

Furthermore, the governors can join with other bodies to form companies and undertake business activities or provide services or facilities to other schools. The consent of the local authority is required and it must ensure that any such companies are kept on a financially firm footing.

(j) **Private Companies and Awarding Bodies:** In 2003 Pearson, a multinational company, bought the Edexcel awarding body for £20 million. A new body called London Qualifications was duly established to run all Edexcel's examinations, though the brand name "Edexcel" is being retained for the time being. Pearson has a seventy-five per cent stake in London Qualifications with the Edexcel Foundation charity owning the remaining twenty-five per cent.

IX: EDUCATION IN WALES

In 1970 the Secretary of State for Wales assumed responsibility for certain aspects of education in Wales. In practice, however, policy in Wales was virtually indistinguishable from that implemented by the Department of Education and Science in London. Many of the central government's policies were unpopular in Wales. For example, only 0.5 per cent of Welsh schools ever became grant maintained.

In May 1997 the Labour government was elected with a commitment to devolution, and in July of that year the first White Paper specifically devoted to Welsh education was published - *Building Excellent Schools Together* (Secretary of State for Wales, 1997). Then, in May 1999 the National Assembly for Wales was created, and in July many of the functions of the Secretary of State were transferred to it. Although it could not initially pass primary legislation, the Welsh Assembly Government had a wide range of responsibilities for education within the statutory framework laid down by Parliament, for example, determining the nature of the National Curriculum in Wales, setting targets for schools and deciding assessment arrangements. The Assembly's powers were increased under the Government of Wales Act 2006, which allowed it from May 2007 to make a new category of legislation known as "Measures of the National Assembly for Wales" on matters within its existing remit. The Act also provides for the Assembly to assume primary legislative powers at a future date, subject to a referendum.

Some of the differences between education in England and Wales are:

(a) **Specialist Schools and Academies:** As has been noted, central government expects all schools in England to become either specialist schools or academies. No such system is planned for Wales where the Minister for Education, Lifelong Learning and Skills, Jane Davidson, stated in May 2001 that "the focus of the National Assembly is on local schools that offer the widest opportunities for their children. We could not contemplate a situation where specialisms are concentrated too narrowly" (Passmore, 2001).

(b) **Private Companies:** No private companies have set up schools in Wales with state funding.

(c) **Education Action Zones.** None has been established in Wales.

(d) **Privatisation of Local Authorities:** No private companies have been granted contracts to assume control of the services offered by local authorities.

(e) **Target Setting:** Different national educational targets have been set in Wales.

(f) **The School Curriculum:** Wales has a different National Curriculum from that imposed in England. A play-based foundation phase becomes compulsory for three to five year olds in 2008 and extends to children aged seven by 2010. Moreover, pupils aged between fourteen and nineteen have the opportunity of pursuing the Welsh Baccalaureate (National Assembly for Wales, 2001). A further development has been the Flying Start programme for children up to the age of three. Nor has the literacy hour been prescribed in Wales.

(g) **National Curriculum Testing:** In 2005 the Welsh Assembly resolved that National Curriculum tests would be phased out over the period 2005-2008. Statutory teacher assessment remains and it is being strengthened by tighter moderation and accreditation arrangements.

(h) **School Achievement and Attainment Tables:** In Wales the National Assembly announced in July 2001 that it would stop publishing each school's results in the form of "league tables" with immediate effect, though parents still receive appropriate information in school prospectuses and governors' reports. Furthermore, in 2005 the Assembly government published the results for each secondary school in Wales under the Freedom of Information Act. They included the percentage of pupils reaching the various levels of the National Curriculum core subjects at the end of Key Stage 3, the percentage achieving each grade of the GCSE at the end of Key Stage 4 and AS and A level results including the average points score for each pupil entered for two or more AS or A levels or the vocational equivalents.

(i) **Funding of Schools:** In England section 101 of the 2005 Education Act has ensured that from 2006 the money allocated by central government to local authorities for spending on schools is ring-fenced, and authorities receive budgets covering a three-year period. In Wales, the Assembly Government grants the councils discretion concerning the allocation of their overall budget among the different services, although from 2004 ministers have indicated the amount they expect each council to devote to education. The Welsh Assembly Government also has the power to change its funding system to bring it into alignment with that operated in England.

(j) **Funding of Education for the Sixteen to Nineteen Age Group:** The National Council for Education and Training was set up in 2001 under the Learning and Skills Act 2000 with responsibility for all post-compulsory, non-university education and training in Wales. Many of its functions were similar to those of the Learning and Skills Council in England, but in April 2006 it was incorporated into the Welsh Assembly Government Department for Education, Lifelong Learning and Skills (DELLS), and decision-making power concerning the future of school sixth forms was returned to local authorities.

(k) **School Inspection:** There is a different structure for school inspection in Wales, though the Assembly has the right under section 62 of the Education Act of 2005 to adopt all or part of the English system if it so wishes.

(l) **Induction of Newly Qualified Teachers:** In Wales a system of Early Professional Development has been introduced covering the first three years of a newly qualified teacher's career.

7 Conducting research in the field of Education

I: INTRODUCTION

Students pursuing degree courses in Educational Studies are often required to undertake a small-scale research project or dissertation. This usually consists of:

- a statement of the aims and rationale for the research;

- a review of literature pertinent to the topic;

- an account of the research methods which are employed;

- an analysis of the results obtained;

- a summary of the conclusions reached and the implications for future research.

In this chapter some guidelines are offered on the planning and implementation of an educational research project of this type.

II: SELECTING A TOPIC

(a) **Possibilities:** One helpful starting point is to write down a list of all the ideas and areas of interest the researcher can conceive. Sources include experience, theoretical perspectives and ideas culled from literature. It is useful at this stage to think about current educational innovations and specific issues prominent in the media as well as themes which have been studied or investigated within an academic programme in the field of Educational Studies. Topics which have been encountered but not pursued in any detail can be included. No proposal, however unlikely it may seem, should be ruled out during this initial planning.

Once an exhaustive list has been generated, it is necessary to examine each item in turn and to consider its feasibility for a research project. Checking the availability of the resources needed to undertake each proposed topic is essential, for example, books, periodicals, access to participants, and the availability of photocopying facilities if questionnaires or similar research instruments are likely to be employed. The next step is to prioritise the list and to select two or three areas for more detailed investigation.

(b) **Probabilities:** Having decided the possibilities, the researcher next needs to narrow the choice down to a particular area or small group of topics and to consider the potential of each as a research subject. The most important criterion is viability. As well as being feasible in the light of the resources to hand, its nature should be such that it is likely to yield valid data. To ensure that this is the case, it is beneficial to study relevant literature and to talk to other competent persons. All these steps can be recorded in the methodology section of the dissertation later on, and so it is advantageous to retain notes concerning these activities at this stage. Once the person is confident about the area which will be pursued, then he or she needs to begin by putting into writing a clearly worded research statement. Attention should be paid to the reasons why research into the topic is deemed to be worthwhile.

Time well spent at this point usually saves a great deal of unnecessary work later. Once the research statement has been completed, it can be discussed with colleagues and the student can subsequently arrange a tutorial with his or her supervisor to finalise the details. This does not preclude making alterations at some later phase if this should prove to be necessary.

III: WRITING THE RESEARCH STATEMENT

Usually, a research statement assumes the following format:

(a) **An Introduction:** This sets out the overall purpose of the study in the appropriate educational context, for example, some topical issue or recent government initiative. Thus, one research study on the perceptions of disaffected young people who had been excluded from school on a number of occasions began with reference to an article in *The Daily Mail* dated 25 March 2005, which showed that being out of education, training and employment for six months or more between the ages sixteen to eighteen is the single most powerful predictor of later unemployment and is also associated with high levels of depression and poor health as well as teenage pregnancy and a criminal record serious enough to be a barrier to employment. This article carried a "punch" which was likely to arouse the interest of the reader from the start of the research report.

(b) **A Statement of Aims:** After an introductory paragraph it is conventional to state the precise aims of the study. Sometime it is desirable to have one overall aim and a number of specific sub-aims, for example:

> *The principal aim of the study is to ascertain the views of a sample of school staff in England and Wales and of student teachers upon the state of initial teacher education and training (ITET) under current legislation and upon the direction which it should take in the future.*

More specific aims are:

- *to gauge the views of student teachers upon the extent to which the mentors with whom they are located in schools fulfil their respective roles;.*

- *to record the main advantages which mentors believe are conferred by the system of partnership between schools and higher education institutions;*

- *to identify any difficulties and constraints which mentors have experienced;*

- *to list any strategies suggested by students and mentors for improving the standard of* ITET *in England and Wales.*

(c) **A Statement of Hypotheses:** A hypothesis has been described by Verma and Beard (1981, p. 184) as "a tentative proposition which is subject to verification through subsequent investigation". If any hypotheses are appropriate, they need to be described at this point. In the research project concerned with the perceptions of disaffected pupils important hypotheses were that:

- *these pupils would have a poor grasp of the key skills, especially reading and writing;*

- *they would, partly as a result of this, fail to be motivated by the core and foundation subjects within the National Curriculum;*

- *traditional forms of assessment, based upon National Curriculum tests and the GCSE, would put these pupils at a disadvantage and further alienate them from the educational system;*

- *a suitable programme of vocationally-oriented education would offer them an alternative curriculum which would better promote motivation and build self-esteem.*

(d) **A Rationale for the Study:** The rationale should put the study into its context and justify its value. For example, the project concerned with disaffection among pupils with their education pointed to the extensive amount of interest in this issue in recent years and the vast amount of literature published in this field in the 2000s, for example, *National Curriculum, National Disaster* (Griffith, 2000), *Working With Disaffected Students,* (Riley and Rustique-Forrester, 2002) and *Underachievement in Schools* (West and Pennell, 2003). Reference was also made to pronouncements by OFSTED and Estyn and to current concerns about disaffection in the researcher's school which justified the implementation of a fresh inquiry, for example, the loss of potential on the part of individual children, the difficulties experienced by teaching staff in seeking to motivate these pupils, and the educational aim of promoting pupils' career satisfaction.

(e) **A Research Timetable and List of Resources Employed:** In this initial statement a step-by-step programme can be included of the various stages of the research together with the appropriate dates and a list of the resources necessary for its completion.

IV: THE LITERATURE REVIEW

The review should include all relevant documents and published materials such as books, articles in journals, government publications and electronic sources which relate to the subject under consideration. The treatment of these sources should be critical, analytical and creative; key ideas and themes need to be debated and contrasted, not simply listed and described. It is unlikely that coverage will be exhaustive and consequently reading should be informed, selective and up to date.

The main purposes of the review are to:

- summarise in a logical order what others have written about the subject, thus providing an indication of the originality of the research being undertaken;

■ establish a theoretical framework for the study, which sets it within the context of current thinking about the topic.

Points to note are:

(a) **Relevance:** It is vital to include only those books and articles which are fully relevant. As has been noted, the purpose of the review is to show what other scholars have said in relation to the issue and to make clear the contribution which this new research makes to our understanding about the topic. Sources which do not contribute to these ends should be disregarded.

(b) **Organisation:** Attention must be paid to the organisation of the literature review. Writers need to be careful not merely to report the comments of different authors in a random manner with the result that this section of the research dissertation becomes a long disconnected list of what various people have said in the past: A *says* ...., B *says* ...., C *says* ...., D *says* ... A literature survey of this type gives the impression of being simply a jigsaw of unrelated comments. It is, therefore, essential to consider the best principle for structuring the review.

In some cases a *chronological* approach is suitable. For example, if a student were describing the evolution of the National Curriculum, the review could begin with the 1987 proposals emanating from the Department for Education and Science (DES) and proceed to summarise the relevant documents which have been issued since that time to the present day. Alternatively, a *thematic* approach may be preferable; in a dissertation concerned with the respective merits of streaming, setting and mixed ability teaching, it would be best to cite studies which champion each of these policies in turn.

(c) **Interrelationship of the Arguments:** The relationship of the different arguments should be explored in the review. If two previously published theses reveal contradictory findings, it is necessary that the points of contrast be shown. If one reference supports the findings of an earlier study, this relationship must be made clear. A structure of this type shows that the writer has the ability to use sources and to identify the fundamental issues. He/she is able to do more than just copy or paraphrase mechanically the ideas of others. This could indicate a sequence of arguments which runs as follows:

It *has been argued by* A (2003), B (2004) *and* C (2005) *that* ....

Other researchers, however, have taken a different stance and contend that ...... (D, 1997; E, 2000; F, 2004).

G (2006) *seeks to reconcile certain of these arguments. She* ......

(d) **Significance:** Brief accounts of the chief arguments and conclusions should be given. It is important to show the significance of an article, paper or chapter in a book to the topic under review. Thus, in a PhD study of educational decision making in one local authority a review was undertaken of other similar research concerned with local government policy. If this had merely offered copious details about events in Darlington, Middlesex, East Ham and other areas, the reader would have been overwhelmed with a lengthy concatenation of decisions and understood little about the underlying factors influencing policy making. What was required was to show the *importance* of these studies, for example, the respective influence of the Director of Education, the Chairman of the Education Committee, local politicians, central government, teachers' organisations and pressure groups.

Theories about the political process (e.g. Easton, 1965, Jennings, 1977) also needed to be recounted.

Where the conclusions of a piece of literature directly contradict any of the student's hypotheses, he/she can state in this section of the research report that the opposite view has been taken.

(e) **The Use of Quotations:** It is usually wise to avoid lengthy quotation from the sources discussed in a literature review. Quotations are best confined to major points or conclusions reached by a writer, for example:

> In their study of policy making in Gateshead Batley, O'Brien and Parris (1970, p. 73) conclude that "the role of the Director of Education ... was central".

Otherwise, a paraphrase is more suitable. Long quotations sometimes signal padding and insecurity.

(f) **Value Judgements on the Part of the Writer:** On occasions evaluative terminology can be employed in the review, for example:

> Gross (2004) in a helpful review of the problems experienced by fifteen exceptionally able pupils in mainstream schools in Australia ....

(g) T**he Use of a Synopsis:** Concluding the literature review with a brief synopsis of the main arguments and their relationship to the research being undertaking has the merit that it maintains an overall focus and helps the reader to understand the key points which have been established.

(h) **Checking Publication Dates:** The publication date of any literature reviewed should always be carefully checked. Educational policies change rapidly and problems may be experienced if information contained in some dated book is believed to be as valid now as when it was written under different political conditions many years ago. A dissertation on the role of school governors would quickly run into difficulties if it assumed that those clauses of the Education (No. 2) Act of 1986 which dealt with the constitution, duties and powers of governors were still in force today.

(i) **The Need for Comprehensive Reference:** Writers need to ensure that *all* the sources to which they make reference in their literature review appear in the bibliography at the end of the research report. Similarly, books and articles which are listed in the bibliography must appear in the body of the text. It is conventional today for the Harvard system of referencing to be employed in academic writing.

(j) **The Importance of Keeping Records:** Bell (1999) stresses the value of maintaining a record of every source which is consulted during the literature review. She advises researchers, as soon as they embark upon their programme of reading, to start a card index with the author's name, the date of publication, the title, the place of publication and the publisher. If this information is collected as the literature review is undertaken, the researcher has all the references to hand and does not have to spend time searching for details of publications when the final draft of the report is being written up.

V: RESEARCH METHODOLOGY

(a) **The Nature of Inquiry:** Cohen, Manion and Morrison (2000) state that there are three important approaches to educational inquiry:

(i) *The Positivist and Scientific Approach*, which is based upon the principles of such scholars as Auguste Comte (1798 – 1857) and John Dewey (1859- 1952). It stresses the formulation of hypotheses which are tested in action, and assumes that we learn from direct sense experience such as observation. Dewey's philosophy of Pragmatism has been depicted in the first chapter of this book. Whereas this approach manifestly fits empirical research, its critics have argued that it ignores *human nature*. It is too mechanistic, and does not address such aspects of human experience as creativity, the aesthetic dimension, freedom, choice and moral responsibility. The philosopher Ludwig Wittgenstein (1889-1951) once observed that, when all possible scientific questions have been addressed, they leave untouched the fundamental question of life.

(ii) *Naturalistic Approaches*, which assume that individuals have different perceptions and that reality can be understood only by sharing their viewpoints. Specific research paradigms of this type include approaches derived from the philosophy of *phenomenology* associated with such thinkers as Edmund Husserl (1859-1938) and Alfred Schutz (1899-1959), *ethnomethodology*, which is concerned with the ways people make sense of the everyday world, social episodes being analysed in terms of the outlook of the actors (Burrell and Morgan, 1979), and *social interaction*, which was initially postulated by G.H. Mead (1934) and developed by researchers like Erving Goffman (1969). The underlying assumption of this last group is that human beings act upon their own view of the world as determined by symbols of which language is an example. Hence, researchers in this school are interested in the symbols people use and the dynamics of interaction between them.

Much educational research is of the naturalistic type as it is concerned with the perceptions of people employed within the education service. Hence, questionnaires and interviews are popular research instruments. However, some critics have objected that studies of this type are insufficient to yield valid results (Bernstein, 1974). Social structures, it is argued, are external to the people who exist within them and are not shaped by their perceptions. Naturalists tend to ignore these structures.

(iii) *Critical Theory*: In contrast to the positivist and naturalistic paradigms, critical theory, which has emerged from the work of Jurgen Habermas, focuses upon political and ideological contexts. It is concerned with the issues of equality, repression, ideology, power, participation, representation, inclusion and interests. Unlike the other approaches it is prescriptive (Griffiths, 1998) and aims to promote social democracy. A typical researcher in the critical theory tradition seeks to:

- describe the situation with reference to people's interpretations of reality (What am I doing? What does it mean to me?);

- examine reasons for the situation, focusing upon interests and ideologies (How did I come to be like this?);

- construct a programme for initiating change which will result in a more egalitarian system;

■ implement and evaluate the achievements of the programme in practice.

Some opponents of critical theory have upbraided it for being too value-loaded. The researcher, they feel, ought to be objective and not assume the role of an ideologue.

(b) **Research Strategies:** The following are strategies frequently used by researchers in the field of educational studies:

(i) *Questionnaires*: These can be distributed to a group of people, for example, pupils, who complete them in the presence of the researcher. Respondents can put questions directly to him or her if they are unsure about any of the items in the questionnaire. Alternatively, questionnaires can be sent by post. The advantage is that they are quick to administer compared with interviews and can involve a larger sample. They allow a researcher to attain results from a wider catchment area than many other forms of investigation and they are particularly helpful in gaining factual information, for example, age profiles and experience of work. Above all, they can be useful in gauging opinions and attitudes.

On the other hand, they do not always present opportunities for the pursuit of matters in very much depth, and in the case of postal questionnaires it is not possible to deal with problems directly; if respondents do not understand a question, there is little that the researcher can do to help. Again, response rates can be poor. Sixty per cent is often seen as a very good outcome and forty per cent as satisfactory. Nor is there any guarantee that the people who return the questionnaire represent the target group at large. Often they tend to be people who have strong views on a matter and the halo or Hawthorne effect predominates. A further limitation is that researchers have no guarantee that honest answers are received, and, if a long period of time elapses between the receipt of a set of questionnaires and their analysis, there is the danger that the respondents will have changed their minds on an issue, especially where they have had the chance to read more widely about it or there has been publicity in the press.

Some guidelines on the construction and administration of questionnaires are offered below:

(1) PRINCIPLES OF PROCEDURE: The first consideration in designing a questionnaire is to ensure that it secures the information required. There is always the danger that novice researchers seek too much information and that much of it is irrelevant. Collecting information for its own sake is pointless. Hence, it is necessary to:

■ define the purpose of the investigation and any hypotheses involved;

■ decide the information required and the respective target group which can provide this information;

■ focus only upon what is absolutely vital to achieve the purpose of the investigation and to confirm or refute any hypotheses;

■ avoid wasting waste time by asking questions about information which is readily available elsewhere, for example, in a school prospectus or register.

(2) QUESTIONNAIRE DESIGN: Valuable advice for the design of questionnaires is to:

- keep the document as **brief** as possible. A lengthy questionnaire is not likely to encourage many people to respond, though questionnaires designed for graduates and those used to dealing with them may be longer. Shorter questionnaires are also easier to analyse.

- explain the **purpose** of the research. It is helpful to set out an introductory paragraph to the questionnaire or to send a covering letter. If the questionnaire is given by hand to a class, it is possible at that stage to state the aim of the project. Potential respondents are better motivated to co-operate if they understand the point of the research. In introductory paragraphs or covering letters it is sometimes advantageous to report that the questionnaire has been used in a pilot study and should take only a few minutes to complete. Another strategy is to invite answers only to those questions which respondents feel are applicable to their situation ("I appreciate that time is short, but I should be grateful if you could answer the questions which require the ticking of boxes. This should take only about three minutes of your time. Please disregard any questions which you feel are irrelevant.")

- set out clear **instructions**, for example, about ticking boxes, putting crosses in columns or underlining phrases.

- ensure that all questions are **relevant** to the purpose. They should seek the information needed and no more.

- check that all the language used is **unambiguous**. Questions like "Are you a boy or a girl?" are likely to receive facetious answers. Moreover, terms which can be misinterpreted are best avoided, for example, "often", "occasionally" and "seldom". One person's "seldom" may be another's "often". In this case it is better to use specific terms, such as "one week", "two weeks", "a month", etc. Similarly, "recently" needs to be pinpointed, for example, "in the last five years". In order to detect and remove ambiguous questions a pilot survey can be organised.

- select **vocabulary** which is suited to the cognitive level of the subjects involved in the survey. The language adopted in questionnaires for pupils will differ from that utilised in questionnaires for teachers. The latter may understand the meaning of terms such as "moderation", "formative assessment" and "criterion-referencing", but vocabulary of this nature will be unfamiliar to pupils and will require fuller explanation. Whatever the audience, it is wise to keep the questions as short as possible and to avoid long tedious sentences, especially those with several negatives in them.

- use a **variety** of questions, but, as far as possible, follow the principle that the questionnaire should be **easy to answer**. This means that it is important to use a good number of closed questions where respondents select an answer from a given list. Specific approaches are:

  - *PRECISE CATEGORY ANSWERS:* The following are examples of questions set in a survey concerned with the teaching of Personal and Social Education (PSE) in the curriculum in Wales:

- Does your school have a PSE co-ordinator?

YES ☐　　　NO ☐

- Is any part of the PSE curriculum negotiated with your pupils?

YES ☐　　　NO ☐

- Do you consider that the current Framework for PSE in Wales should be made statutory?

YES ☐　　　NO ☐

- TICKING BOXES: An example is given from research on collaborative teaching in ITET:

At what stage in your school experience did you become involve in collaborative teaching? Please tick the appropriate box(es):

During the first week	
During the second week	
During the third week	
Later than the third week	

- CIRCLING THE ANSWER THE RESPONDENT FAVOURS: Please circle the appropriate response to indicate the people with whom you have engaged in collaborative teaching:

mentor

class teacher

another student in the same year cohort as yourself

more than one student in the same year cohort as yourself

another student from a different year cohort

more than one student in a different year cohort.

- PUTTING A CROSS IN ONE OF A SERIES OF COLUMNS: This strategy is useful for ascertaining opinions, for example: Please indicate your views on the arrangements made at your school for each of the following items. Please put a cross in the appropriate box, using the scale 1 = highly satisfactory, 2 = satisfactory, 3 = unsatisfactory, 4 = highly unsatisfactory.

Item	1	2	3	4
a tour of the school				
provision of a staff/student handbook				
provision of a school policy on discipline				
provision of a school policy on the curriculum				
provision of a school policy on assessment				
an introduction to the management structure of the school				
an attachment to a form tutor				
provision of an opportunity to learn from the SENCO				
an attachment to staff outside your specialism to observe examples of good practice.				
an invitation to attend curriculum planning meetings				
provision of an opportunity to attend PSE lessons				

- *UNDERLINING A NUMBER*, for example: *How would you rate your subject mentor in relation to the following aspects of his/her role? Please underline the appropriate number: (1 = excellent, 2 = satisfactory, 3 = unsatisfactory, 4 = very poor).*

   providing you with departmental schemes of work   1   2   3   4

   providing you with a timetable which enabled you to experience a range of ages and abilities   1   2   3   4

   modelling good practice in their teaching   1   2   3   4

- ◼ ensure that any lists set out in questionnaires given are **exhaustive**. For instance, in a survey of children's reading strategies in the 1970s one researcher set the question:

Which method of teaching English do you use? Please circle the appropriate answer(s):

   phonics;

   colour scheme;

   initial teaching alphabet.

   This question poses several problems, since the category "phonics" covers a range of techniques (e.g. synthetic phonics, analytic phonics), and other valid answers (e.g. look and say) are excluded.

- ◼ offer opportunities for **longer responses**: Closed questions have the advantage that they are usually quick to answer and easy to analyse. They do, however, limit the respondent's choice, and it is often helpful to supplement them with open-ended questions which allow for further explanation and comment. In order to assure participants that the time taken to complete the questionnaire will not be inordinate, it is important to make it clear that these open-ended questions are not obligatory, for example:

Were you able to attend a formal review meeting with the senior mentor towards the end of your school experience to discuss your general progress?

YES ☐   NO ☐

If YES, did you find the comments you received in the review to be helpful?

YES ☐   NO ☐   NOT SURE ☐

If you would like to make any other comments on the role of the senior mentor (e.g. any additional courses of action which you feel should be taken by the senior mentor), please enter them below:

> Open-ended questions allow people to answer freely. They can be very valuable as they are sometimes the source of ideas which can be included in the final recommendations of a research report. Of course, they take longer to answer and can be harder to analyse, especially where the meaning is not clear.

■ avoid answering **leading questions**. The question *What advantages are there in changing from community to foundation status?* presupposes that respondents favour a political system whereby a school's governors employ the staff, own the site and buildings and control the admissions policy.

■ ask for only **one response** in each question. Two discrete questions should never be combined in one question. *Have you taught English and mathematics in the last two years?* needs to be expressed as two separate questions:

Have you taught ENGLISH in the last two years?

Have you taught MATHEMATICS in the last two years?

■ set questions **which respondents can reasonably be expected to answer**. It is unlikely that a subject teacher will have any immediate knowledge about details of the school's budget and it is pointless to ask such a question of this person. Again, in putting a question on some complex educational innovation the researcher cannot assume that the respondent will have a knowledge of the initiative. It is, therefore, necessary to provide an analysis of the issues at stake. For example, few teachers would be able to answer the following question without guidance:

Please indicate your views of the recommendations of the Tomlinson Report of 2004.

The researcher would need to spell out the issues on which an opinion was invited, for example, a framework of diplomas embracing all four levels from entry to advanced, a common structure of core learning and main learning, a grading system at three levels and changes proposed to the current modes of assessment. This would require a large number of highly structured questions.

■ exclude any questions which put participants **at a disadvantage**. If this is not the case, it is unlikely that many will reply. Similarly, personal questions involving such items as income can be controversial. Where such information is essential to a research project, helpful techniques include:

- giving a clear explanation why such a question is important to the research;

- offering an assurance of confidentiality;

- leaving such questions to the end of the questionnaire in the hope that the person will at least complete the earlier sections which will then increase the number of responses to those questions.

■ conclude the questionnaire by giving the subject the opportunity to add any **further comments** which he/she feels to be relevant. Thus, the final section may read: *If there are any further comments you would like to make about the issues raised in this questionnaire, please enter them below.*

■ insert at the end of the document some **statement of thanks**, for example, *Thank you for taking the time to answer this questionnaire.*

■ add a final column for **coding responses**:

How often do you attend the teachers' centre?	Please tick	Coding
Daily		(a)
Weekly		(b)
Other		(c)

(3) QUESTIONNAIRE TECHNIQUES: Useful techniques include:

■ MULTIPLE CHOICE QUESTIONS, for example: *Does this innovation offer*:

	Please tick
greater scope for the teaching of your subject?	
less scope for the teaching of your subject?	
about the same scope for the teaching of your subject?	

Such questions do not offer the opportunity for reasons to be given and can be supplemented with appropriate open questions.

- **CHECKLISTS**, where a person ticks those responses which apply to her/him, for example, a list of qualifications: BA; BSc; BEd; MEd; PhD.

- **CATEGORIES**, where a person is given a series of categories such as ages and is asked to indicate the one which is relevant: 20-29; 30-39; 40-49; 50-59.

- **RANKING**, where the subject is asked to place items in rank order, for example:

When you offer students debriefing on their teaching what are your aims? Please rate the following in order of priority (1 = most important, 10 = least important):

to have students imitate the teaching strategies demonstrated by teachers at your school	
to offer tips and guidelines on classroom practice	
to assess students' performance in relation to the standards for qualified teacher status	
to encourage students to review their progress in relation to the standards	
to encourage students to consider fundamental moral and ethical assumptions underlying their teaching	
to encourage students to modify their views about their teaching through reflection on experience	
to encourage students to reflect critically upon a range of educational issues beyond those relating purely to the classroom	
to encourage students to relate their classroom experience to principles and concepts which they have studied in relevant textbooks and research reports	
to relate students' thinking to issues covered during the college course	
to build students' confidence in their teaching ability	

- **RATING SCALES**, where a series of statements is printed and participants are requested to indicate their views on each. Examples of scales commonly used in questionnaires are:

  - **Likert Scales**, also known as summated ratings, where a list of statements is printed and the subject is asked to make a judgement on each, using a scale. In a six-point scale 1 will indicate "I strongly agree", 2 "I agree", 3 "I probably agree", 4 "I probably disagree", 5 "I disagree' and 6 'I strongly disagree'. The number of points in the scale can vary; where a "don't know" or "undecided" category is important to the research, an odd number of categories must be utilised. An example is given:

The term "reflective practitioner" is used in much literature concerned with initial teacher education and training. Please indicate on the 4-point scale your views on the following approaches to "reflective practice". (1= I consider this approach to be of considerable value, 2= I consider it to be of some value, 3 = I am unsure about the value of this item, 4 = I consider it to be of limited value, 5 = I consider it to be of very little value).

Item	1	2	3	4	5
Identifying problems in teaching, forming hypotheses to solve these problems and testing the hypotheses in action					
Considering moral and ethical issues underlying teaching					
Interpreting a situation, taking action in the light of that interpretation, reviewing the consequences of the action and reinterpreting the situation in the light of the review					
Being able to put into words thoughts about courses of action taken in the classroom					
Relating analysis of teaching experiences to the actions of qualified teachers					
Relating analysis of teaching experiences to theories derived from reflection on practice					
Relating analysis of teaching experiences to educational theories derived from reading					
Analysing teaching capability in relation to the standards for qualified teacher status					
Using data received from pupils to help analyse performance					
Thinking critically about all aspects of teaching and education					

- **Guttman Scales** where a short list of statements is given, usually six to eight, each offering a slightly different position on a scale of attitude. The respondent then marks that statement which most accurately expresses his or her opinion (1 = "I hate English"; 8 = "English is my favourite subject").

- **Thurstone Scales** where a larger number of statements – between twenty and twenty-five - is set out, each expressing some attitude to the topic under investigation. The statements are usually collected from a survey of literature together with others gathered in preliminary discussion with the type of subject who will be approached in the survey. For example, during research concerning the attitudes of undergraduates to teaching as a career, an initial meeting was organised with a sample of students to ascertain most of the commonly held attitudes and these were included in the questions. In a Thurstone scale the aim is to produce as comprehensive a series of statements as possible. Then, before the questionnaire is administered "judges" are appointed to sift through the statements and arrange them in nine groups representing shades of opinion ranging from extremely favourable to extremely hostile. Each statement is numbered and some twenty to twenty-five selected to cover all nine points of the scale. They are arranged in random order and respondents mark those with which they agree.

- **Paired Comparisons** where the subject is compelled to make a choice between pairs of statements, recording a vote in favour of one or the other. In a research project into attitudes towards study skills pupils were to choose one statement from a set of paired statements to indicate which was "more nearly true of them" :

1(a) *I don't care much about my marks.*

1(b) *I don't mind not having sport, if there is work to be done.*

■ *BRANCHING QUESTIONS*, which can save respondents much time:

Please tick the relevant box to indicate how Personal and Social Education (PSE) is organised in your school. More than one category may be relevant.

	Tick	
As discrete timetabled lessons		IF YES, PLEASE ANSWER QUESTIONS 2 AND 6-7
As part of a carousel, rotating with other subjects		IF YES, PLEASE ANSWER QUESTIONS 3 AND 6-7
Offered within a blocked timetable (e.g. a whole day or week devoted to PSE)		IF YES, PLEASE ANSWER QUESTIONS 4 AND 6-7
Integrated into a number of subject disciplines		IF YES, PLEASE ANSWER QUESTIONS 5 AND 6-7
As part of the tutorial programme within the school's system of pastoral care		IF YES, PLEASE ANSWER QUESTIONS 6-7

■ *GRIDS*, which allow two or more questions to be answered at the same time:

Since the age of eighteen how many years have you spent on the following? Ignore periods of less than one academic year:

Courses	1-2 years	3-4 years	5-6 years	More than 6 years
GCE O level or GCSE				
GCE A level				
Access/return to study course(s)				
No formal study				
Other (please specify)				

(4) CONDUCTING A SURVEY:

It is sound policy to conduct a pilot scheme to help eliminate problems of design, instructions which are not clear and difficulties created by the order of the items. Some researchers have argued that a pilot should consist of about ten per cent of the total sample.

The questionnaire should be organised in such a way that it is easy to analyse. This can be achieved by using numbers corresponding to the various answers and circling the appropriate number according to the subjects's response. The coding system illustrated in the earlier paragraph can be beneficial.

Where questionnaires are dispatched to schools, it is necessary first to secure the permission of the headteacher and other parties (See the comments under the heading of Research Ethics below). Accompanying letters should explain the aims of the research, its value and its importance. Some education authorities, if they approve the topic, are prepared to distribute questionnaires to local schools, which saves the researcher considerable expense. All letters should be well written, have a personal signature and, in most cases, promise anonymity. In order to help secure a satisfactory response rate, it is normal practice to set a date by which the completed questionnaire should be returned and to enclose a stamped addressed envelope.

In order to follow up any interesting replies for personal interviews or further, more detailed questionnaires it is advantageous to ask respondents to enter their names and to supply a contact telephone number or address. This also assists the researcher in the process of checking those institutions from which no reply has been received. Another strategy is to number questionnaires so that responses can be readily noted.

Attention should be paid to timing. Few teachers are likely to complete and return a lengthy questionnaire which arrives in the midst of the examination period. It is necessary to consider a time of the year when people working within the educational system are most likely to have the time to cope with a document of this type.

Where replies are slow to arrive, it is possible to send reminders. In some cases it may be desirable to send a second copy of the questionnaire "in case the first copy was lost in the post". If the response rate is low, steps that can be taken are:

- to try to contact people who were approached and who have not yet replied.

- to check if there is any significance between respondents and non-respondents, for example, age, locality, qualifications or role. Sometimes inferences for research can be drawn from non-responses. For example, the failure of many smaller firms to return a questionnaire focusing upon government initiatives in the field of new vocational qualifications may suggest that they have little knowledge of these developments.

- to contact a sample of those who have not answered and to try to ascertain their attitudes towards the topic. Possibly, telephone or personal interviews can be organised to supplement the information obtained by means of questionnaires.

If staff at schools or other organisations have expressed an interest in receiving a copy of the results, a summary of the findings should be sent to them as soon as possible.

(ii) *Interviews*: Unlike questionnaires, interviews involve the gathering of data face-to-face. They have the advantage that the researcher can go into far more detail than is true of questionnaires and put supplementary questions according to need. Some researchers have found that interviews can be especially useful in the early stages of research where they are seeking to clarify matters and to obtain a picture of the overall context.

Interviews allow the researcher to explain the purpose of the study more precisely than is possible with a postal questionnaire, to deviate from the planned interview schedule, and to ensure that the interviewee fully understands the meaning of every question. Moreover, if the interviewee tends to wander from the topic under investigation, it is a relatively simple matter to remind him or her of the aim of the research and to ensure that the requisite information is gleaned. Furthermore, data can often be attained which would be difficult to acquire by means of a postal questionnaire, for example, from children or people whose literary abilities are less impressive than their oral skills. Again, questions on the same events can be varied to cater for the perceptions of different role incumbents, for example, Education Officers, members of an Education Committee, headteachers and parents.

One restriction on the value of the interview as a research instrument is that it can be more time-consuming than sending out a postal questionnaire. Sometimes, it can lead to greater expenditure, especially where considerable distances are involved in travelling. Preparation is certainly time-consuming as each interview needs individual planning and the outcomes have to be recorded. Analysis of the content of a series of interviews can be complex. A further problem is that some people may be unwilling to be interviewed, particularly if they think that the research will involve controversial material.

There are several types of interview:

- those seeking information which is *factual* - what the subject *knows*;

- those concerned with *beliefs, attitudes and opinions* - what the subject *feels*;

- *standard/structured interviews* where the procedure to be followed is determined in advance of the interview. The same questions are given to each subject and there is no rephrasing or alteration of the questions. In this type of interview there will be a precise interview schedule with the same pattern, wording, instructions, alternatives and methods of recording and categorisation.

- *non-standardised interview* where procedure is decided beforehand but interviewers can deviate from it as the situation demands. Wording and order can be altered in the light of unexpected comments. This can be useful in studies dealing with issues where the perceptions of participants may differ considerably. In this type of research, however, the data obtained cannot always be easily compared.

Some guidelines on preparing and conducting interviews are offered:

(1) PREPARATION: As with questionnaires it is necessary to plan the objectives of the investigation very carefully, to decide the information needed to achieve these objectives and to identify the people who can most readily supply it. The next step is to draw up the requisite questions. Much of the advice

given above about the construction of questionnaires is equally valid in determining the format of an interview. It is, for example, essential to avoid including an excessive number of questions. Powney and Watts (1987, p. 145) warn against trying to collect too much data in the hope that this information will prove to be useful at some future date. It is best to ensure that the interview schedule focuses precisely upon the research aims, though it can, of course, allow respondents the opportunity to contribute other observations where appropriate. For many people an interview of an hour is quite sufficient. It is sometimes useful to rehearse an actual interview and to test the time it will take to put the questions.

The researcher next needs to write to the potential interviewee, stating the purposes of the research and giving an indication of the type of questions which will be put. Some people, especially in research of a controversial nature, may stipulate that they see the questions before they agree to grant an interview.

If the same interview is to be conducted with a number of subjects, organising a pilot with a sample from the respective group can be valuable. On the basis of the experience gained, the schedule can be redesigned, perhaps by the removal of ambiguities or the insertion of more prompts.

(2) INTERVIEWING TECHNIQUES:

- In order to secure the co-operation and trust of the interviewee a friendly manner is necessary. Sometimes a brief chat at the outset on another topic of general interest can help to "break the ice". The researcher must, of course, avoid appearing to be superior, patronising or aggressive.

- In most cases it is important to stress at the very beginning that confidentiality will be maintained.

- An interview will often commence with a statement of the context, for example, a short statement of the main events which form the focus of the questions or an outline of the topic. This is preferable to starting the interview "from cold".

- It is valuable to start with the questions which are concerned with relatively simple, factual issues so that rapport can gradually be built up. More intricate and controversial questions are better left until a later stage in the interview.

- The interviewer needs to show that he/she has thoroughly researched the area under investigation in terms of subject matter and review of the literature.

- Questions should be written in full. Many of the points pertinent to the construction of questionnaires will again be relevant, for example, avoiding technical jargon, ambiguities and biased questions.

- Whereas all important questions which were initially planned should be asked, there are in interviews opportunities for deviations, and it is often useful to put supplementary questions which add details and perhaps lead the researcher to conclusions which were not previously contemplated. These will be put according to his/her judgement in response to the comments offered by the interviewee.

- Prompting may be necessary in some cases; that is to say, the interviewer puts additional questions to guide the subject to the point under discussion or to clarify a response. For example, in a study of undergraduates' attitudes to teaching as a career the following dialogue took place:

Q: *What occupation do you intend to enter after you have graduated?*

A: *It depends on the type of degree I receive.*

Q: *Assuming that you receive the kind of degree you are expecting at the present.*

A: *Post-graduate study.*

Q: *What type of study do you have in mind?*

- The efficient interviewer is one who listens carefully rather than one who talks incessantly.

- Interviewers should avoid giving hints by facial expression or tone of voice about the type of answer they require.

- Care should be taken not to be distracted by irrelevancies. Some interviewees like to talk in a rambling, uncoordinated manner and it is necessary to bring them back to the point at hand. The researcher has to prevent a garrulous flow of information of dubious value, while at the same time remaining polite and tactful.

- At the end of an interview it can be helpful briefly to summarise to the interviewee the main points and the conclusions drawn. This gives the opportunity to correct any errors or misconceptions.

(3) STRATEGIES FOR RECORDING THE INFORMATION RECEIVED: The principal strategies are:

- **To take notes during the interview:** Notes can be written manually or be entered on a laptop word processor. This has the advantage that the information is recorded at the time it is provided. If anything is unclear it is possible immediately to ask supplementary questions. Where the transcript is rather unstructured, it is desirable to re-write it tidily in a simple "question and answer" format as soon as possible after the interview while the points are still relatively clear in the interviewer's mind. The act of redrafting a transcript also helps to consolidate understanding of the main issues. If anything requires further clarification, it is necessary to contact the interviewee by telephone or e-mail so that the matter can be resolved without delay.

  The main problem with this strategy is that writing during an interview may inhibit the fluency of the subject.

- **writing notes after the interview:** This helps to obviate the difficulties encountered when notes are taken during the interview but there is the drawback that the interviewer may only partially remember the comments received.

- **using a tape recorder:** This secures an accurate record with all the emotional character of the responses given. However, the presence of a tape recorder can be inhibitive and it is still essential that a transcript or at least a summary of the main conclusions be completed at a later stage. It is also necessary to ask the person concerned whether he or she has any objections to the use of a tape recorder.

(iii) *Classroom Research*: This can take many different forms. Two examples are given:

(1) OBSERVATION OF CLASSROOM PRACTICE: In research of this type the following stages are commonly adopted:

- *data collection and generation of categories or hypotheses*: The researcher collects the appropriate data, using a videotape recorder or some other method to gather information about the classroom activities which are taking place. (S)he then formulates ideas ("categories" or "hypotheses") about what is happening. In one project described by Hopkins (2002) a teacher used a camera to record her lessons with a class. She formed the hypothesis that she was too abrupt in her questioning technique and did not give pupils enough time to answer.

- *validation of the categories or hypotheses*: Some validation is sought for these hypotheses. In the study mentioned by Hopkins the teacher asked a colleague to watch her teach in order to corroborate or refute her hypothesis. In addition, she issued a questionnaire to certain pupils. This gave her three sources for validating her hypothesis that she was too abrupt with her questioning technique.

  Alternatively, the strategy of *saturation* can be employed, whereby the hypothesis generated from observation is tested repeatedly. On subsequent occasions it may be refined or discarded. Thus, in the case cited by Hopkins the teacher videotaped herself with several classes on different occasions and felt that her initial hypothesis was confirmed.

- *interpretation*: This involves fitting validated categories or hypotheses into a frame of reference to give them meaning. In other words, the findings are linked to formal theory, for example, principles of good practice derived from textbooks, the policies of the school or the teacher's own thoughts about what constitutes effective teaching. As Hopkins writes, "In doing this, the classroom teacher is creating meaning out of hitherto discrete observations and constructs" (p. 137).

- *action*: The research leads to planning within the school with a view to taking future action. This action can again be the subject of review and further research. The following matrix can be employed in planning research of this type:

ANALYSIS	Surveys	Questionnaires	Observations	Interviews	Documents
Data collection and generation of categories or hypotheses					
Validation of categories or hypotheses					
Interpretation by reference to theory, established practice or teacher judgement					
Action plan for development					

Other forms of classroom observation include the use of: tally systems; rating scales; timelines; frequency counts; logs; and studies which focus upon the activities of a specific group of pupils (Wragg, 1999).

(2) ACTION RESEARCH: The term "action research" has frequently been used in different contexts (Bryant, 1996; Hopkins, 2002; McNiff, Lomax and Whitehead, 2003). In one popular model the elements are:

- the identification of a problem;

- the establishment of objectives for resolving the problem;

- the planning of a suitable strategy to meet these objectives;

- the establishment of success criteria to determine the desired outcomes of the strategy;

- the implementation of the strategy;

- the testing of the strategy by matching the outcomes against the success criteria;

- deciding the extent to which the strategy has in fact solved the problem.

In action research analysis of the data collected centres around the question: *to what extent did the strategy adopted meet the objectives?* One way of reaching a decision on this question is to use the following chart:

Objectives	Strategies Employed	Success criteria (i.e. the desired outcomes)	Outcomes	Did the outcomes match the success criteria?
(i)				YES/NO
(ii)				YES/NO
If NO to the last column: • Why were the desired outcomes not achieved? • What action needs to be taken to achieve the desired outcomes in future research?				

(iv) *Other Forms of Research in the Field of Educational Studies* include: historical reports (Burns, 2000, pp. 481 - 490); case studies, for example, of the characteristics of a child, class or school (Freebody, 2003, pp. 80-84); surveys "to obtain information which can be analysed and patterns extracted and comparisons made" (Bell, 1999, p. 13); and statistical analyses (Horowitz, 1974).

(c) **Research Ethics:** Researchers have a commitment to advancing knowledge and understanding. They must not trick people, make false promises or use subjects merely as a means to an end. In conducting research they should at all times respect human dignity. Furthermore, they have a duty to undertake honest inquiry and rigorous analysis. Under no circumstances should there be deliberate falsification of results. Specific ethical principles include:

(i) *securing permission for the research to be carried out*: As was noted in the section concerning questionnaires, it is necessary to approach the headteacher of any schools involved in research and possibly to secure the permission of the local authority. Where children are involved, the consent of parents or guardians must be sought.

(ii) *respect for justice and inclusiveness, fairness and equity*: The benefits of the research should be evenly distributed, and no segment of a school or class should be unfairly burdened. It is wrong for researchers to approach the same people on a regular basis just because they have co-operated in earlier projects.

(iii) *respecting people's right not to participate in the research*: Individuals who are asked to take part in planned research have the right to terminate proceedings at any time. Whereas this right can easily be exercised by those completing postal questionnaires, it is more difficult for a "captive" group in a classroom. In certain contexts covert observation need not necessarily be objectionable. For example, it can be used to conduct a frequency count in the case of playground behaviour and those who are unaware of the nature of the research will act more naturally. On the whole, however, deception is seldom warranted.

(iv) *making contract with research subjects*: Where venues, timetables and specific research strategies have been agreed, researchers must adhere to them and not cause participants unnecessary inconvenience.

(v) *respect for privacy and confidentiality*: It is important to protect the dissemination of personal information. Participants in research have the right to decide which aspects of their lives they wish to disclose to others. Confidentiality and anonymity need at all times to be respected. Unless there are good reasons why people should be named –when, for example, their names appear in public records - the final draft of a research report should make it difficult for the reader to deduce their identity.

(vi) *respect for vulnerable persons*: Care must be taken where research involves those whose diminished competence and/or decision-making capacity make them vulnerable, for example, children with special educational needs or those who are entitled to specific protection against abuse, exploitation or discrimination. Consideration must be given to procedures which protect their interests. The researcher, like the teacher, is in a position of authority and trust.

(vii) *the law*: Laws governing privacy, confidentiality, intellectual property and discrimination must be observed when planning and conducting educational research.

(viii) *keeping respondents informed*: Subjects should be aware of the motives of the researcher and the purposes of the research. They should be given a summary of the results if this has been promised and be permitted to see the records of any interviews in which they have participated.

(ix) *making findings public*: Burns (2000, p. 21) argues that educational researchers should be open with their results and allow disinterested colleagues to examine and criticise the outcomes of their work. As he rightly comments, no-one wishes to see politicians rushing off to create new policies before research conclusions have been verified and replicated by other competent members of the academic community.

McNiff, Lomax and Whithead (2003, pp. 54-57) suggest that, when researchers contact any possible participants, they include within their letter an *ethics statement*, for example, "This statement is to assure you that I will observe agreed ethical practice throughout the research".

(d) **Validity, Triangulation And Reliability:**

(i) *Validity*: The term "validity" is used to indicate that a particular research instrument does in fact measure what it purports to measure. In *quantitative* research, concerned with "definable and quantifiable social facts" (Burns, 2000, p. 11), it may be achieved through careful sampling, the application of suitable methodology and appropriate statistical treatment. In *qualitative* research, where there is greater emphasis upon the subjective experience of individuals, it may be achieved through the depth and scope of data, lack of bias and triangulation which is described in paragraph (ii) below. Types of validity listed by Cohen, Manion and Morrison (2000) include:

(1) INTERNAL validity where conclusions are supported by the data.

(2) EXTERNAL validity or the degree to which the findings can be generalised with respect to the wider population.

(3) CONTENT validity: The research relates to the areas which were established in the original statement of aims.

(4) CONSTRUCT validity, where the conclusions reached correlate with generally accepted findings in other research literature.

(5) ECOLOGICAL validity: The portrayal of social situations is accurate. Activities identified by the researcher do actually take place in an educational setting.

(6) CATALYTIC validity: The research leads to change in educational practice. This is important in the context of research conducted in accordance with the tenets of critical theorists.

(7) CRITERION-RELATED validity: The data obtained in the first round of a research project correlate with data collected at a later stage.

(ii) *Triangulation*: This refers to two or more methods of collecting data within the same research project. It is derived from a metaphor used in the military and in surveying whereby three points are used to identify a precise location. In research concerned with human behaviour it may involve using both quantitative and qualitative data. Examples are:

(1) METHODOLOGICAL triangulation, where the same method is employed on several occasions with different subjects;

(2) INVESTIGATOR triangulation, where more than one observer is used;

(3) TIME triangulation where the same research is conducted at different times;

(4) CROSS-CULTURAL triangulation, where, for example, a specific teaching strategy is implemented in schools in Europe, North America and Africa and its outcomes are assessed;

(5) THEORETICAL triangulation, which draws on more than one educational theory.

(iii) *Reliability*: The term "reliability" implies that, if the research were carried out on further groups of comparable subjects by another competent researcher, then similar results would be obtained. In quantitative research this involves the concepts of:

(1) STABILITY: A reliable research instrument yields similar data from similar respondents over time. The analogy is drawn with a leaking tap which always loses one litre of water a day.

(2) EQUIVALENCE: If a different but equivalent type of research instrument were to be adopted, it would produce similar results. Alternatively, if several people conducted the research, they would all arrive at much the same conclusions.

(3) INTERNAL CONSISTENCY: For example, test items are divided into halves and each half is marked separately. The results are then compared to check consistency.

Reliability in qualitative research is a little harder to achieve than in quantitative research. As Oppenheim (1992) comments "the problem of validity remains one of the most difficult in social research and one to which an adequate solution is not yet in sight" (p. 78). The usual strategies are:

(1) STABILITY OF OBSERVATIONS: The same conclusions would be drawn if observations were conducted at different times.

(2) PARALLEL FORMS: The researcher would have interpreted observations in the same manner if attention had been paid to other phenomena during the period of observation.

(3) INTER-RATER RELIABILITY: Another competent researcher observing the phenomena would reach the same conclusions.

(iv) *Validity and Reliability in Questionnaires*: Commons strategies of securing validity are to supplement the data obtained in questionnaires with information acquired in interviews and to plan the sample so that the people selected are those who are most likely to yield the information required. Validity can sometimes be checked by comparing results against external criteria, for example, examination results collated nationally or census figures.

One way of ensuring reliability in the case of specific events is to ask the same question in different ways. For example, a question about attendance at in-service courses may be followed by another question at a later stage about the number of times a person has attended any such courses. This can also be utilised in research designed to ascertain attitudes, though in these cases it is more difficult to assess reliability. Again, it is possible to put questions to test the extent to which people are telling the truth, guessing or answering carelessly. In a questionnaire concentrating on the views of employers about vocational qualifications, subjects were asked: *Do you understand the operation of the GNVQ system?* Later on questions were added to test their knowledge, as they were required to explain the meaning of concepts associated with this qualification (e.g. "verification"). Another form of checking is the split ballot where the respondents are divided into two or more equivalent sub-samples and each is given a questionnaire with slightly different wording. The average of the responses given by the groups is then used by the researcher.

(v) *Reliability And Validity In Interviews*: Since interviewees can provide incorrect and biased information, the researcher needs to contemplate validity of the type discussed by Cohen, Manion and Morrison; he/she has to check that the outcomes of the interview correlate with other proven valid measures. Avoiding leading comments, having a highly structured interview schedule with the same wording for all participants and employing closed questions also increase validity and reliability, though, as has been argued above, open-ended questions do allow researchers to explore respondents' perceptions in some depth. In all types of interview there is the need to guard against "the problem of power" whereby the interviewee says what (s)he thinks the researcher wants to hear. Having two or more interviewers can be helpful in this respect. Attention also needs to be paid to the conduct of interviews involving children, particularly strategies for gaining their trust, overcoming reticence on their part, finding the appropriate level of vocabulary and keeping their comments to the point. Finally, it is always valuable to undertake a pilot survey to test an interview schedule. In this way difficulties can be eliminated before the full research initiative is launched.

(vi) *Validity And Reliability In Observations*: Issues of which students need to be aware when they use observations as their principal research instrument are: first, that they not always aware of events which have taken place in the classroom before their arrival; second, that the information they obtain may not be representative of the normal situation; and, third, that their presence may cause different behaviour patterns in the subjects being observed. There is always the additional danger that they become too attached to the group forming the research sample with the consequence that objectivity is lost. Once again, the organisation of a pilot study can help safeguard against some of these shortcomings.

VI: ANALYSING THE RESEARCH DATA

(a) **Collection Of Data:** As has been shown, common means of collecting data include questionnaires, interviews and classroom research. Some surveys may involve the collection of statistics, for example, test scores and examination results. The information gathered from these sources needs to be collated so that all the results can be analysed in such a way that the researcher is able to make clear to the reader the significance of the findings. This process of analysis is essential because key issues rarely "jump out" at the researcher. It is also vital, as Bell (1999, p. 172) warns, to avoid the problem of making sweeping generalisations which the data do not warrant. Some procedures for the analysis of information acquired from the research methods described in this chapter are suggested below.

(b) **Questionnaires:**

(i) *Analysing Questionnaires*: The mode of analysis depends upon the format of the questions which have been set. Examples of the most common types of question are:

1. CLOSED QUESTIONS: Where closed questions are asked and no further opportunity is available to offer comments, the researcher needs to construct a summary sheet for the responses. S(h)e then marks off the number of replies received in each category of answer, for example:

after *every* lesson	
after the *majority* of lessons	
after only a *minority* of lessons	
after *no* lessons	

In this example it is easiest to arrange the questionnaires into four piles, each containing the responses to one of the four categories. The number of questionnaires in each pile is then counted and the results entered onto the sheet. It may be necessary to add a fifth category headed: No Response (N/R).

Every lesson	Majority	Minority	No lessons	N/R
25	35	12	9	1

These findings can be represented in the final report as simple percentages calculated to represent either the total sample or the number actually replying to each question. Different ways of presenting these results are discussed in paragraph (ii) below.

2. RATING SCALES: These can be analysed in various ways. The main principle is to allocate the highest scores to positive statements and the lowest scores to negative statements. The totals for each statement are then calculated and they are arranged in rank order. For example, where a 5 point Likert scale is used, (e.g. 1 = "very true of me", 2 = "partly true of me", 3= "cannot say", 4 = "partly true of me", 5 = "very untrue of me") and the statement is *positive*, 1 may be valued at 5 points, 2 at 4 points, 3 at 3 points, 4 at 2 points and 5 at 1 point. Thus, in a study designed to ascertain a respondent's academic motivation the first statement "I feel ashamed when I get a poor mark" would be valued at 5. For *negative* statements (e.g. "I think homework is a bore") the scoring would be reversed (1 would score a rating of 1).

3. OPEN-ENDED QUESTIONS: These replies are more difficult to analyse than closed questions

because of the variety of answers which can be received and their possible length. A good example of a question which produced thirty-six different responses is: What does SPIRITUALITY mean to you? Approaches which can be used to analyse multifarious responses are:

- *to list all comments in order of priority*. For example, in one research project the aim was to ascertain the view of school mentors concerning the standards for qualified teacher status which student teachers are expected to reach. Many different views were received, and so in collating the responses the researcher began with the most positive comments, then listed those which indicated general satisfaction with the standards but expressed some doubts about their value and finally recorded those which were most hostile. Examples of these comments are:

POSITIVE COMMENTS:

"It is important that students are aware of the standards and that procedures are in place to try to ensure that these standards are met."

"Concrete requirements ensure that common goals are specified and greater consistency achieved."

"These standards are valuable not only for students, but for experienced teachers as well."

COMMENTS WHICH ARE FAVOURABLE BUT WHICH EXPRESS SOME RESERVATIONS:

"The standards are important, but I do not feel that they should be used at the very beginning of students' school experience. Students need to gain confidence. Then they should concentrate on improving their skills and comparing them with the standards."

"The idea is good, but we also need training in assessing students according to the standards."

COMMENTS EXPRESSING MANY RESERVATIONS:

"We have found that some of our students lack good English, especially spelling. Our most recent student, who was otherwise excellent, has peppered exercise books with the words 'Please complet this !' The standards do not really provide for this problem."

"The standards result in too much bureaucracy and complex form filling."

This system makes easier the task of calculating the numbers of respondents in favour of or opposed to some proposition.

- *to note the most common replies and to give each a number*. Thus, we may allocate 1 to all those who strongly favour the system of the standards, 2 to those who generally favour them but have some reservations, 3 to those who disagree with them but see some advantages and 4 to those who are totally opposed to the whole concept of competence-based training. Then the number of responses received for each can be calculated and the results set out in a table. This was the best procedure for dealing with the question on the meaning of spirituality, where answers were coded in terms of respondents who defined "spirituality" as a set of underlying principles derived from:

a = religion;

b = personal philosophy;

c = moral principles and values;

d = relationships with other people.

Each response was then appropriately coded and the numbers in each of the four categories counted.

(ii) *Interpreting the Findings*: In some studies it may be advantageous for researchers to report the results obtained in reply to each question in the order set in the questionnaire. However, there is the danger that the findings are presented in a *descriptive* rather than an *analytic* manner. They are set out in a mechanistic fashion in which the researcher merely reports the outcomes of each question ("Ninety per cent of teachers agreed that Personal and Social Education was a valuable subject in the curriculum and ten per didn't.") In these cases it is difficult for the reader to identify the fundamental issues and the report is boring to read. It is far preferable to start with the findings which are most important for that study. How does a researcher decide? The following guidelines may be helpful:

(1) What were the original *aims* of the study? In many instances it is beneficial to report the findings of the research in such a way that they match the aims:

> *The aims of this study were to ascertain the standards for qualified teacher status in which a sample of ITET students were strong and those in which they needed more help. The survey specifically asked students for their views on the ability of their mentors in helping them cope with the standards concerned with assessing pupils' achievements.*

In this example, the aims determined the order in which the findings were reported, and this differed from the order of the actual questions put to mentors and students.

(2) Was there a *hypothesis*? If so, this can be reiterated in the section of the research report which sets out the main findings. The results can be used to show whether or not the hypothesis was confirmed:

> *The hypothesis of this study was that most teachers in South-East Wales would welcome the framework on Personal and Social Education issued by ACCAC, the advisory body on the curriculum to the Welsh Assembly Government.*

Irrespective of the order of questions in the research instrument, it is necessary to state at the outset whether or not the hypothesis has been confirmed. A possible order for setting out the results of a survey into the views of teachers concerning the framework for Personal and Social Education is:

- the fact that the hypothesis was confirmed;
- the percentage of teachers in the total sample agreeing with the proposition;
- the reasons why teachers welcomed the ACCAC framework;
- the percentage of teachers who did not agree with the proposition;
- their reasons for not welcoming the framework.

(3) Sometimes it is useful for a researcher to ask him/herself the question: "If someone enquired what the main findings of this survey were, how would I reply?" The answer to this question can be employed

as the starting point for reporting the results. In one survey students on an ITET course were asked about the quality of the mentoring they received in schools. It was apparent that the subject mentors were seen to be highly efficient, but students expressed some concerns about the role of their senior mentors. In many schools they failed to offer a weekly seminar on a whole school policy, to act as quality control agents with respect to subject mentors' judgements, or to provide summative feedback to students. Although these issues related to questions which were posed at different points in the student questionnaire, when the results were analysed, the problems reported with the senior mentor role were so prominent that they needed to be discussed at an early stage of the section of the report which was concerned with the interpretation of data.

(4) Once the order of the findings has been established, the main points need to be illustrated and interpreted by drawing upon the responses received from the various sections of the questionnaire. In the survey cited above, reasons could be found, often in reply to open ended questions, which helped to explain why senior mentors were deemed by students to be less effective than subject mentors. Factors included their workload and responsibilities as members of the senior management team, the lack of time available to them for the organisation of tutorials with students and the inadequacy of funding within the system of school-based initial teacher training and education. All these points needed to be brought together in order to present a coherent, structured account of the results of the survey, irrespective of their location within the questionnaire.

(5) One final issue for consideration concerns the light which the results shed upon general thinking about the topic selected for the research, for example, their significance for arguments and conclusions mentioned in the literature review. In constructing the questionnaire about the meaning of "spirituality" the researchers examined views on the meaning of the concept in current literature. The replies received from respondents - students and qualified teachers – indicated that they believed "spirituality" to consist of a set of principles for guiding a person through life and that these principles were usually derived from religion, a personal philosophy, moral principles and values, or relationships with other people. In reporting the findings, they therefore showed how these results related to the work of other researchers in this field. For example, the conclusion that a person could be spiritual without being religious correlated with the arguments put by Hay (1990) and Hay and Nye (1998) but contradicted the outcomes of a small-scale study by Watson (2001).

(iii) *Mode of Presentation*: Results can be presented in percentage form in the text or illustrated graphically. There is no one correct form. In deciding which mode of presentation to use the researcher's main consideration should be to adopt that format which best illustrates the findings. Examples are:

- TABLES, which can be used to report most of the results obtained in questionnaires;

- BAR CHARTS and HISTOGRAMS, which are often employed to illustrate the outcomes of rating scales;

- PIE CHARTS, which are helpful in illustrating the *proportion* of respondents who fall into various categories;

- GRAPHS, which can chart results along two axes for example, the relationship between students' coursework and examination results;

- SCATTERGRAMS, where the data are random with no discernible pattern.

For other examples of presentational modes the reader is referred to the twelfth chapter of *Doing Your Research Project* (Bell, 1999).

(c) **Interviews:**

(i) *Clarity of Purpose*: In analysing interview responses data need to be elicited which answer the questions forming the basis of the research. These findings should be presented in ways which clearly indicate the most important features, relationships and patterns.

(ii) *Content Analysis*: This is the process of sifting through transcripts to list common themes or patterns of belief. It is helpful at an early stage to look for emerging issues and to organise responses into specific categories on a chart. Anne Edwards (1990) gives an example of categorising interview data in research into people's capacity for planning:

NAME	Planning	Use of Time	Future Ambitions	Support from Others	View of Current Employment
Fred J.	"I need to know what I'm doing. I always plan."				
Pete M.					
Etc.					

All the information gathered from each interview is entered onto this sheet under the respective categories.

(iii) *Use of Coding Criteria*: The researcher can save time by establishing coding criteria. In the above example, under the heading of "planning" it is possible to utilise codes for the different responses received:

plans a lot = 1;

plans a little = 2, *etc.*

This information is then entered onto a sheet such as the one shown below or into a computer programme:

Respondent identification number	Planning	Use of Time	Future Ambitions	Support from Others	View of Current Employment
33	1	1	2	3	3
34	2	3	2	1	3

(iv) *Use of Summaries*: With interviews there is the danger that the researcher is overloaded with information and fails to see the wood for the trees. One useful technique for resolving this problem is to write a short summary of each interview with reference to the principal themes or aims of the research. In the project focusing upon decision making within a local authority the researcher conducted seventy interviews, including local authority officers, councillors and headteachers. A one-page summary of each transcript with respondents' comments on the respective roles played by the people involved in the policy making process was found to be extremely valuable:

Interview with . . . .

ROLE:	KEY POINTS:
central government	
local political parties/ councillors	
the Chief Education Officer	
teachers' organisation	
parents' groups	
other interest groups	

(v) *Writing up the Outcomes*: The outcomes should be reported in as "reader friendly" a manner as possible. To identify references and quotations from interviewees which may appear in the final draft, it is advantageous to employ coloured text highlighter pens when analysing transcripts. Where appropriate, tables, graphs and diagrams can be inserted along the lines suggested for reporting the results of questionnaires. Lengthy extracts from interviews or whole interview transcripts are best set out as separate appendices to which reference is made in the text.

(d) **Statistical Analysis:** There are various processes available for analysing statistical data within quantitative research. Examples are:

(i) *Arithmetic Mean*: The mean is the average and is found by adding together each item and dividing the total by the number of items. If we take the example of an age profile of a sample of teachers and there are ten respondents whose ages are: 25, 26, 27, 28, 29, 30, 31, 32, 33 and 34, then the total is 295. Divided by the number of items (ten), the mean is 29.5.

(ii) *Median* (or mid point). To find the median the researcher puts the items in order of size (*rank order*). Where there is an odd number of items, the median is the middle item. Where there is an even number, it is the average of the two middle numbers. For example, if the ages were 21, 22, 29, 30, 30, 33, 33, 33, 36 and 40, then the median would be the average of 30 and 33 which is 31.5.

(iii) *Standard Deviation* refers to the degree to which items differ from the mean. It is used where a researcher wishes to show by how much scores are spread out. It is found by taking the square root of the sum of the square of the deviation of each score from the mean divided by the number of items.

(iv) *Chi-squared Tests* are used to chart the differences between statistically expected scores and actual scores.

(v) *The Spearman Rank Order Correlation* is a statistic to measure the degree of association between two ordinal variables. It can, for instance, be used to decide whether the results from one rating scale correlate with the results from another.

(vi) *The Mann-Whitney U-Test* measures any significant difference between two independent samples, for example, whether there is a significant difference in the results of a rating scale for two independent samples - males and females.

(vii) *Kruskal-Wallis Analysis* is a method of determining any significant differences between three or more independent samples.

(viii) *Statistical Package for Social Sciences* (*SPSS*): This is a set of related computer programmes for storing, analysing and reporting statistical results.

VII: DRAWING CONCLUSIONS AND MAKING RECOMMENDATIONS:

Usually, the concluding section of a research study makes reference to:

(a) **An Overall Evaluation of the Research Initiative:** An evaluation is offered of the way in which the chosen methodology was actually implemented. This could include any changes which were made in the light of experience, any problems which were encountered and issues of reliability and validity.

(b) **The Principal Conclusions Emanating from the Survey:** A summary of the main points needs to be presented. Conclusions should be justified from the evidence of the research findings and must not go beyond it.

(c) **The Light which the Findings Shed on the Initial Aims of the Study:** It is important to relate the findings to the aims which were outlined in the research statement. **None** of the aims listed at the outset should be ignored in the discussion of the results and the overall conclusions. Similarly, if some hypothesis were discussed at the commencement of the survey, the reader needs to be informed whether or not it was confirmed. There is sometimes the danger that inexperienced researchers set aims at the outset which are not always developed as the research proceeds and are forgotten when the results are recorded. For example, one student proposed to examine the views of teachers concerning an educational innovation introduced by central government. Within a long sequence of aims she resolved to investigate whether younger teachers would welcome this initiative whereas the older generation would resent the changes it imposed. Yet, when the research was completed, although many of the key areas were addressed, no further mention was made of the perceptions of teachers of different age ranges.

(d) **Any Implications of the Outcomes of the Research**, for example, theoretical models which can be applied in other situations and the relationship of the findings to themes raised in the literature review.

(e) **Recommendations for Future Policy**, for example, changes which should be made to current practice in the light of the results of the research. Unless the research design warrants it, the recommendations should avoid being too dogmatic in putting forward policies for change.

(f) **Suggestions for Future Research and Study Emanating from the Conclusions.**

Bibliography

ABBOTT L. (2002) *Birth to Three Matters: A Framework to Support Children in their Earliest Years*, DFES

ABRAMS F. (2005) No Bog Standard Solution, *Times Educational Supplement (TES)*, 8 July

ACCAC (AWDURDOD CYMWYSTERAU CWRICWLWM AC ASESU CYMRU) (2000a) *English in the National Curriculum in Wales*, ACCAC

ACCAC (2000b) *Framework for Personal and Social Education*, ACCAC

ACCAC (2004) *The Foundation Phase in Wales: A Draft Framework for Children's Learning*, ACCAC

ACCAC (2005) *Foundation Phase Guidance Material*, ACCAC

ADAMS H. & WALLACE B. (1991) TASC: A Model for Curriculum Development, *Gifted Education International*, 7/3

AITCHISON J. (2003) *Teach Yourself Linguistics*, Hodder Education

ALEXANDER H. & McLAUGHLIN T. (2002) Education in Religion and Spirituality, in: BLAKE N., STANDISH P. & SMEYERS P., *The Blackwell Guide to the Philosophy of Education*, Blackwell

ALEXANDER W. (1954) *Education in England: The National System and How it Works*, Newnes

ALVES C. (1991) Just a Matter of Words? The Religious Education Debate in the House of Lords, *British Journal of Religious Education*, 13/3

ANDERSON P. (1998) *The Origins of Post-Modernity*, Verso

ANDREWS R. (2006) The Effect of Grammar Teaching on Writing Development, *British Educational Research Journal*, 32/1

ANTIDOTE (2003) *The Emotional Literacy Handbook*, David Fulton

ARENDS R. (1998) *Learning to Teach*, McGraw-Hill

ARISTOTLE (1953) *The Ethics*, Penguin

ARISTOTLE (1962) *The Politics*, Penguin

ARNOLD M. (1978) *Culture and Anarchy*, Cambridge University Press

ASSESSMENT REFORM GROUP (2002a) *Assessment for Learning: Ten Principles: Research-based Principles to Guide Classroom Practice*, Assessment Reform Group and Nuffield Foundation

ASSESSMENT REFORM GROUP (2002b) *Testing, Motivation and Learning*, Assessment Reform Group and Nuffield Foundation

AYER A. (1971) But This is to Misconceive the Problem, in: FLEW A. *Body, Mind and Death*, Macmillan

BAILEY C. (1984) *Beyond the Present and the Particular*, Routledge and Kegan Paul

BAILY E. (2002) Introduction, *Implicit Religion*, 5/2

BAINBRIDGE B. (2005) *The Front Row: Evenings at the Theatre*, Continuum

BALL C. (1994) *Start Right: The Importance of Early Learning*, Royal Society of Arts

BAKER K, (1993) *The Turbulent Years*, Faber and Faber

BAKHTIN M. (1981) *The Dialogic Imagination: Four Essays*, University of Texas Press

BAKHTIN M. (1986) *Speech Genres and Other Late Essays*, University of Texas Press

BANTOCK G. (1971) Discovery Methods, in: COX B. and DYSON A. *The Black Papers on Education*, Davis-Poynter

BANTOCK G. (1980) *Studies in the History of Educational Theory: Artifice and Nature*, Allen and Unwin

BARNARD N. & DEAN C. (2001) Poised to Unite for Workload Crusade, *TES*, 20 April

BARNEKOW RASMUSSEN V. & RIVETT D. (2000) The European Network of Health Promoting Education and Democracy, *Health Education*, 100/2

BARTHOLOMEW L. & KENNEDY C. (2006) Look At Me, *Nursery World*, 6 April.

BARTLETT S., BURTON D. & PEIM N. (2001) *Introduction to Education Studies*, Paul Chapman

BARTON J., BEECHER T., CANNING T., ERAUT E. & KNIGHT J. (1980) Accountability and Education, in: BUSH T., GLATTER R., GOODEY J. and RICHES C. *Approaches to School Management*, Harper and Row

BASTIDE D. (1992) *Good Practice in Primary Religious Education 4-11*, Falmer

BATLEY R., O'BRIEN O. & PARRIS H. (1970) *Going Comprehensive*, Routledge and Kegan Paul

BAYLES E. (1966) *Pragmatism and Education*, Harper and Row

BEARD R (1998) *National Literacy Strategy: Review of Research and Other Related Evidence*, DFEE

BEAUDOIN T. (1998) *Virtual Faith: The Irreverent Spiritual Quest of Generation X*, Sage

BECK J. (1999) Spiritual and Moral Development and Religious Education, in: THATCHER A. *Spirituality and the Curriculum*, Cassell

BEECHER T. & MACLURE S. (1978) *Accountability in Education*, NFER

BELL J. (1999) *Doing Your Research Project*, Open University Press

BERNSTEIN B. (1971) *Class, Codes and Control*, Routledge and Kegan Paul

BERNSTEIN B. (1974) Sociology and the Sociology of Education: A Brief Account, in: REX J. *Approaches to Sociology: An Introduction to Major Trends in British Sociology*, Routledge and Kegan Paul

BEST R. (1996) *Education, Spirituality and the Whole Child*, Cassell

BEST R. (2000) *Education for Spiritual, Moral, Social and Cultural Development*, Continuum

BIBBY R. (2002) *Restless Gods: The Renaissance of Religion in Canada*, Stoddart

BIBER D. (1988) *Variation Across Speech and Writing*, Cambridge University Press

BLACK P., HARRISON C., LEE C., MARSHALL B. & WILIAM D. (2003) *Assessment for Learning: Putting it into Practice*, Open University Press

BLACK P. & WILIAM D. (1998) *Inside the Black Box: Raising Standards through Classroom Assessment*, King's College London School of Education

BLOOMFIELD L. (1933) *Language*, Holt, Rinehart and Winston

BLUNKETT D. (2001) *Respect for All*, Commission for Racial Equality

BOTTERY M. & WRIGHT N. (2000) *Teachers and the State: Towards A Divided Profession*, Routledge

BOUD D. (2000) Sustainable Assessment; Rethinking Assessment for the Learning Society, *Studies in Continuing Education*, 22/2

BOWKER J, (1995) *Sense of God*, Oneworld

BOWLBY J. (1951), *Maternal Care and Mental Health*, World Health Organisation

BOWNESS C. & CARTER M. (1999) Bread Not Stones – Nurturing Spirituality, in: THATCHER A. *Spirituality and the Curriculum*, Cassell

BOYSON R. (1975) *The Crisis in Education*, Woburn Press

BRADFORD J. (1995) *Caring for the Whole Child: A Holistic Approach to Spirituality*, The Children's Society

BRITISH BROADCASTING COPERATION (BBC) (2000) *The Soul of Britain*

BROOKS J. & BROOKS M. (1993) *In Search of Understanding: The Case for Constructivist Classrooms*, Association for Supervision and Curriculum Development

BROWN A. (1997) Teaching Not Just Facts, but Values, *Church Times*, 3 October

BRYANT I. (1996) Action Research and Reflective Practice, in: SCOTT D. & USHER R. *Understanding Educational Research*, Routledge

BUCKLEY M. (1987) *At the Origins of Modern Atheism*, Yale University Press

BULLOCK A. & TROMBLEY S. (1999) *The New Fontana Dictionary of Modern Thought*, Harper Collins

BURNS R. (2000) *Introduction to Research Methods*, Sage

BURRELL G. & MORGAN C. (1979) *Sociological Paradigms and Organisational Analysis*, Heinemann

BUZAN T. (2000) *Use Your Head*, BBC Worldwide Ltd.

BUZAN T. (2003) *Brain Child: How Smart Parents Make Smart Kids*, Thorsons

CARR D. (1994) Knowledge and Truth in Religious Education, *Journal of Philosophy of Education*, 28/2

CARR D. (1995) Towards a Distinctive Conception of Spiritual Education, *Oxford Review of Education*, 21/1

CARR D. (1996) Rival Conceptions of Spiritual Education, *Journal of Philosophy of Education*, 30/2

CARR D. & HALDANE J. (2003) *Spirituality, Philosophy and Education*, Routledge Falmer

CARR M. & CLAXTON G. (2002) Tracking the Development of Learning Dispositions, *Assessment in Education Journal*, 9/1

CARR W. & HARTNETT A. (1996) *Education and the Struggle for Democracy: Politics of Educational Ideas*, Open University Press

CARSON D. (1996) *The Gagging of God: Christianity Confronts Pluralism*, Apollos

CARTER R. (1992) *Knowledge About Language in the Curriculum: The LINC Reader*, Hodder and Stoughton

CASSELLS J. (2003) Central Control Damages Teaching, *TES*, 12 December

CENTRAL ADVISORY COUNCIL FOR EDUCATION (ENGLAND) (1954) *Early Leaving*, (the Gurney-Dixon Report), HMSO

CENTRAL ADVISORY COUNCIL FOR EDUCATION (ENGLAND) (1959) *Fifteen to Nineteen*, (the Crowther Report), HMSO

CENTRAL ADVISORY COUNCIL FOR EDUCATION (ENGLAND) (1963) *Half Our Future*, (the Newsom Report), HMSO

CENTRAL ADVISORY COUNCIL FOR EDUCATION (ENGLAND) (1967) *Children and Their Primary Schools* (the Plowden Report), HMSO

CENTRAL ADVISORY COUNCIL FOR EDUCATION (WALES) (1965) *Science in Education in Wales Today* (the Llewellyn-Jones Report), HMSO

CENTRAL ADVISORY COUNCIL FOR EDUCATION (WALES) (1968) *Primary Education in Wales* (the Gittins Report), HMSO

CHAMBERS J. (2003) *Sociolinguistic Theory*, Blackwell

CHILTON PIERCE J. (2002) *The Biology of Transcendence: A Blueprint of the Human Spirit*, Park Street Press

CHITTY C. & DUNFORD J. (1999) *State Schools, New Labour and the Conservative Legacy*, Woburn

CLARK L. (2006) The Children of Eleven Who Cannot Spell the Simplest Words, *The Daily Mail*, 28 January

CLARKE S. (1998) *Targeting Assessment in the Primary Classroom*, Hodder and Stoughton

CLARKE S. (2003) *Enriching Feedback in the Primary Classroom*, Hodder and Murray

COBBAN A. (1957) The Enlightenment, *The Cambridge Modern History*, Cambridge University Press

COHEN L., MANION L. & MORRISON K. (2000) *Research Methods in Education*, Routledge Falmer

COLES R. (1992) *The Spiritual Life of Children*, Harper Collins

COMMITTEE OF INQUIRY APPOINTED BY THE SECRETARY OF STATE FOR EDUCATION AND SCIENCE UNDER THE CHAIRMANSHIP OF SIR ALAN BULLOCK (1975) A *Language for Life* (the Bullock Report), HMSO

COMMITTEE OF INQUIRY INTO THE TEACHING OF ENGLISH LANGUAGE (1988) *Report* (the Kingman Report), HMSO

COMMITTEE ON HIGHER EDUCATION (1963) *Higher Education* (the Robbins Report), HMSO

CONNER C. (1991) *Assessment and Testing in the Primary School*, Falmer

CONSULTATIVE COMMITTEE TO THE BOARD OF EDUCATION (1931) *The Primary School* (the Hadow Report), HMSO

CONSULTATIVE COMMITTEE TO THE BOARD OF EDUCATION (1933) *Infant and Nursery Schools* (the Hadow Report), HMSO

CONSULTATIVE COMMITTEE TO THE BOARD OF EDUCATION (1938) *Secondary Education with Special Reference to Grammar Schools and Technical High Schools*, (the Spens Report), HMSO

COPLEY T. (2000) *Spiritual Development in the State School*, University of Exeter Press

COTTINGHAM J. (2003) Spirituality, Science and Morality, in: CARR D. & HALDANE J. *Spirituality, Philosophy and Education*, Routledge Falmer

COTTON K. (2003) *Classroom Questioning*, Northwest Regional Education Laboratory

COUPLAND N. & JAWORSKI A. (1997) *Sociolinguistics: A Reader and Coursebook*, Macmillan

CROMPTON M. (1998) *Children, Spirituality, Religion and Social Work*, Ashgate-Arena

CRYSTAL D. (1997) *The Cambridge Encyclopedia of the English Language*, Cambridge University Press

CRYSTAL D. (2005) http://news.bbc.co.uk/1/hi/uk/4152394.stm

CUNNINGHAM H. (2006) *The Invention of Childhood*, BBC Books

CURTIS A. (2002) A *Curriculum for the Pre-School Child: Learning to Learn*, Routledge Falmer

CZERNIEWSKA P. (1985) The Experience of Writing, in: OPEN UNIVERSITY *Every Child's Language: An In-Service Pack for Primary Teachers*, Open University Press

D'AQUILI E. & NEWBERG A. (2001) *Why God Won't Go Away: Brain Science and the Biology of Belief*, Ballantine Books

DARWIN C. (2004) *On Natural Selection*, Penguin

DAVIE G. (1994) *Religion in Britain since 1945: Believing Without Belonging*, Blackwell

DEARDEN R. (1968) *The Philosophy of Primary Education*, Routledge and Kegan Paul

DEARING R. (1993) *The National Curriculum and its Assessment: An Interim Report*, School Curriculum and Assessment Authority

DE BONO E. (1986) *CORT Thinking Programme*, Pergamon

DEMAINE J. (2002) *Education Policy and Contemporary Politics*, Palgrave

DENT H. (1961) *The Educational System of England and Wales*, University of London Press

DEPARTMENT FOR EDUCATION (DFE) (1992) *Choice and Diversity: A New Framework for Schools*, London, HMSO

DFE (1994) *Religious Education and Collective Worship*, DFE

DEPARTMENT FOR EDUCATION AND EMPLOYMENT (DFEE) (1997a) *Excellence in Schools*, DFEE

DFEE (1997b) *The National Literacy Strategy*, DFEE

DFEE (1998) *Nursery Education: Desirable Outcomes for Children's Learning on Entering Compulsory Education*, DFEE

DFEE (2000) *The Role of the LEA in School Education*, DFEE

DEEE (2001) *National Strategy: Framework for Teaching English: Years 7, 8 and 9*, DFEE

DEPARTMENT FOR EDUCATION AND SKILLS (DFES) (2003) *Every Child Matters*, DFES

DFES (2004a) *Assessment for Learning: Guidance for Senior Leaders*, DFES

DFES (2004b) *Five Year Strategy for Children and Learners*, DFES

DFES (2005a) *14-19 Education and Skills*, DFES

DFES (2005b) *Higher Standards, Better Schools for All: More Choice for Parents and Pupils*, DFES

DEPARTMENT OF EDUCATION AND SCIENCE (DES) (1972) *Education: A Framework for Expansion*, HMSO

DES (1977) *Education in Schools: A Consultative Document*, HMSO

DES (1985) *Better Schools*, HMSO

DES (1990) *Starting with Quality* (the Rumbold Report), HMSO

DES (1991) *The Charter for Parents*, DES

DES (1994) *The Charter for Parents*, DES

DES & HER MAJESTY'S INSPECTORATE (HMI) (1977a) *Curriculum* 11-16, HMSO

DES & HMI (1977b) *Supplement to Curriculum 11-16*, HMSO

DEVEREAUX J. & MILLER L. (2003) *Supporting Children's Learning in the Early Years*, David Fulton

DEWEY J. (1921) *Reconstruction in Philosophy*, University of London Press

DEWEY J. (1938) *Experience and Education*, Collier

DICKENS C. (1859) *Oliver Twist*, Gawthorn

DONALDSON M. (1978) *Children's Minds*, Fontana

DRIVER R & BELL B. (1986) Students' Thinking and the Learning of Science: A Constructivist View, *School Science Review*, 67

DRYDEN L., FORBES R., MUKHERJI P. & POUND L. (2005) *Essential Early Years*, Hodder and Stoughton

DU BOULAY S. (1999) *Beyond the Darkness: A Biography of Bede Griffiths*, Rider

EASTON D. (1965) *A Systems Analysis of Political Life*, John Wiley

EAUDE T. (2001) Exploring How Schools Promote the Spiritual Dimension of Young Children's Experience, Paper at Eighth Annual International Conference, Education, Spirituality and the Whole Child, University of Surrey, Roehampton, 21-23 June

EDGINGTON M. (2004) All About ...The Outdoors Curriculum, *Nursery World*, 2

EDWARDS A. (1990) *Practitioner Research*, University of Lancaster

EDWARDS R. (1997) *Changing Places? Flexibility, Lifelong Learning and a Learning Society*, Routledge

ELTON-CHALCRAFT S. (2001) Empty Wells? How Well Are We Doing at Spiritual Well-being? Paper at Eighth Annual International Conference, Education, Spirituality and the Whole Child, University of Surrey, Roehampton, 21 - 23 June

ERRICKER C, (1998) Spiritual Confusion: A Critique of Current Educational Policy in England and Wales, *International Journal of Children's Spirituality*, 3/1

ERRICKER C. & ERRICKER J (1997) Hearing Voices: Taking Account of Children in Understanding Spiritual and Moral Development, *Engaging the Curriculum*, 5

ERRICKER C. & ERRICKER J. (2001) *Meditation in Schools*, Continuum

ERRICKER C., ERRICKER J., OTA C., SULLIVAN D. & FLETCHER M. (1997) *The Education of the Whole Child*, Cassell

FENWICK I. (1976) *The Comprehensive School 1944-1970: The Politics of Secondary School Reorganisation*, Methuen

FERGUSON, M. (1981) *The Aquarian Conspiracy: Personal and Social Transformation in the 1980's*, Routledge and Kegan Paul

FEUERSTEIN R., RAND Y., HOFFMAN M. & MILLER R. (1980) *Instrumental Enrichment: An Intervention for Cognitive Modifiability*, University Park Press

FISHER J. (1999) Helps to Fostering Students' Spiritual Health, *International Journal of Children's Spirituality*, 4/1

FISHER R (1998) *Teaching Thinking*, Cassell

FISHER R. (1990) *Teaching Children to Think*, Blackwell

FLANAGAN G. (1996) *Beginning Life*, Dorling Kinersley

FLEER M. (1992) Introducing Technology Education to Young Children: A Design, Make and Appraise Approach, *Research in Science Education*, 22

FORUM ON VALUES IN EDUCATION AND THE COMMUNITY (1998) *Draft Guidance for Pilot Work*, QCA

FREEBODY P. (2003) *Qualitative Research in Education*, Sage

FREIRE P. (1972) *Pedagogy of the Oppressed*, Penguin

FROEBEL (1887) *The Education of Man*, Appleton

FROST J. (2006) *Ask Super Nanny*, Hodder and Stoughton

FOWLER H. (1906) *The King's English*, Clarendon Press

GARDNER H. (1993) *Frames of Mind: The Theory of Multiple Intelligences*, Basic Books

GARDNER H. (1999) *Intelligence Reframed: Multiple Intelligences for the Twenty-First Century*, Basic Books

GAY B. (2000) Fostering Spiritual Development through the Religious Dimension of Schools: the Report of a Pilot Study in Seventeen Independent Schools, *International Journal of Children's Spirituality*, 5/1

GAY D. (1998) Millennium Dome Reflects our "Spiritual Wasteland", *The Times*, 7 March

GAY P. (1967) *The Enlightenment: The Rise of Modern Paganism*, Weidenfeld and Nicholson

GEEN A. (1986) *Decision Making and Secondary Education: A Case Study*, University of Wales Press

GEEN A. (2005) *Effective Teaching for the Twenty-First Century: Priorities in Secondary Education*, UWIC Press

GENERAL TEACHING COUNCIL FOR WALES (GTCW) (2004) The Daugherty Review of Assessment at Key Stage 2 and 3, *Teaching Wales*, 4

GILBERT R. (1998) *Mysticism*, Element

GILLIAT P. (1996) Spiritual Education and Public Policy 1944-1994, in: BEST R. *Education, Spirituality and the Whole Child*, Cassell

GIPPS C. McCALLUM B. & BROWN M. (1996) Models of Teacher Assessment Among Primary School Teachers in England, *The Curriculum Journal*, 7/2

GIPPS C, McCALLUM B. & HARGREAVES E. (2000) *What Makes a Good Primary Teacher? Expert Strategies*, Routledge Falmer

GIPPS G. (1997) Using Assessment Strategically to Change the Way Students Learn, in: BROWN S. and GLASNER A. *Assessment Matters in Higher Education: Choosing and Using Diverse Approaches*, Open University Press

GIROUX H. (1997) Crossing the Boundaries of Educational Discourse: Modernism, Postmodernism, and Feminism, in: HALSEY A., LAUDER H. BROWN P. and WELLS A. *Education: Culture, Economy, and Society*, Oxford University Press.

GOFFMAN E. (1969) *The Presentation of Self in Everyday Life*, Allen Lane

GOLD K. (2004) Goodbye to Testing, Long Live Assessment, *TES*, 15 October

GOLEMAN D. (1995) *Emotional Intelligence*, Bantam Press

GOLEMAN D. (1998) *Working with Emotional Intelligence*, Bloomsbury

GOLLNICK J. (2003) Is Implicit Religion Spirituality in Disguise? *Implicit Religion*, 6/2

GOODY J. (1987) *The Interface between the Written and the Oral*, Cambridge University Press

GORDON P. & WHITE J. (1979) *Philosophers as Educational Reformers*, Routledge and Kegan Paul

GRIFFITHS B. (1954) *The Golden String*, Harvill

GRIFFITH R. (2000) *National Curriculum: National Disaster: Education and Citizenship*, Routledge

GRIFFITHS M. (1998) *Educational Research for Social Justice*, Open University Press

GROSS M. (2004) *Exceptionally Gifted Children*, Routledge Falmer

HALDANE J., (2003) On the Very Idea of Spiritual Values, in: CARR D. & HALDANE J. *Spirituality, Philosophy and Education*, Routledge Falmer

HALLIDAY M. (1989) *Spoken and Written Language*, Oxford University Press

HAMER D. (2005) *The God Gene: How Faith is Hardwired into our Genes*, Doubleday

HAMMOND J., HAY D., MOXON J., NETTO B., RABAN K., STRAUGHEIR G. & WILLIAMS C. (1990) *New Methods in Religious Education Teaching. An Experiential Approach*, Oliver and Boyd

HARDING L. & BEECH J. (1991) *Educational Assessment of the Primary School Child*, National Foundation for Educational Research and Nelson

HARDY A. (1979) *The Spiritual Nature of Man*, Clarendon Press

HARRISON C. (2002) *Key Stage 3 English: Roots and Research*, DFES

HART L. (2000) Human Brain and Human Learning, in: LAZEAR D. *Pathways of Learning: Teaching Students and Parents about Multiple Intelligences*, Zephyr Press

HARVEY D. (1990) *The Condition Of Postmodernity. An Enquiry into the Origins of Cultural Change*, Blackwell

HAWKING S. (1988) A *Brief History of Time*, Bantam Press

HAY D. (1987) *Exploring Inner Space*, Mowbray

HAY D. (1990) *Religious Experience Today: Studying the Facts*, Cassell Mobrays

HAY D. & HAMMOND J. (1992) "When You Pray, Go To Your Private Room.": A Reply to Adrian Thatcher, *British Journal of Religious Education*, 14/3

HAY D. & NYE R. (1998) *The Spirit of the Child*, Fount

HEADINGTON R (2000) *Monitoring, Assessment, Recording and Accountability: Meeting the Standards*, Fulton

HEAFFORD M. (1967) *Pestalozzi*, Methuen

HEFFERN R. (2001) Exploring the Biology of Religious Experience, *National Catholic Reporter*, 20 April

HEIMBROCK H. (2004) Beyond Secularisation: Experiences of the Sacred in Childhood and Adolescence as a Challenge for Religious Education Development Theory, *British Journal of Religious Education*, 26/2

HER MAJESTY'S INSPECTORATE (HMI) (1985) *The School Curriculum from 5 to 16*, HMSO

HICK J. (1999) *The Fifth Dimension: An Exploration of the Spiritual Realm*, Oneworld

HILBOURNE N. (2005) Governors Quit in Faith Row, *TES*, 16 December

HILL F. (1995) Managing Service Quality in Higher Education: The Role of the Student as Primary Consumer, *Quality Assurance in Education*, 3/3

HIRST P. (1967) The Logical and Psychological Aspects of Teaching a Subject, in: PETERS R. *The Concept of Education*, Routledge and Kegan Paul

HIRST P. (1971) The Logic of the Curriculum, in: HOOPER R. *The Curriculum: Context, Design and Development*, Open University Press

HIRST P. (1972) Liberal Education and the Nature of Knowledge, in: DEARDEN R., HIRST P. and PETERS R. *Education and the Development of Reason*, Routledge and Kegan Paul

HIRST P. (1974) *Knowledge and the Curriculum*, Routledge and Kegan Paul

HIRST P. & PETERS R. (1970) *The Logic of Education*, Routledge and Kegan Paul

HOAD T. (1989) *The Oxford Library of Words and Phrases III: The Concise Oxford Dictionary of Word Origins*, Oxford University Press and Guild Publishing

HOLMES J. (1992) *An Introduction to Sociolinguistics*, Longman

HONDERICH T. (1995) *The Oxford Companion to Philosophy*, Oxford University Press

HONEY J. (1997) *Language is Power: The Story of Standard English and its Enemies*, Faber

HOPKINS D. (2002) *A Teacher's Guide to Classroom Research*, Open University Press

HOROWITZ L. (1974) *Elements of Statistics*, McGraw Hill

HUDSON R. & HOLMES J. (1995) *Children's Use of Spoken Standard English*, School Curriculum and Assessment Authority

HUGHES R. (1996) *English in Speech and Writing: Investigating Language and Literacy*, Routledge

HUTCHINS R. (1936) *The Higher Learning in America*, Yale University Press

HUXLEY A. (1971) *The Doors of Perception and Heaven and Hell*, Penguin

HUXLEY T. (1868) *Liberal Education: Where to Find It*, Macmillan

ISAACS S. (1954) *The Educational Value of the Nursery School*, Nursery School Association of Great Britain and Northern Ireland

ISHERWOOD L. (1999) Liberating Spirituality: Empowered for a World in Need of Passion, *British Journal of Religious Education*, 2/2

ISHERWOOD L. & McEWAN D. (1993) *Introducing Feminist Theology*, Sheffield Academic Press

IZARD C., ROBERTS R., ZEIDER M. & MATTHEWS G. (2001) Emotional Intelligence or Adaptive Emotions, *Emotion*, 1/3

JACKSON M. (1997) Benign Schizotypy? The Case of Spiritual Experience, in: CLARIDGE G. *Schizotypy: Implications for Illness and Health*, Oxford University Press

JACKSON M. & GRETTON J. (1976) *William Tyndale: Collapse of a School or A System?* Allen and Unwin

JACOBS J. (2003) Spirituality and Virtue, in: CARR D. & HALDANE J. *Spirituality, Philosophy and Education*, Routledge Falmer

JAFFE A. (1989) *Was C.J. Jung a Mystic? And Other Essays*, Daimon

JAMES M. (2003) Supporting Assessment for Learning: From a Perspective of Hope to a Climate of Trust, ACCAC Conference on Assessment for Learning

JENNINGS R. (1977) *Education and Politics*, Batsford

JESPERSEN O. (1946) *Language: Its Nature, Development and Origin*, W.W. Norton

JOHNSON S. (1755) *The Dictionary of the English Language*, W. Strahan

JOHNSON S. (1954) *Lives of the Poets*, Everyman

JONES L., HOLMES R. & POWELL J. (2005) *Early Childhood Studies: A Multi-Professional Perspective*, Open University Press

JUWAH C., MacFARLANE-DICK D., MATTHEW B., NICOL D., ROSS D. & SMITH B. (2004) *Enhancing Student Learning Through Effective Feedback*, The Higher Education Academy

KANT I. (1892) *The Critique of Judgement*, Macmillan

KANT I. (1956) *The Critique of Practical Reason*, Bobbs-Merrill

KANT I. (1964) *The Doctrine of Virtue*, Harper and Row

KANT I. (1970) On Education, in: CAHN S. *The Philosophical Foundations of Education*, Harper and Row

KEATING R. (2001) Spirituality and the Rite of Passage from Adolescence into Adulthood: Using Comparative Wisdom Literature to facilitate this Passage in the Final Year of Schooling, Paper at Eighth Annual International Conference, Education, Spirituality and the Whole Child, University of Surrey, Roehampton, 21-23 June

KERSWILL P. (1996) Milton Keynes and Dialect Levelling in South-Eastern British English, in: GRADDOL D., LEITH D. & SWANN J. *English: History, Diversity and Change*, Routledge

KERSWILL P. & WILLIAMS A. (2005) New Towns and Koineisation: Linguistic and Social Correlates, *Linguistics*, 43/5

KING U. (1997) Spirituality, in: HINNELLS J. *The Penguin Dictionary of Religions*, Penguin

KLUGER A. & DENISI A. (1996) The Effects of Feedback Interventions on Performance: A Historical Review, a Meta-analysis, and a Preliminary Feedback Intervention Theory, *Psychological Bulletin*, 119/2.

KNIGHT P (1995) *Assessment for Learning in Higher Education*, Kogan Page

KOGAN M. (1978) *The Politics of Educational Change*, London, Fontana-Collins

KOGAN M. (1986) *Education Accountability*, Hutchinson

KOGAN M., BOYLE E. & CROSLAND A. (1971) *The Politics of Education*, Penguin

KOGAN M. & PACKWOOD T. (1974) *Advisory Councils and Committees in Education*, Routledge and Kegan Paul

KOHLBERG L. (1986) *Essays on Moral Development*, Harper and Row

KOHLBERG L. (1987) *Child Psychology and Childhood Education: A Cognitive View*, Longman

KOHLBERG L. (1994) *Moral Development: A Compendium*, Garland

KOHN A. (2005) *Moving from Rewards and Punishment to Love and Reason*, Atria Books

KRESS G. (1982) *Learning to Write*, Routledge and Kegan Paul

KWON Y-I. (2002) Changing Curriculum for Early Childhood Education in England, *Early Childhood Research and Practice*, 4/2

LABOV W. (1972a) *Language in the Inner City: Studies in the Black English Vernacular*, University of Pennsylvania Press

LABOV W. (1972b) *Sociolinguistic Patterns*, University of Pennsylvania Press

LANGER J. (2001) *Excellence in English in Middle and High School: How Teachers' Professional Lives Support Student Achievement*, National Research Centre on English Learning and Achievement

LAW NOLTE D. (1998) *Children Learn What They Live*, Workman Publishing

LAWRENCE E. (1952) *Friedrich Froebel and English Education*, Routledge and Kegan Paul

LAWTON D. (1968) *Social Class, Language and Education*, Routledge and Kegan Paul

LAZEAR D. (2000) *Pathways of Learning: Teaching Students and Parents about Multiple Intelligences*, Zephyr Press

LEALMAN B. (1982) The Ignorant Eye: Perception and Religious Education, *British Journal of Religious Education*, 4/2

LEATON GRAY S. (2006) *Teachers Under Siege*, Trentham Books

LEE V. (1979) *Language Development*, Croom Helm

LEECH K. (1985) *True God: An Exploration in Spiritual Theology*, Sheldon Press

LESTER SMITH W. (1965) *Government of Education*, Penguin

LEWIS C. & SHORT C. (1966) *A Latin Dictionary*, Clarendon Press

LE XUAN H. & LOEVINGER J. (1996) *Ego Development*, Lawrence Erlbaum

LEYSER H. (1995) *Medieval Women: A Social History of Women in England 450-1500*, Weidenfield and Nicolson

LINDON J. (2005) *Understanding Child Development: Linking Theory and Practice*, Hodder Arnold

LIPMAN M., SHARP A. & OSCANYAN F. (1980) *Philosophy in the Classroom*, Temple University Press

LITTLEDYKE M. & HUXFORD L. (1998) *Teaching the Primary Curriculum for Constructivist Learning*, David Fulton

LLOYD D. (1976) *Philosophy and the Teacher*, Routledge and Kegan Paul

LOCKE M. (1974) *Power and Politics in the School System*, Routledge and Kegan Paul

LONGAKER C. (1998) *Facing Death and Finding Hope*, Arrow

LORENZ, K. (1979) *The Year of the Greylag Goose*, Harcourt Brace

MacLEAN P. (1990) *The Triune Brain in Evolution: Role in Paleocerebral Functions*, Plenum

MacNAUGHTON, G. & WILLIAMS, G. (2004) *Teaching Young Children Choices in Theory and Practice*, Open University Press

MANSELL W. (2005) Unions Sign Up to Academy Pay Deal, *TES*, 25 March

MARKHAM I. (1999) Response to Clive and Jane Erricker, in: THATCHER A. *Spirituality and the Curriculum*, Cassell

MARTIN, P. (2005) *Making Happy People: The Nature of Happiness and its Origins in Childhood*, Harper Perennial

MASLOW A. (1964) *Religions, Values and Peak Experiences*, Viking

MAYBIN J. & MERCER N. (1996) *Using English, from Conversation to Canon*, Routledge

McCARTHY M. & CARTER R. (1996) *Exploring Spoken English*, Cambridge University Press

McCOURT F. (1996) *Angela's Ashes*, Harper Perennial

McCREERY E. (1996) Talking to Young Children about Things Spiritual, in: BEST R. *Education, Spirituality and the Whole Child*, Cassell

McCREERY E. (2001) Approaching the Spiritual: the Significance of Teachers' Life Experiences, Paper at Eighth Annual International Conference, *Education, Spirituality and the Whole Child*, University of Surrey, Roehampton, 21-23 June

McDONALD B. & BOUD D. (2003) The Impact of Self-assessment on Achievement: the Effects of Self-assessment Training on Performance in External Examinations, *Assessment in Education*, 10/2

McGHEE M. (2003) Making Spirits Attentive: Moral and Spiritual Development, in: CARR D. & HALDANE J. *Spirituality, Philosophy and Education*, Routledge Falmer

McGUINESS C. (1999) *From Thinking Skills to Thinking Classrooms: A Review and Evaluation of Approaches for Developing Pupils' Thinking Skills*, HMSO

McMILLAN M. (1919) *The Nursery School*, Dent

McNIFF J., LOMAX P. & WHITEHEAD J. (2003) *You and Your Action Research Project*, Routledge Falmer

MEAD G. (1934) *Mind, Self and Society*, University of Chicago Press

MICHAELS S. (1981) Sharing Time: Children's Narrative Styles and Differential Access to Literacy, *Language in Society*, 10/1

MILLER J. (2002) Book Review of Erricker and Erricker "Meditation in Schools", *British Journal of Religious Education*, 25/1

MILNE J. (2006) High-Class but Poor Quality, *TES*, 14 July

MINISTRY OF EDUCATION (1951) *Education 1900-1950*, HMSO

MINISTRY OF EDUCATION OF NEW ZEALAND (1996) *Te Whariki: Early Childhood Curriculum*, Ministry of Education

MONTESSORI M. (1912) *The Montessori Method*, Heinemann

MORRIS V. (1966) *Existentialism in Education*, Harper and Row

MOYLES J. (2005) *The Excellence of Play*, Open University Press

MURRAY N. (2002) *Aldous Huxley: An English Intellectual*, Little, Brown

MURSELL G. (2001) *The Story of Christian Spirituality*, Lion

MYERS B. & MYERS M. (1999) Engaging Children's Spirit through Literature, *Childhood Education*, 76/1

NAISBITT J. & ABURDENE P. (1999) *Megatrends* 2000, Morrow

NATIONAL ASSEMBLY FOR WALES (NAW) (2001) *The Learning Country: A Paving Document*, NAW

NATIONAL COMMISSION ON EDUCATION (2003) *Learning to Succeed: The Next Decade*, National Commission on Education

NATIONAL CURRICULUM COUNCIL (NCC) (1993) *Spiritual and Moral Development*, NCC

NATIONAL CURRICULUM TASK GROUP ON ASSESSMENT AND TESTING (TGAT) (1988) A *Report*, DES and Welsh Office

NAYLOR F. (2001) *Is Education for Spirituality Compatible with a Managerial Approach to Schooling?* Prospero, 7/2

NEUMARK V. (1996) Thinking About Thinking, *TES*, 13 September

NEWMAN E (2005) Lads and English, *English in Education*, 39/1

NEWMAN J. (1852) *Idea of a University*, Longmans

NICOL D. (1997) *Research on Learning and Higher Education Teaching*, Universities and Colleges Staff Development Agency

NIETZSCHE F. (1969) *Thus Spoke Zarathustra*, Penguin

OFFICE FOR STANDARDS IN EDUCATION (OFSTED) (1993a). *Boys and English*, OFSTED

OFSTED (1993b) *Framework for School Inspection*, OFSTED

OFSTED (1994) *Spiritual, Moral, Social and Cultural Development*, OFSTED

OFSTED (1996) *Gender Divide: Performance Differences between Boys and Girls at School*, OFSTED and Equal Opportunities Commission

OFSTED (2001) *Inspecting English 11-16*, OFSTED

OFSTED (2003a) *Boys' Achievement in Secondary Schools*, OFSTED

OFSTED (2003b) *Excellence in Cities and Education Action Zones: Management and Impact*, OFSTED

OFSTED (2004) *Promoting and Evaluating Pupils' Spiritual, Moral, Social and Cultural Development*, OFSTED

OLKOWSKI W. (2006) Divine DNA, *Skeptic*, 12/3

OLSON D. (1994) *The World on Paper: The Conceptual and Cognitive Implications of Writing and Reading*, Cambridge University Press

OPPENHEIM A. (1992) *Questionnaire Design, Interviewing and Attitude Measurement*, Continuum

PARIS S., LAWTON T., TURNER J. & ROTH J. (1991) A Developmental Perspective on Standardised Achievement Testing, *Educational Researcher*, 20

PASSMORE B. (2001) Happy To Do It Their Way, *TES*, 18 May

PEARSON H, (1998) *The Life of Oscar Wilde*, Senate

PEI M. (1965) *Invitation to Linguistics*, George Allen and Unwin

PELZER D. (2002) *Dave Pelzer's Life Lessons*, Element

PENN H. (2005) *Understanding Early Childhood: Issues and Controversies*, Open University Press

PERERA S. (1994) *Children's Reading and Writing*, Blackwell

PETERS R. (1966) *Ethics and Education*, George Allen and Unwin

PETERS R. (1969) *Perspectives on Plowden*, Routledge and Kegan Paul

PETRE J. (2005) Public "Shop" for Religion in Latest Reality TV Show, *The Daily Telegraph*, 4 June

PHENIX P. (1964) *Realms of Meaning*, McGraw-Hill

PIAGET J. (1977) *The Essential Piaget*, Basic Books

PICARD L. (2000) *Dr Johnson's London, Everyday Life in London* 1740-1770, Phoenix

PINKER S. (1994) *The Language Instinct*, Harper Collins

PLATO (1954) *The Last Days of Socrates*, Penguin

PLATO (1974) *The Republic*, Penguin

POLLACK D. (1996) Zur Religios-kirchlichen Lage in Deutschland nach der Wiedervereinigung: Eine religionssoziologische Ananyse, *Zeitschrift fur Theologie und Kirche*, 93

POLLARD A. (1997) *Reflective Teaching in The Primary School*, Cassell

PORTILLO M. (2001) *Art that Shook the World: Richard Wagner and the Ring Cycle*, BBC Television

POUND L. (2005) *How Children Learn, Practical Pre-School*, Step Forward Publishing

POWNEY J. & WATTS M. (1987) *Interviewing in Educational Research*, Routledge and Kegan Paul

PRICE C. (1994) A New Vice Anglaise, *TES*, 14 January

PRIESTLY J. (1985) Towards Finding the Hidden Curriculum: A Consideration of the Spiritual Dimension of Experience in Curriculum Planning, *British Journal of Religious Education*, 7/3

PRING R. (1983) *Personal, Social and Moral Education*, Falmer

PRING R. (2005) Labour Government Policy 14-19, *Oxford Review of Education*, 31/1

PRZEDLACKA J. (2001) Estuary English and RP: Some recent findings. www.phon.ox.ac.uk/~joanna/sap36_jp.pdf

QUALIFICATIONS AND CURRICULUM AUTHORITY (QCA) (1997) *The Promotion of Pupils' Spiritual, Moral, Social and Cultural Development – Draft Guidance for Pilot Work*, QCA

QCA (2000) *Curriculum Guidance for the Foundation Phase*, QCA

RADFORD M. (1999) Religious Education, Spiritual Experience and Truth, *British Journal of Religious Education*, 21/3

RAFFERTY F. (1998) Blunkett Delivers a Beefy Doorstep, *TES*, 2 January

RAVN B. (2006) *Parents in Education – European Perspectives*, School of Education, Copehagen University, Denmark

RHODES B. (2005) http: DialectEnglishvarieties of the BritishIsles. Htmwww.universalteacher.org.uk/lang/britishisles.htm

RICHARDSON A. (1997) Dyslexia and Schizotypy, in: CLARIDGE G. *Schizotypy: Implications for Illness and Health*, Oxford University Press

RILEY D. (1979) War in the Nursery, *Feminist Review*, 2

RILEY K. & RUSTIQUE-FORRESTER E. (2002) *Working With Disaffected Students*, Paul Chapman

RINPOCHE S. (1992) *The Tibetan Book of Living and Dying*, Rider

ROBINSON T. (2005) *The Worst Children's Jobs in History*, MacMillan

RODGER A. (1996) Human Spirituality: Towards an Educational Rationale, in: BEST R. *Education, Spirituality and the Whole Child*, Cassell

ROGERS A. (1946) A *Student's History of Philosophy*, Macmillan

ROMAINE S. (1994) *Language in Society: An Introduction to Sociolinguistics*, Oxford University Press

ROOF W. (1993) A *Generation of Seekers: The Spiritual Journeys of the Baby Boom Generation*, Harper and Row

ROOF W. (1999) *Spiritual Marketplace: Baby Boomers and the Remaking of American Religion*, Princetown University Press

ROSE S. (1976) *The Conscious Brain*, Penguin

ROUSSEAU J. (1974) *Emile*, Everyman

ROUSSEAU J. (2004) *The Social Contract*, Penguin

ROWE M. (1974) Pausing Phenomena: Influence on the Quality of Instruction, *Journal of Psycholinguistic Research*, 3/3

ROWE M. (1996) Science, Silence, and Sanctions, *Science and Children*, 34/1

RUSSELL B. (1992) An Outline of Intellectual Rubbish: A Hilarious Catalogue of Organised and Individual Stupidity, in: EGNER R. & DENONN L., *The Basic Writings of Bertrand Russell*, Routledge

SADLER R. (1989) Formative Assessment and the Design of Instructional Systems, *Instructional Science*, 18

SAUSSURE F. (1983) *Course in General Linguistics*, Duckworth

SAYEED Z. & GUERIN, E. (2002) *Early Years Play: A Happy Medium for Assessment and Intervention*, David Fulton

SCHEFFLER I. (1960) *The Language of Education*, Charles Thomas

SCHMIDTCHEN G. (1997) *Wie weit ist der Weg nach Deutschland? Sozialpsychologie der Jugend in der postsozialistischen Welt*, Leske and Budrich

SCHOOL CURRICULUM AND ASSESSMENT AUTHORITY (SCAA) (1995) *Spiritual and Moral Development*, SCAA

SCAA (1996a) *Desirable Learning Outcomes*, SCAA

SCAA (1996b) *Education for Adult Life: The Spiritual and Moral Development of Young People*, SCAA

SECONDARY SCHOOL EXAMINATIONS COUNCIL (1943) *Curriculum and Examinations in Secondary Schools* (the Norwood Report), HMSO

SECRETARY OF STATE FOR WALES (1997) *Building Excellent Schools Together*, The Stationery Office

SHAW G. (2003) *Pygmalion*, Penguin

SHAW M. (2005) King's Praised as Unity Fails, *TES*, 5 June

SHAW M. (2006) Angry Heads Pull the Strings, *TES*, 5 May

SHAW M. & MANSELL W. (2006) "Mixed Messages" Undermine Progress, *TES*, 10 March

SHAW S. & HAWES T. (1998) *Effective Teaching and Learning in the Primary Classroom: A Practical Guide to Brain Compatible Learning*, Optimal Learning

SHELDRAKE P. (1999) Spirituality as an Academic Discipline, in: THATCHER A. *Spirituality and the Curriculum*, Cassell

SHERMAN N. (2003) Stoic Meditations and the Shaping of Character: the Case of Educating the Military, in: CARR D. & HALDANE J. *Spirituality, Philosophy and Education*, Routledge Falmer

SHERMER M. (2000) *Why People Believe Weird Things*, Freeman

SIRAJ-BLATCHFORD I., SYLVA K., LAUGHARNE J., MILTON E. & CHARLES F. (2005) *Monitoring and Evaluation of the Effective Implementation of the Foundation Phase (MEEIFP) Project Across Wales*, Welsh Assembly Government

SLATER J. (2006) Decorous Delegates Raise Eyebrows, But Not the Roof, *TES*, 14 April

SLOAN-CHESTER E. (1925) The Angel Child: The Study of Good Little Girl: The Quiet Child May be Unhealthy, *The Nursery World for Mothers and Nurses*, 1

SMITH A. (2000) *Accelerated Learning in Practice*, Network Educational Press

SMITH A. (2002) *The Brain's Behind It*, MPG Books

SMITH A. & CALL N. (1999) *The ALPS Approach: Accelerated Learning in Primary Schools*, MPG Books

SMITH D. (1999) *Making Sense of Spiritual Development*, Stapleford Centre

SOCKETT H. (1980) *Accountability in the English Educational System*, Hodder and Stoughton

SPENCER H. (1878) *Education: Intellectual, Moral and Physical*, Williams and Norgate

SPOCK B. (1946) *The Common Sense Book of Baby and Child Care*, Duell, Sloan and Pearce

SPOCK B. & PARKER S. (1998) *Dr Spock's Baby and Child Care*, Pocket Books

SPURLING H. (2006) A Summary of *The Royal Literary Fund's Report on Student Writing in Higher Education*, Royal Literary Fund, www.rlf.org.uk/fellowshipscheme/documents/launchtalk.pdf

STERNBERG R. (1985) *Beyond IQ: A Triarchic Theory of Human Intelligence*, Open University Press

STERNBERG R. (1988) *The Triarchic Mind: A New Theory of Human Intelligence*, Viking

STERNBERG R. (1996) *Successful Intelligence: How Practical and Creative Intelligence Determine Success in Life*, Plume

STEVENS D. (2005) Showing the Strategy Where to Go: Possibilities for Creative Approaches to Key Stage 3 Literacy in Initial Teacher Education, *English in Education*, 39/1

STEWART R. (1997) *Ideas That Shaped Our World*, Marshall

STEWART W. (2005a) Cameron Gives Four Minutes to Schools, *TES*, 7 October

STEWART W. (2005b) Doubts Cast on Academies, *TES*, 18 February

STEWART W. (2006a) Heads Back Private Duo, *TES*, 24 February

STEWART W. (2006b) Primaries Spared "Rip-Off" PFL Deals, *TES*, 17 March

STIERER B. & MAYBIN J. (1994) *Language, Literacy and Learning in Educational Practice*, Open University Press

STONE M. (1992) *Don't Just Do Something, Sit There*, St, Martin's College Lancaster

STREIB H. (2005) Lifestyle and Religious Orientation of Adolescents in Germany, in: FRANCIS L., ROBBINS M. & ASTLEY J. *Religion, Education and Adolescence*, University of Wales

STRONG J. (2002) Reviewing the Literacy Hour, *Literacy Today*, 31

SUTHERLAND S. (1995) *The Spiritual and Moral Development of Children, in Future Progress in Religious Education*, The Templeton London Lectures at the RSA

SUTTON R. (1995) *Assessment for Learning*, RS Publications

SYLVA K., MELJUISH E., SAMMONS P., SIRAJ-BLATCHFORD I. & TAGGART B. (2004) *The Effective Provision of Pre-School Education (EPPE) Project: Technical Paper 12: The Final Report*, DFES

TACEY D. (2002) Student Spirituality and Educational Authority, *International Journal of Children's Spirituality*, 7/2

TAGGART G. (2002) Micky Mouse Spirituality? Children's Worldviews and the Culture Industry, *British Journal of Religious Education*, 25/1

TAGLIAMONTE S. (2005) Female Adolescents: Trendsetters in Teen Talk, *Journal of Pragmatics*, 15 June

TALBOT M. & TATE N. (1997) Shared Values in a Pluralist Society, in: SMITH R. & STANDISH P. *Teaching Right and Wrong: Moral Education in the Balance*, Trentham Books

TATE N. (1996) Education for Adult Life: Spiritual and Moral Aspects of the Curriculum, Paper delivered to SCAA Conference on Education for Adult Life, 15 January

TEMKO N and CAMPBELL D (2006). Classroom Revolution in Bid to Boost 3Rs, *The Observer*, 20 August

THATCHER A. (1991) A Critique of Inwardness in Religious Education, *British Journal of Religious Education*, 14/1

THATCHER A. (1999) *Spirituality and the Curriculum*, Cassell

THOMPSON H. (2006) *This Thing of Darkness*, Headline Review

THORNTON K. (1998) Byers Tells Secondaries to Set Exam Targets, *TES*, 26 June

THORNTON K. (2002) Fear Grows over Power of Academy Sponsors, *TES*, 26 August

TIBBLE J. (1966) *The Study of Education*, Routledge and Kegan Paul

TOON P. (1990) *Spiritual Companions*, Marshall Pickering

TORRANCE H. (2004) *Do Summative Assessment and Testing Have a Positive or Negative Effect on Post-16 Learners' Motivation for Learning in the Learning and Skills Sector?* Shaftesbury Learning and Skills Research Centre

TORRANCE H. & PRYOR J. (1998) *Investigating Formative Assessment: Teaching, Learning and Assessment in the Classroom*, Open University Press

TRUDGILL P. (1974) *Sociolinguistics: An Introduction*, Penguin.

TRUSS L. (2003) *Eats, Shoots and Leaves: The Zero Tolerance Approach to Punctuation*, Profile Books

UNGOED-THOMAS J. (1986) *Personal and Social Education: Religious and Spiritual Development in Perspectives*, Christian Education Movement (CEM)

USHER R. & EDWARDS R. (1994) *Postmodernism and Education*, Routledge

VAN DOREN (1943) *Liberal Education*, Holt

VERMA G. & BEARD R. (1981) *What is Educational Research ? Perspectives on Techniques of Research*, Gower

VYGOTSKY L. (1986) *Thought and Language*, MIT Press

WALLER J. (2005) *The Real Oliver Twist, Robert Blincoe: A Life that Illuminates an Age*, Icon Books

WARDHAUGH R. (1993) *An Introduction to Sociolinguistics*, Blackwell

WATSON J. (2000) Whose Model of Spirituality Should Be Used in the Spiritual Development of School Children? *International Journal of Children's Spirituality*, 5/1

WATSON J. (2001) Experience of Spirituality, Experience of School, Paper presented at the Eighth Annual International Conference, Education, Spirituality and the Whole Child, University of Surrey, Roehampton, 21-23 June

WEBSTER D. (1996) Spiders and Eternity: Spirituality and the Curriculum, in: BEST R. *Education, Spirituality and the Whole Child*, Cassell

WEIKART D., EPSTEIN A., SWEINHART L. & BOND J. (1978) *Ypsilanti Pre-school Curriculum Demonstration Project: The Pre-school Years and Longitudinal Results Through Fourth Grade*, High Scope Press

WEIMANN K. (1995) *Einfuhrung ins Altenglische*, Quelle and Meyer

WEINSTOCK A. (1976) I Blame the Teachers, *TES*, 23 January

WELLS B. (1973) *Psychedelic Drugs: Psychological, Medical and Social Issues*, Penguin

WELLS G. (1979) Variation in Child Language, in: FLETCHER P. & GARMAN M. *Language Acquisition: Studies in First Language Development*, Cambridge University Press

WELSH ASSEMBLY GOVERNMENT (WAG) (2003) *The Foundation Phase 3-7*, WAG

WELSH ASSEMBLY GOVERNMENT DEPARTMENT FOR EDUCATION, LIFELONG LEARNING AND SKILLS, (2007) *Foundation Phase Foundation for Children's Learning*, WAG

WEST A. & PENNELL H. (2003) *Underachievement in Schools*, Routledge Falmer

WHALLEY M. & THE PEN GREEN CENTRE TEAM (2004) *Involving Parents in their Children's Learning*, Paul Chapman

WHEATLY G. (1991) Constructivist Perspectives on Science and Mathematics Learning, *Science Education*, 75

WHITAKER P. (1997) *Primary Schools and the Future: Celebration, Challenges and Choices*, Open University Press

WHORF B. (1956) *Language, Thought and Reality*, MIT Press

WILBRINK B. (1997) Assessment in Historical Perspective, *Studies in Educational Evaluation*, 23

WILCE H. (2005) Shaking Up the Neighbours, *TES*, 8 April

WILDE O. (1997) De Profundis, in: GAYNOR T. *The Works of Oscar Wilde*, Senate

WILDE S., WRIGHT S., HAYWARD G., JOHNSON J. & SKERRETT R. (2005) *Nuffield Review Higher Education Focus Groups: Preliminary Report*, Department of Educational Studies, University of Oxford

WILKINSON A. (1965) *Spoken English*, University of Birmingham

WILLAN J., PARKER-REES R. & SAVAGE J. (2004) *Early Childhood Studies*, Learning Matters

WILLIAMS A. & KERSWILL P. (1999) Dialect Levelling: Change and Continuity in Milton Keynes, Reading and Hull, in: FOULKES P. & DOCHERTY G. *Urban Voices*, Arnold

WILLIAMS R. (1997) Educating the Spirit, *The National RE Festival – Inaugural Address*, Christian Education Movement, Wales

WOLFE P. (2001) *Brain Matters: Translating Research into Classroom Practice*, Association for Supervision and Curriculum Development

WOLFENDALE S. (1983) *Parental Participation in Children's Development and Education*, Gordon and Breach

WOOD D. (1988) *How Children Think and Learn*, Blackwell

WOODS G., O'NEILL M. and WOODS P. (1997) Spiritual Values in Education: Lessons from Steiner? *International Journal of Children's Spirituality*, 2/2

WRAGG E. (1999) *An Introduction to Classroom Observation*, Routledge

WRAGG E. & BROWN G. (1993) *Questioning*, Routledge

WRAGG E. & BROWN G. (2001) *Questioning in the Primary School*, Routledge

WRIGHT A. (1999) *Discerning the Spirit: Teaching Spirituality in the Religious Education Classroom*, Culham College Institute

WRIGHT A. (2000) *Spirituality and Education*, Routledge Falmer

WRIGLEY E.A. (1997) *English Population History from Family Reconstitution*, Cambridge University Press

WRINGE D. (1976) The Curriculum, in: LLOYD D. *Philosophy and the Teacher*, Routledge and Kegan Paul

WYSE D. (2002) *Becoming a Primary School Teacher*, Routledge Falmer

WYSE T. (1837) *Educational Reform: The Necessity of a National System of Education*, Longman

YORKE M. (2003) Formative Assessment in Higher Education: Moves Towards Theory and the Enhancement of Pedagogic Practice, *Higher Education*, 45/4

ZAEHNER R. (1972) *Drugs, Mysticism and Make-Believe*, Collins

ZOHAR D. & MARSHALL I. (2000) SQ: *Spiritual Intelligence: The Ultimate Intelligence*, Bloomsbury